NEWS LITERACY AND DEMOCRACY

News Literacy and Democracy invites readers to go beyond surface-level fact checking and to examine the structures, institutions, practices, and routines that comprise news media systems.

This introductory text underscores the importance of news literacy to democratic life and advances an argument that critical contexts regarding news media structures and institutions should be central to news literacy education. Under the larger umbrella of media literacy, a critical approach to news literacy seeks to examine the mediated construction of the social world and the processes and influences that allow some news messages to spread while others get left out. Drawing on research from a range of disciplines, including media studies, political economy, and social psychology, this book aims to inform and empower the citizens who rely on news media so they may more fully participate in democratic and civic life.

The book is an essential read for undergraduate students of journalism and news literacy and will be of interest to scholars teaching and studying media literacy, political economy, media sociology, and political psychology.

Seth Ashley, PhD, is an associate professor of journalism and media studies at Boise State University. His research on media literacy, media sociology, and communication policy has been published in a range of scholarly outlets, including the *Journal of Media Literacy Education*; *Communication Law and Policy*; *Journalism & Mass Communication Educator*; *Communication and the Public*; *Media, War & Conflict*; and the *Journal of Broadcasting & Electronic Media*. Ashley received his PhD and MA from the University of Missouri School of Journalism. He has worked as a writer and as an editor for newspapers and magazines and as a designer and technician for film, theater, and music productions.

"Seth Ashley's book on news literacy provides a refreshing, original and long overdue treatment of the matter, making media literacy a vibrant political and intellectual issue for our times."

–Robert W. McChesney, *University of Illinois at Urbana-Champaign*

"In *News Literacy and Democracy*, Seth Ashley offers a refreshing holistic approach to news literacy that goes far beyond so-called 'fake news' and one that is deeply aligned with the key concepts of media literacy. This book provides a rich knowledge base to help people understand how the news is constructed and why it has become more sensational and more partisan over time. Timely and responsive to the current media environment, this book helps people understand how changing business models for journalism are influencing the depiction of news and current events that we encounter online. This book should be required reading for every citizen as they reflect upon and consider what new forms of media policy and regulation may be needed to ensure that journalism can fulfill its social obligations in sustaining the democratic process."

–Renee Hobbs, *University of Rhode Island*

"With great care and clarity, Seth Ashley maps out key challenges facing our society today, from the decline of journalism to the rise of misinformation. In doing so, he underscores the need for a critical approach to news literacy that considers contextual factors such as market fundamentalism and monopoly power. This timely and invaluable book should be required reading for anyone who is concerned about the future of democracy."

–Victor Pickard, *University of Pennsylvania*

"In a time of increasing distrust in civic institutions, and specifically the news industry, Seth Ashley provides a poignant look at the challenges to our contemporary news ecosystem. Ashley's critical insight shows an understanding of the impacts of digital technologies on our news industries, and also explores some of the potential ways that citizens can become meaningfully engaged in news processes. Seth Ashley has provided a text that is necessary reading for those interested in the future of vibrant, diverse, and equitable democracy."

–Paul Mihailidis, *Emerson College*

"Pulling from media sociology, political science, social psychology, and other fields, this book distills rich theoretical concepts and wide-ranging empirical findings into clear and helpful insights. In the process, Seth Ashley expands the scope of what news literacy is and what it can do for democratic life."

–Tim P. Vos, *Michigan State University*

"Ashley provides a timely, engaging discussion of the need for critical news literacy in contemporary democracies. He brings a nuanced and historical perspective to modern problems and avoids hyperbole surrounding 'fake news.' This book is perfect for students and others looking to understand news literacy and its applicability to our lives."

–Melissa Tully, *University of Iowa*

NEWS LITERACY AND DEMOCRACY

Seth Ashley

Routledge
Taylor & Francis Group

NEW YORK AND LONDON

First published 2020
by Routledge
52 Vanderbilt Avenue, New York, NY 10017

and by Routledge
2 Park Square, Milton Park, Abingdon, Oxon, OX14 4RN

Routledge is an imprint of the Taylor & Francis Group, an informa business

© 2020 Taylor & Francis

Library of Congress Cataloging-in-Publication Data
A catalog record for this book has been requested

ISBN: 978-1-138-62505-1 (hbk)
ISBN: 978-1-138-62506-8 (pbk)
ISBN: 978-0-429-46022-7 (ebk)

Typeset in Bembo
by Apex CoVantage, LLC

For Amanda, Will, and Ben, with love and hope.

CONTENTS

PREFACE

This book represents what I've learned about news and democratic life over the past two decades, and it has been gratifying to sit and write much of it down. Through my personal and professional experience, I've come to care deeply about the news media environment because of the ongoing education it offers to all of us and the impact it has on our shared perceptions, beliefs, and behavior. Although the news we consume constitutes only a part of what shapes our worldview, it plays a central role in what we do separately as individuals and together as a society. By learning to navigate the complex news media environment, I hope we can make better decisions for ourselves and each other and improve the conditions of democracy for all. I hope this book can help.

Whom is this book for? Everyone! I wanted to write an accessible overview of a broad range of topics that I see as central to the news literacy education everyone needs to be a successful citizen and participant in democratic life. This book represents my best attempt to catalog and explore what I consider the most significant elements of news literacy and to make the case that my approach is a good one. I strive to use as much jargon-free, non-academic language as possible, but I do cover a range of academic concepts that are helpful for unpacking and examining the news media landscape. Where possible, I've also tried to offer citations to widely accessible books and articles, which contain references to academic sources for readers who want to dig deeper.

Who am I to write this book? I've spent the past decade pursuing a research agenda focused on better understanding the news media system and figuring out what the public should know about it. I've spent more time in classrooms than newsrooms over the past 20 years, but I do have first-hand knowledge of what goes into the production process for news and other media, and, more importantly, I have a profound appreciation for the hard work that journalism requires, particularly in the current information environment. I also spend hours each week working with students in a college media outlet, and I constantly learn as much from them as I hope to impart. Along with my respect and appreciation for the practice and products of journalism, I bring a critical lens to my analysis of the field. I see many scenarios where even good journalism does not live up to its full potential, and I see ways it could be better under the right structural conditions.

News literacy is an issue for a global agenda, to be sure, and I've attempted to show how news trends have played out worldwide. However, my context is primarily the United States, as that's the environment I know best. But even for international readers, I think the American experience is instructive for the rest of the developed and developing worlds. There is much to learn from our experience, both positive and negative.

Throughout the book, I've relied on the imperfect metaphor of "environment" or "landscape" to describe the news media around us, as if the mediated world is something we merely walk through like a forest or desert. It's a label that lacks precision because the environment is so vast and the terrain so varied. But that's sort of the point. That's what we're facing when we talk about "news" today, and that's what makes the present moment so challenging. We should think of the vast news environment as one to be not merely observed but rather explored and experienced with attention to all its subtle variations.

As you read, I hope you'll bring your own critical faculties to bear on what I have to say, and even if you don't like my perspective, I hope you approach the book as an invitation to learn more. Mine certainly is not the last word on news literacy or the modern news environment, so I hope this is just a stop along your journey to a better, more complex understanding of the world around us.

ACKNOWLEDGMENTS

I'm deeply indebted to all who have been part of my ongoing education, beginning with my parents, Andy and Linda, who made sure I had every possible opportunity in life. Many wonderful teachers helped open my eyes and showed me what's possible; I'd like to go back and tell each of these unsung heroes how much I appreciate their time and effort. That's especially true for my professors and mentors in graduate school at the University of Missouri, particularly Stephanie Craft, Tim Vos, Don Ranly, Charles Davis, and Victoria Johnson. I've been lucky to have all kinds of amazing peers and colleagues and to work with great coauthors and friends, especially Stephanie Craft and Adam Maksl, who have helped make my academic journey possible. I'm also grateful to a host of inspirational scholars and journalists who make me want to go further and do more. Thanks also to my friends, colleagues, and students at Boise State University, where I get to learn more every day. For this book, in particular, I'm thankful to everyone who helped me bounce ideas around and gave me feedback on various components and iterations, especially Melissa Tully, Paul Mihailidis, Brian Stone, Mike Sickels, and other anonymous reviewers. And thanks to Erica Wetter at Routledge for taking on this project. Ultimately, I alone am responsible for the perspective I offer here and for any errors. Lastly, I dedicate this to my wife, Amanda, without whom this book—and much more—would not be possible. Thanks for being on this roller coaster with me. Thanks also to Will and Ben, who deserve the brightest of futures.

PART I
Why News Literacy?

1

WHAT IS NEWS LITERACY?

Content and Context

"The World Outside and the Pictures in Our Heads" was the title Walter Lippmann gave to the introduction of his 1922 book, *Public Opinion*, about one of
the central problems of democracy. A leading political journalist and media critic,
Lippmann began the book by describing an island in the ocean and its inhabitants
who, in 1914, received news of the outside world by way of a British mail steamer
that came only once every 60 days. For more than six weeks, the Englishmen,
Frenchmen, and Germans who lived there did not receive word of the fight-
ing that had broken out in Europe, now known as World War I. "For six strange
weeks, they had acted as if they were friends, when in fact they were enemies,"
Lippmann wrote. "There was a time for each man when he was still adjusted to
an environment that no longer existed."[1]

How we get news and information and where it comes from are just as important as the news itself. Today, most of us don't sit around waiting for the mail ship
to arrive, but we still experience the same gaps between the world as we see it
and the world as it really is. What we read or see on Facebook or CNN provides
the "pictures in our heads," but the perceptions generated for us by the powerful
purveyors of our news environment don't always match the world outside. Some
things have certainly changed since Lippmann's day. Knowing our environments
is no longer a question of simply accruing information; instead, we are bombarded
with it. The more significant interval has become the one between information
and knowledge, between ideas and understanding. Lippmann's century-old point
about these gaps is as relevant as ever: "Looking back we can see how indirectly
we know the environment in which we nevertheless live. We can see that the
news of it comes to us now fast, now slowly; but that whatever we believe to be a
true picture, we treat as if it were the environment itself."[2] The connection news

gives us to the world around us may be indirect, but the news we consume and share is central to shaping our perceptions of that world and of our place in it.

Democracy has always been a bit of a tenuous proposition, but I don't think it's an overstatement to say we now live at a crossroads for democratic life. Democracy is ultimately about citizen participation in the organization of society. We are governed by elected representatives, and because representative government requires an informed citizenry, we need news that gives us an accurate picture of our environment. But the morass of information out in the world today poses a real threat to our ability to govern our societies. As individuals, we now have more control than ever over what we see and hear, which is a good thing, but it also puts a lot of pressure on each of us to know what we're doing. We each curate our own news consumption based on the seemingly limitless options provided in the digital era, and the picture of the world we end up seeing has enormous power to shape our perceptions of reality, which in turn shape our behavior and our attitudes. So the job of curating our own news consumption is an important one, and it's become harder than ever. Where should we direct our limited attention? Whom should we trust and why? What should we believe? Why should we tune into news at all? Trying to find the good and avoid the bad is a daunting task. Faced with a sea of infinite "content," many of us have just stopped trying, preferring to tune out altogether, while the rest of us often flounder in shallows. As author David Foster Wallace once wrote, "to really try to be informed and literate today is to feel stupid nearly all the time, and to need help."[3]

News literacy can be the help we need. While there is much to fix in our information environment, an easy place to start is with ourselves. We all need a holistic education in how and why news and information are produced and consumed, and we need it now. Not only are we forced to contend with the rise of so-called fake news and online hoaxes, but we face a host of arguably bigger problems. Journalism and press freedom are declining around the world, and authoritarianism is on the rise. Commercial media systems often put profits ahead of public service, and news is constrained by market forces. In the online environment, once heralded as the levelest of playing fields, power has been usurped by a small handful of monopolies that sell our personal lives for private profit and take advantage of our worst human tendencies toward tribalism and emotionalism. As a result, we fail to engage our critical reasoning skills, we retreat to the worlds we know and are most comfortable in, and we lose our capacity for empathy and compassion.

Calls for news literacy have surged in the 21st century. As misinformation swirls around the internet, news literacy is viewed by many as the antidote. Indeed, the ability to analyze news content is vital to getting accurate information and preserving democratic practices. But many people have tended to approach news literacy with a narrow web-based focus on hoax spotting and fact checking. These are vital skills, but equally and perhaps more important are the political, economic, historical, and cultural contexts in which news and information are produced and consumed. A critical, sociological approach—with an emphasis on the institutions and structures of news media systems—is essential for anyone who wants to develop meaningful news literacy. A narrow focus on news content cannot adequately address or explain patterns of news coverage, the influence of markets and audiences, the pressures created by algorithmic sorting, the monopoly power of digital giants, or the role of human cognition. A critical approach to news literacy seeks to examine the mediated construction of the social world and the processes and influences that allow some news messages to materialize and proliferate, while others fade from view or are omitted entirely. Drawing on research across a range of fields including sociology, psychology, political science, economics, and communication and media studies, this book presents a context-oriented approach to the critical analysis of the production and consumption of news and information. The ultimate goal is to inform and empower the citizens who rely on news media to participate effectively in democratic and civic life and to get more out of their own lives at the same time.

And the stakes could not be higher. A host of issues ranging from climate change and inequality to potential nuclear war and cyberterrorism to public health and human rights will only be addressed if we have accurate understandings of the realities we face. None of the important issues of the day will have a fair shot in a polluted and toxic information environment. So it's hard to overstate the significance of the current moment. Will we take advantage of the amazing potential of the digital revolution to inform and enlighten ourselves and each other, or will we squander it through willful ignorance and mindless consumption? The silver lining in today's dark clouds is the opportunity we have to examine and reshape our information environment and to make the improvements to ourselves and our societies that will help ensure a bright future.

Are We Really Living in a Post-Truth World?

In the United States, the idea that we are living in a "post-truth" society gained traction in the context of the 2016 presidential election, where many saw facts take a backseat to falsehoods. Around the world, swirls of misinformation online and in traditional news media made the idea so popular that Oxford Dictionaries named "post-truth" the "word of the year" and defined it as "relating to or denoting circumstances in which objective facts are less influential in shaping public opinion than appeals to emotion and personal belief."[4] Indeed, the emotional parts of our brains can be far more powerful than the reasoning parts of our brains, and that's nothing new. Our basic human tendencies to feel with our guts more than we think with our heads go back much further than the 21st century and are well documented in psychological research.[5] Thousands of years ago, our survival as a species depended on our ability as individuals to trust our guts and stick with our tribes without taking time to carefully analyze the facts. Our primitive brains are wired for this behavior, and it would be naïve of us to think this has changed just because we have come to control our environment in other ways.

After "post-truth" became a word of the year, the late-night television host Stephen Colbert jokingly complained that it was just a rip-off of his term "truthiness," which he coined in 2005 in the pilot episode of his satirical Comedy Central show "The Colbert Report." "Truthiness" also became a "word of the year," defined as "the quality of preferring concepts or facts one wishes to be true, rather than concepts or facts known to be true." Colbert's blowhard character (modeled largely after Fox News opinionator Bill O'Reilly) explained his disdain for fact-based reasoning: "I don't trust books. They're all fact, no heart. And that's exactly what's pulling our country apart . . . We are divided between those who think with their head and those who know with their heart." In this comedic context, Colbert noted that the rationale for the 2003 invasion of Iraq was not supported by evidence, but for many, it *felt* like the right thing to do.

It's fun to joke about having a penchant for feelings over facts, but this silliness reflects the deep misgivings many people have about the information environment we face and the ease with which many people are being taken in by falsehoods. This tendency was evident surrounding the 2016 U.S. presidential campaign and election, where Americans were inundated with "fake news" and other misinformation—both homegrown and from foreign sources—but it doesn't stop there. Fake news and misinformation also made the rounds surrounding the Brexit referendum campaign in Britain, which contributed to the chaos over Britain's exit from the European Union. Fake news was invoked in Myanmar, where state officials flat out denied the existence of hundreds of thousands of members of the Rohingya minority. In Syria, President Bashar al-Assad wrote off the deaths of thousands of military prisoners as fake news. And the disinformation provided by Russian influence campaigns has been used against pro-Western forces in Eastern Europe for years.[6]

To be sure, misinformation abounds on the web, and the intention by some to use digital media in this way illustrates some of our darker human tendencies. It may seem that fake news poses an immediate threat that can be defused by teaching people to sort real from fake. That's partly true, but fake news is only a symptom of larger problems with the news media environment, and to be truly news literate, we need to know more. In fact, some evidence suggests that although many people have been exposed to fake news, and many people have trouble telling that it's fake, most people's news consumption is actually broad enough that they are not heavily influenced by fake news.[7]

Our perceptions of reality are just as likely to be based on the traditional and alternative news sources we consume, which can range from *The New York Times* and *The Wall Street Journal* to Fox News and CNN to our local television news, NPR, the BBC, the *Today Show, Yahoo! News*, the *Huffington Post, Vice, Breitbart, Buzzfeed, Vox, Town Hall, The Daily Beast*, and so on. And "news" today can also be anything we see on social media, from Facebook and Twitter to Snapchat and

Instagram. So while it's tempting to view news literacy simply as the antidote to fake news, a narrow focus on fake news, hoaxes, and misinformation keeps us from gaining a broad understanding of the news media environment. Fake news may be a good place to start, but it's just the visible tip of an enormous iceberg below the surface.

We are living in an age of misinformation, but it began at least 500 years ago. The invention of the printing press in the 1450s made it easier than ever to pass along fiction as fact. As Mark Twain once wrote about the printing press, "It found truth astir on earth and gave it wings; but untruth also was abroad, and it was supplied with a double pair of wings."[8] In 17th-century England, pamphlets were written and distributed for profit and power with little regard for fact or expertise. Information was hard to verify, and "news" about sea monsters and witches spread widely. The American founding fathers made up stories about the savage brutality of Native Americans to encourage support for revolution. False reports of slave uprisings stirred up racist sentiments and led to violence against African-Americans.[9] And fake stories about Jewish rituals were part of the Nazi propaganda machine that led to the Holocaust.[10]

Humans didn't need the internet for any of this. Journalists in 19th-century America routinely published fake interviews and sensationalized dull stories. On the radio, many 1938 listeners were duped by Orson Welles' famous "War of the Worlds" broadcast about a fake alien invasion in New Jersey. Reports of panic and chaos were widespread, and the tale lives on as "fake news" legend. Actually, it's more likely that the reports of panic and chaos were the actual "fake news," exaggerated chiefly by newspapers that wanted to demonstrate their superior reliability over the emerging competitor of radio broadcasting.[11] Fake news about fake news!

Imagine what Mark Twain would have to say today. We know all too well that misinformation travels faster than the truth online. A 2018 MIT study found that, on Twitter, where people tend to trust what their friends have to say, lies are 70 percent more likely to be retweeted than facts.[12] It's one thing to be taken in by fake news and misinformation, but the bigger problem is the consequences that can result. Fake reports and images of 2012's Hurricane Sandy destruction over the East Coast were shared widely on Twitter, causing confusion and panic as they were passed on by traditional news outlets. (One image that proliferated was a promotional still from the 2004 disaster movie *The Day After Tomorrow*. Talk about life imitating art!) Stock prices can be manipulated by fake and false news, as when a fake 2013 report of an explosion at the White House led to a $130 billion loss in value. "Fake news in the financial market has been a problem for a long time, we just didn't call it fake news," said one analyst in *Forbes*.[13]

And sometimes fake news leads to violence. When the 2016 "Pizzagate" conspiracy theory spread about a child sex trafficking operation at a Hillary Clinton campaign center, an armed man went in to free the captives and fired an AR-15.

Of course, there were no captives, and the man was arrested. "The intel on this wasn't 100 percent," the shooter said later.[14] And in 2015 a young man named Dylann Roof searched Google for information about "black on white crime," and by his own account, he found "pages upon pages of these brutal black on White murders," which helped establish his racist worldview and led him to murder nine innocent congregants in a South Carolina church.[15] Of course, the results he found were full of misinformation—most violent crimes are committed by people who are the same race as their victims—but Roof's search history and other factors would have encouraged Google's algorithms to lead him down a racist rabbit hole on the web.

False information also can affect how we deal with our biggest problems, particularly when coupled with a lack of accurate information. According to the Yale Program on Climate Change Communication, as of March 2018, only 49 percent of Americans were "extremely" or "very" sure global warming is happening, and that's a significant improvement over recent years. Only 58 percent understand that humans are the primary cause of global warming. Nearly all climate scientists agree that human-caused global warming is happening, but only 15 percent of Americans understand this scientific consensus.[16] These numbers represent significant progress over the past decade, as news coverage has increasingly reflected the scientific evidence about climate change instead of treating it like a legitimate controversy with two equal and opposite sides. But we still have a long way to go, and the problem of climate change requires a global policy solution, which is less likely to come when people are misinformed.

Will this swirl of misinformation be the end of us? Is the messy digital environment created by the technological tools we have now—and those yet to come— too much for our primitive brains to handle, or will we master the tools and tame the wild beasts of the digital age? Will we find common ground and resolve our major differences, or will we get to a point where no one trusts anyone? The jury is still out. Even experts, who are often grouped as technology celebrants and skeptics, are evenly divided. The Pew Research Center surveyed more than 1,000 technology experts and scholars and found them equally split over whether the information environment will improve or get worse over the next ten years. The pessimistic "no" side suggested that our basic survival instincts and inclination toward comfort and convenience will make things worse, especially as malicious actors continue to manipulate the information environment. Our brains simply aren't wired to keep up with the pace of technology, and many will simply give up on trying to be informed. The more optimistic "yes" side suggested that technology is what will allow us to solve these problems, and it is human nature to band together during tough times and successfully adapt to our changing environments. And widespread news and information literacy education will help people learn to navigate the digital world.[17]

So are we living in a post-truth world? Despite the swirl of misinformation, the answer should be a definitive "no." While some things truly are up for debate, on many matters, there is an objective reality that can be described with facts and evidence. Generally, for example, national debts and deficits can be accurately recorded and projected; votes can be reliably counted; government spending on military or social programs can be tallied; scientific questions can be investigated; and even difficult policy questions—such as those surrounding global warming, public health, and inequality—can be addressed with evidence and reason rather than emotion and denial. It's also true that evidence can change over time. Even the once-accepted view of Earth as the center of the universe had to give way to the better-supported theory of a heliocentric solar system. But at the moment, especially as we consider the needs of day-to-day decision making, we should commit to working with the best available evidence we have. We should always leave room to improve on "the truth" by seeking new evidence, but it's untenable to simply toss aside the well-established methods of verification that have gotten us this far.

But surviving the chaos of our news and information environment will require more than checking our facts. We'll need to understand how and why misinformation is spread in the first place and that the news landscape is structured in ways that make it much harder than necessary to get accurate, reliable information. While it's important to be able to sort fact from fiction, it's just as important to understand how even "real news" can fall short, how computer algorithms can mislead us, how news media can propagate falsehoods while omitting relevant truths, and how use of social media can lead to polarization and discord. If we are to overcome the challenges posed by the modern information landscape, we need to take a holistic view.

What Is News Literacy and Why Do We Need It?

News literacy is the critical evaluation of information content as well as the contexts where it is produced and consumed. We can think of news literacy as the set of knowledge, skills, and attitudes that a person brings to their personal consumption of information and to their understanding of the structure of the news media landscape. If we develop our news literacy, especially our knowledge about the news environment, the job of navigating that environment becomes far more manageable. We can go from passive to active consumers of information, where we learn to mindfully direct our attention at news sources that help us meet our personal consumption goals and allow us to become empowered and engaged as citizens in complex societies. We can learn to bring to our news consumption a critical and curious perspective that will help us ask good questions about what we are getting—and what we are not getting. We can also learn the value of consuming useful information, and we can enjoy the sense of confidence that we gain from feeling informed and being able to reconcile competing ideas. Most of all, we can experience the thrill of participating in public life as competent citizens working to make the world a better place.

To do this, news literacy requires more than just an analysis of news content—checking facts, spotting hoaxes, and so on. A critical approach to news literacy examines the contexts in which news is produced and shared—the how and the why more than the who and the what. To become truly news literate, citizens need a holistic education in the institutions and structures of the news media system as well as the economic, technological, social, and psychological forces that influence how news is created and shared. We need to know about the forces that influence this process, which can include the daily routines of hard-working journalists, the roles of media owners and policymakers, the computer algorithms operating behind the scenes, and the profit motives that drive most news production. Individuals need a range of knowledge to be able to judge the quality of the information before them as well as the quality of the overall news media environment.

It is a lot to ask of ordinary citizens. Who has the time or energy to work this hard just to have access to reliable information and be an engaged citizen? The demands placed on citizens in the digital age can be daunting, and the task at hand can feel overwhelming. In some ways, it's unfair, and that's part of the point. Information systems are often structured in ways that make it hard to be well informed. But it doesn't have to be this way. Armed with contextual knowledge and a critical perspective, citizens can learn to navigate the information environment with relative ease. After reading this book, students and citizens should be better prepared to find the information they need and remain above the fray of the struggle we face as citizens in self-governing societies. This book aims to help you develop your critical perspective by lifting the veil that conceals many of the inner workings of the news media environment, and you should gain a sense of how the news landscape could be improved through changes to the institutions and structures that influence it.

Why does this matter and why should people care? In a word, democracy! The democratic societies of the Western world are made possible by citizen governance. As individuals, we might not write laws or punish wrongdoers directly, but we do have the privilege of exercising our collective voice about who will lead us and how we will organize our societies. Many of us are able to do this at the voting booth every so often, but we also can speak freely to our representatives and our fellow citizens, and we can influence the policy-making process through a number of ways. To do any of this well, we need access to reliable information. As the challenges presented by the digital environment grow (and it will almost certainly get worse before it gets better), we need to develop our news literacy to become effective participants in democratic life.

But wait—there's more! While effective participation in democratic life might be a central goal of news literacy education, our ability to understand and evaluate the news media environment has significant consequences for other areas of daily life. Like all media products, news plays a major role in determining how we perceive ourselves and each other, how we communicate, how we focus our limited attention, and ultimately how we choose to live our lives. A holistic education in news literacy can help us achieve a range of goals when it comes to gaining a better understanding of ourselves and the world around us. Ultimately, news literacy can help us create and share a world that is more democratic, equal, and just, where the benefits of power and progress are enjoyed by the many, not just the few.

Some people might groan at the idea of all this civic responsibility. "I'm just not very political," some say, or "I'm not a political person." The reality is we are all political. We are all affected by the resources made available to us, which is only possible through politics and policy making. The word "politics" comes from a Greek word meaning "affairs of the cities," and while we might not outwardly advocate for our preferences or even vote, our daily decisions reflect our politics. When we drive gas-powered cars, for example, we are indirectly supporting private rather than public transportation, a fossil-fuel economy, and publicly funded roads, and we are showing our willingness to accept the pollution most cars produce as a necessary cost of getting around. This is not necessarily a bad thing, especially if we're just trying to get to work or school, but it does show how we all are involved in the "affairs of the cities." We are also political when we choose what to eat, what to buy, whom to work for, and where to live. Even choosing not to vote is a political decision to opt out of representative government, which is still a luxury for many on planet Earth in the 21st century. We might eschew organized politics, which can certainly be ugly at times, but our involvement in political life is unavoidable. We need to be well informed so we can make good decisions for ourselves and our societies. If we enjoy freedom and privilege, our informed participation in civic life is our responsibility to those who have helped us get this far and to those who have less. Through the lottery of birth, some of us were lucky enough to have been born into conditions that others would relish, and it's important not to take our privileges for granted.

If we want to wield our privilege and power responsibly, we need to be informed. As we begin to learn to navigate the news media environment, each time we encounter a piece of information, we should start by asking a simple question: who is sending this message, and why are they sending it? Eventually, our questions will get bigger as our examination expands and our focus broadens to the sets of institutions and structures that influence the news environment: whose interests are served by a given set of arrangements? Does the current organization of the news landscape serve citizens broadly or does it mainly serve the interests of the powerful few? What changes could be made to improve on the status quo? Quite simply, who benefits?

This can be touchy stuff. Asking hard questions about power and privilege can be uncomfortable and can even seem unfair at times. But a meaningful approach to news literacy should invite these tough questions—even if different people reach different conclusions. Let's try to start from the premise that ignoring big questions and simply accepting the world as it is no different from questioning, challenging, and even working to change it. For students and citizens, this type of critical inquiry is the essence of education—asking questions, examining conventional wisdom, solving problems—and is part of their growth as lifelong learners. For teachers, scholars, policy makers, and parents, anything less than an open invitation for students to question and challenge the world around us is an abdication of our responsibilities if we truly believe in education and its power for liberation and human flourishing.

One final note here: it's easy to critique fake news and lies. These have no value and, once identified, can be readily discarded. But when directed at legitimate news, the critical lens we bring to news literacy can make it seem like we are also here to bash the hard work of serious journalists. Taking a critical look at news can have the effect of undermining the very thing we want to save! To the contrary, I think it's fair to say that anyone who cares about news literacy generally cares deeply about news and journalism and wants to see this essential institution of democracy succeed and thrive. Some proponents of news literacy tend to focus on the importance of the traditional news business and the role it plays in democracy. They are not wrong to want to do this, and perhaps this approach is the best we can hope for in these challenging times. But there is more to the picture, and many of us who have studied the problems with modern news and journalism have a hard time promoting its strengths without also considering its weaknesses. This puts us in a difficult position of wanting to defend the traditional practice while also being free to discuss the problems. Certainly, the very thing that sets journalism apart from all the other "content" online is the high standard it aspires to meet. I'm confident that the practice of journalism—when done well—is central to the success of democracy, and I want to make sure that message is clear throughout this book. At the same time, we must acknowledge the flaws of news and journalism so we can continue to hold it to a high standard and make it better. Call it "tough love."

The Role of News in Democracy

Anyone reading this book probably does not need to be told that news plays a significant role in our lives. News of some kind touches all of us, and we tend to have mixed feelings about our options. According to the Pew Research Center, as of 2016, 81 percent of U.S. adults get news online, and 62 percent get news from social media.[18] Young adults prefer social media and the web, while older Americans mostly watch television. Americans turn to professional news outlets far more than they rely on family and friends, and 70 percent of Americans say they follow local and national news somewhat or very closely. Most people say they trust national and local news organizations even though they say most news outlets tend to favor "one side." Only half of news consumers say they feel loyal toward their news sources, but most people return to the same sources over and over anyway. These figures vary internationally, but overall, citizens around the world have similar experiences with news.[19] News and our relationship with it may be changing, but clearly, interest in news remains high.

Whether our feelings about the news are warm or not, we spend a fair amount of time with it. But for something we spend so much time with and rely on so heavily, we're not encouraged to do much thinking or learning about how it works. News literacy asks us to do just that. Think about the news you've consumed in the past 24 hours. Compare what you've learned about the world through news media to what you've learned from your own first-hand experience. As we live more of our lives on our computers and devices, our experience of the world is increasingly *mediated*, which means it comes to us through one or more media formats or platforms rather than our own first-hand experience. For instance, most of us do not know personally the president of the United States or the chancellor of Germany or a player in the National Football League or any of the famous Kardashian sisters. Most readers here probably did not personally witness a Black Lives Matter protest or attend a campaign rally for Donald Trump. We did not watch our food as it was being grown, and we did not see how our car was assembled. And most of us lack the scientific expertise to evaluate ice core samples for evidence of warming temperatures or the medical knowledge to identify the best cancer treatments. What we learn about the world and how we come to perceive reality is often limited to the news we receive, and our perceptions of reality are increasingly influenced by the media we consume.

News literacy is particularly important because of the role news plays in democratic society. We rely on news to become informed and make decisions about how government should work and how society should be structured. At least that's the idea. Without good information provided by a vigilant and vibrant press, government by the people would be impossible. But what's so great about democracy in the first place? Who says citizens should have a say in how our societies are governed? The idea of democracy goes back to at least the ancient Greeks, and the term "democracy" comes from Greek words that literally mean "people power." The basic idea of democracy is shared governance. Instead of a monarch or dictator making all the decisions, power is decentralized and shared. Democracy can take different forms and allow for different levels of participation, but the various flavors of representative government that have existed over time have aimed to break up concentrated power and the abuses that typically come with it. Democracy can be limited and indirect, where only certain citizens can participate and simply choose representatives to manage public affairs on their behalf. Democracy can also be inclusive and direct, where many citizens participate and have the opportunity to weigh in on specific policy debates like whether to expand Medicare, legalize drugs, or raise taxes to pay for schools or parks. Either way, rather than be ruled by monarchs and dictators, humans have fought for generations for the opportunity to have at least some say in how our societies are organized.

Democratic rule aims to promote both *liberty* and *equality*, two values that are often in tension with each other.[20] Individual liberty allows people to express themselves and generally live as they please. Equality aims to give all citizens similar opportunities to make their voices heard and to share in the benefits of civilization. In elections, liberty means all eligible citizens get to vote, and equality means each vote carries the same weight. This gets tricky with other issues, such as owning property or running a business or providing public education or subsidizing health care. When preference is given to liberty, people have freedom to do what they want without government getting in the way. It's often assumed that this is the best way to give everyone the same chance to succeed and thrive without getting into thorny questions of when and how government should intervene. But because not everyone is born with the same resources and privileges, democratic governments also have an interest in promoting equal opportunities for all. When preference is given to equality, some sort of thoughtful distribution of resources is required to level the playing field and provide equal opportunities. The essential challenge of democracy is finding the right balance between these competing tendencies.

Like all human endeavors, democracy is imperfect. It's far from efficient and does not always achieve its stated aims. Since its invention at least 2,500 years ago, democracy has been viewed skeptically and even disdainfully by many political theorists and elites. But this book proceeds from the position that the values of democracy generally embody commonly held human desires and offer the best path forward for the effective management of public affairs and an equitable and just organization of society. As Winston Churchill supposedly quipped, "Democracy is the worst form of government, except for all the others."

If we can agree that some form of shared governance is a good thing, we can start to see that citizens need good information in order to understand the tensions of civic life and to weigh in on the policy questions they raise. That's why viable democracies have at least some legal guarantees and protections to ensure a free press. Thomas Jefferson, one of the American founding fathers, was as an ardent defender of the press—at least until he wasn't. Writing from Paris on the eve of the French Revolution, Jefferson emphasized the importance of protecting unfettered speech and press rights. "The basis of our governments being the opinion of the people, the very first object should be to keep that right," Jefferson wrote in a letter in 1787.[21] One of the first principles of government should be to protect individual expression, he argued. He even went so far as to suggest that the press and its ability to express popular opinion would be more important than the government itself: "And were it left to me to decide whether we should have a government without newspapers, or newspapers without a government, I should not hesitate a moment to prefer the latter." But he did not stop there. The mere existence of newspapers would not be enough, he added: "But I should mean that every man should receive those papers and be capable of reading them." That means broad distribution of information and high levels of literacy would be prerequisites for an effective free press.

By 1807, near the end of his presidency, Jefferson's views had shifted. In another letter, he suggested that a useful newspaper should be restrained to "true facts and sound principles only."[22] He also realized the difficulty of reaching a broad audience with such restraint: "Yet I fear such a paper would find few subscribers," Jefferson wrote. "It is a melancholy truth, that a suppression of the press could not more completely deprive the nation of its benefits, than is done by its abandoned prostitution to falsehood." In other words, the press was already doing such a bad job that government censorship couldn't possibly make it any worse. He went on:

> Nothing can now be believed which is seen in a newspaper. Truth itself becomes suspicious by being put into that polluted vehicle. The real extent of this state of misinformation is known only to those who are in situations to confront facts within their knowledge with the lies of the day. I really look with commiseration over the great body of my fellow citizens, who, reading newspapers, live & die in the belief, that they have known something of what has been passing in the world in their time.[23]

In other words, consuming news gives the false impression that we know anything about the real world.

Wow, that's dark! Suspicious truth? Polluted vehicle? State of misinformation? In some ways, it's comforting to know that the founding fathers and the early American colonials faced some of the same issues we are dealing with today. Their situation was certainly different as they worked to keep a fragile republic from falling apart. But nonetheless, it's significant that guarantees of speech and press freedom were enshrined in the First Amendment to the U.S. Constitution and have stood the test of time as one of the major successes of the American experiment. Even with all the garbage that poses as news and information, the theory goes, it's still better to let most of it out instead of attempting to crack down and restrict these broad rights. Some Americans and others around the world have actually come to believe that news and other media have too much freedom and deserve a more restrictive approach that would aim to curtail tendencies toward lies, falsehoods, and bias. Such restrictions could eventually come, but for now, media content generally remains well protected by law. With any such regulations, the difficulty is always in determining where to draw the lines between what's allowed and what's not. Who among us should be the arbiters of truth for all of us?

The idea that it's best to "let it all out" emerged in the 16th through 18th centuries in Europe in the context of the Renaissance, the Scientific Revolution, and the Age of Enlightenment. Noting his opposition to the British practice of requiring publications to be licensed, or approved, by the king, John Milton famously wrote in 1644, "Let [Truth] and Falsehood grapple; who ever knew

Truth put to the worse, in a free and open encounter?"[24] When you put it all out there, how could truth not win out over falsehoods? Similarly, Voltaire, the French Enlightenment thinker, was an ardent supporter of free speech. A biographer in 1906 summarized his view that even unpopular speech deserves strong protections: "I disapprove of what you say, but I will defend to the death your right to say it."[25] Today, free expression advocates often suggest that the best answer to "bad speech" is "more speech." Rather than censoring those who mislead or offer unpopular views, it's better to respond with speech that draws attention to and corrects or challenges offensive speech. This basic philosophy, which still guides the general approach to speech and press freedom in democratic societies, shows why dealing with fake news, misinformation, and other falsehoods is so difficult. Picking and choosing what's allowed and what's not is an early step on the road to authoritarianism. And so liberty is preserved by allowing unfettered speech and press freedom.

Well, sort of. Just because there are few legal restrictions on news content doesn't mean other forces don't have a major impact in shaping the information environment. In the United States, the chief regulating body of the communication system is the Federal Communications Commission (FCC), which was created by the Communication Act of 1934. With a few exceptions such as regulating obscenity, the FCC doesn't rule on content directly. But they do grant and renew the free licenses that allow news stations to broadcast over the public airwaves, and, in doing so, the FCC has significant influence over what voices will be heard.[26] The FCC is also at the center of the ongoing debate over "net neutrality," or the idea that all websites and web content deserve equal treatment from internet service providers.[27] The FCC made net neutrality a rule in 2015 but then repealed it in 2018. This is not a direct influence on content, but it does have an indirect effect on the operations of internet service providers and their obligations to consumers. Another example of an indirect effect on content is the role the U.S. Department of Justice plays in approving or denying the consolidation of communication companies, as in the case of Comcast's acquisition of NBCUniversal or AT&T's merger with Time Warner. A decline in the diversity of ownership of media companies and the consolidation of content creators (like NBC) with content providers (like Comcast) often means fewer choices for consumers as competition is reduced. This decline began in the 1980s and has accelerated rapidly over the decades since.[28]

Because of the difficulty of directly regulating news and information content in democratic societies, we can only understand news and information by looking to the systems and structures in which content is created and consumed. And the demands of democracy should make it clear why this is so important. Although news media are far from perfect, they have an essential role to play in the practice and preservation of democratic life. Beyond media in general, news deserves special attention because of its central importance.

Different Approaches to News Literacy

The idea of sorting good information from bad is nothing new. News and media literacy have gotten a lot of attention in recent years, but learning to evaluate information through critical questioning can be traced back (like most things) to the ancient Greeks, whose instructional practices centered on rhetoric, public speaking, and the art of politics. Modern media education has been around since at least the 1920s, when the advent of motion pictures brought concerns about the effects of visual imagery on moviegoers. As radio and television developed in the mid-20th century, media education examined the emerging culture industries and the messages they produced. By the 1970s and 1980s, many scholars and educators, especially in Europe, saw media education as a component of citizenship with a focus on questions of power and culture.[29]

The critical analysis of news messages has been a key part of media education for decades, but only in the early 21st century has news literacy emerged as a domain of its own. Although still rooted in the broad framework of media literacy—the ability to access, analyze, evaluate, and create media messages in a variety of forms—news literacy targets news and information rather than other types of media messages such as movies, television, advertising, and magazines. News literacy is premised on the idea that news plays a central role in creating a self-governing citizenry, and so news deserves special attention in education. On this point there is broad agreement. But the precise goals and methods of news literacy education are subject to some debate.

For starters, how we approach news literacy depends on how we define "news" and "literacy." The notion of "news" means different things to different people, and these days, can include any headline or meme that appears online regardless of source. One effect of getting news from social media has been to smooth over the information landscape as one undifferentiated mass of content, each piece having its own sense of validity and legitimacy (or lack thereof). Also, news has traditionally been viewed as a type of mediated communication where messages travel from a single sender (like NBC News) to a large, diverse mass audience. Today, news is just as likely to be tailored and customized for niche audiences and can be transmitted and shared in a variety of ways. "Literacy" is also a complex idea that has traditionally been limited to one's ability to read and write but now can refer to competence or knowledge in a number of specific domains—think of "health literacy" or "financial literacy." In the context of news, literacy can focus narrowly on the comprehension of news content, but it also can take a broader view of the political, economic, cultural, and social environments in which news is produced and consumed. Table 1.1 shows some of the different possible outcomes of examining news content and contexts.

As the field of news literacy has developed, so too have a variety of approaches to teaching, studying, and practicing news literacy. The narrower conception of

TABLE 1.1 News literacy knowledge, skills, and attitudes for content and contexts.

	Content	*Contexts*
Knowledge	• Not all information is created equal. • Reliable information is necessary for democratic self-governance. • News messages are constructed and have embedded meanings.	• News content constructs reality and influences democratic life. • Structural, institutional, and individual forces influence news content. • Legal, economic, and historical trends create the news media system.
Skills	• Use evidence-based reasoning to analyze content and spot misinformation and bias. • Consume and share information responsibly.	• Examine content based on historical, political, economic, and social contexts. • Identify personal biases and preconceptions. • Challenge and resist media structures that allow misinformation to spread.
Attitudes	• Develop a desire to consume and share accurate and useful information. • Develop a healthy news media diet.	• Develop a personal commitment to critical inquiry. • Engage with public affairs and democratic life.

news literacy centers on the analysis of specific pieces of information content. This process has always been one of the foundations of critical or analytical thinking, which used to get more attention from educators than it does today. Many educators, especially librarians, have always worked to teach methods for evaluating information for its quality, relevance, and usefulness. These basic approaches to evaluating content offer a great starting point, especially for young learners. As we review a few of these, it helps to consider the strengths and weaknesses of these tools, which can guide us toward the knowledge, skills, and attitudes that inform a broader conception of news literacy.

One common approach to teaching information literacy and evaluation of sources is the CRAAP test. This is an excellent tool to get students and citizens thinking about the quality of their information. The test asks a variety of questions centered around five domains, which form the "CRAAP" acronym: currency, relevance, authority, accuracy, and purpose (see Table 1.2). These domains provide excellent criteria for examining specific pieces of content, but of course, the test is not designed to get at the broader influences of the information environment, and it does not specifically address prior beliefs and the relativity of perspectives,

TABLE 1.2 The CRAAP test.

Currency: the timeliness of the information.	• When was the information published or posted? • Has the information been revised or updated? • Does your topic require current information, or will older sources work as well? • Are the links functional?
Relevance: the importance of the information for your needs.	• Does the information relate to your topic or answer your question? • Who is the intended audience? • Is the information at an appropriate level (i.e., not too elementary or advanced for your needs)? • Have you looked at a variety of sources before determining this is one you will use? Would you be comfortable citing this source in your research paper?
Authority: the source of the information.	• Who is the author/publisher/source/sponsor? • What are the author's credentials or organizational affiliations? • Is the author qualified to write on the topic? • Is there contact information, such as a publisher or email address? • Does the URL reveal anything about the author or source? examples:. com,. edu,. gov,. org,. net
Accuracy: the reliability, truthfulness, and correctness of the content.	• Where does the information come from? • Is the information supported by evidence? • Has the information been reviewed or refereed? • Can you verify any of the information in another source or from personal knowledge? • Does the language or tone seem unbiased and free of emotion? • Are there spelling, grammar, or typographical errors?
Purpose: the reason the information exists.	• What is the purpose of the information? Is it to inform, teach, sell, entertain, or persuade? • Do the authors/sponsors make their intentions or purpose clear? • Is the information fact, opinion, or propaganda? • Does the point of view appear objective and impartial? • Are there political, ideological, cultural, religious, institutional, or personal biases?

Source: Developed by Sarah Blakeslee at California State University, Chico, Meriam Library.

where one person's "fact" could be another person's "propaganda." The American Library Association has embraced the CRAAP test for years but since 2016 has emphasized the contextual nature of authority; a position of power alone does not necessarily equal a qualified source.[30] This gray area is important given the erroneous and misleading statements often made by politicians and pundits, but it puts the learner in a difficult position where trust and reliability become difficult to establish even with what you might think are qualified experts. Of course, no test or method of evaluation is perfect, but this one is a great starting point. Every student should be familiar with it no later than junior high school.

The lessons of the content-based approach to news literacy also are well modeled in Bill Kovach and Tom Rosenstiel's 2010 book, *Blur: How to Know What's True in the Age of Information Overload*. According to these veteran journalists, news literacy is about "the skills of how to 'read' the news—the discipline of skeptical knowing."[31] The authors call for the introduction of civic and news literacy into middle and high school curricula in order to improve the skills of citizens. Their "skeptical way of knowing" is based on six questions:

1. What kind of content am I encountering?
2. Is the information complete, and if not what is missing?
3. Who or what are the sources, and why should I believe them?
4. What evidence is presented, and how was it tested or vetted?
5. What might be an alternative explanation or understanding?
6. Am I learning what I need to?[32]

For news literacy beginners, these questions help to address important concerns about bias, fairness, accuracy, and completeness.

Another approach has been popularized by the Center for News Literacy at Stony Brook University. The Stony Brook approach packages a journalist's view of the world for regular news consumers. In their reporting, journalists themselves typically rely on multiple, authoritative independent sources who can support their claims with verifiable evidence. And most journalists prefer to avoid using anonymous sources whenever possible. This approach helps journalists produce accurate, reliable information, so it makes sense that these skills would translate well to news consumers who want to access accurate, reliable information. As leaders of the Center for News Literacy have written, "every student in America should acquire the critical thinking skills of a journalist."[33]

The Stony Brook Center offers its own acronym—IM VAIN—to help students remember how to think like journalists as they encounter news content (see Table 1.3).[34] Like the CRAAP test, this approach is a great starting point for learners. This kind of test can keep citizens oriented toward news they can trust, and it can help offer an understanding of how journalists do their jobs, which can help build an appreciation for the kind of serious, evidence-based reporting a democratic society requires. Also like the CRAAP test, this approach is focused

TABLE 1.3 The IM VAIN chart.

I: Independent sources are better than self-interested sources
M: Multiple sources are better than single sources.
V: Sources who **Verify** with evidence are better than sources who assert.
A/I: Authoritative/Informed sources are better than uninformed sources.
N: Named sources are better than unnamed sources.

Source: Stony Brook University Center for News Literacy.

on analyzing individual pieces of content and doesn't get at the larger contexts in which news is produced and consumed.

A similar approach to news literacy is offered by the News Literacy Project, which also aims to teach students to think like journalists. The nonprofit organization does so by sending professional journalists into classrooms to explain their methods to students. Journalists, teachers, and students all report the benefits of these interactions for the students who participate: deeper thinking about the quality of information, an increased interest in current events, and a more skeptical orientation to news in general.[35] These are excellent outcomes and should be encouraged, especially for young learners. Thinking like a journalist is a great thing to be able to do, and learning these criteria for news can do a lot to inform and empower news consumers.

At the same time, journalists can have their own flaws and blind spots about their profession and their practices. For example, while many journalists abhor the idea of government-funded news media and the influence it might wield over their news content, they often have no problem with the advertising that subsidizes most of their work and pays for their salaries. If news funded by government would be subject to influence and control, is it possible that news funded by advertising could have some of the same problems? Another problem with professional journalism is its heavy reliance on official sources, which can create a distorted view of who matters and what's important. Also, offering fair and balanced reporting can be a good general goal, but aiming to avoid bias by simply offering "both sides" of an issue can create false equivalencies even when one side is supported by overwhelming evidence while the other side is based on empty assertions (e.g., global warming and vaccine safety). In general, journalists are some of the best experts at being skeptical about the world around them, but sometimes they have difficulty applying that same critical lens to the prevailing industry practices.

Another way of providing instruction on information sources is to portray the news landscape as a spectrum of political bias and reliability and to indicate which sources are liberal or conservative or which are trustworthy or not. Like the tests described previously, this kind of guidance can be a useful starting point, but it is problematic for a few reasons. First, bias is relative. The political left and right differ from one country or one region to another. For example, "left" in the

United States is often thought to be more centrist than "left" in Europe. Second, bias appears in the eye of the beholder. For a liberal or conservative die-hard, their preferred information sources might seem neutral to them but could appear highly polarized to a more moderate observer. Third, this approach can be overly prescriptive. Rather than encouraging students and citizens to do their own critical thinking about news, it prescribes a view of the information environment from a position of authority. Think of the old Chinese proverb: catch a person a fish and feed them for a day; teach a person to fish and feed them for a lifetime. Like catching a fish for someone, telling people which sources are legitimate or centrist might be useful in the short term, but it avoids the broader lessons that would help learners do the necessary task of sorting information on their own.

In sum, the emerging field of news literacy has tended to focus narrowly on the analysis of content: checking facts, spotting hoaxes, verifying claims, and recognizing authoritative sources. These are excellent goals, especially for young learners. The basics of this approach can be summed up in a few pithy points:

1. Be familiar with your sources and know where your information is coming from.
2. Verify facts, especially if they seem surprising or unusual or stir your emotions.
3. Get information from a variety of sources.
4. Read beyond headlines, which are often oversimplified.
5. Know the difference between news, opinion, commentary, and propaganda.
6. Look for the original sources of reporting instead of trusting someone else's interpretation.
7. Follow a story over time and evaluate sources based on trends in coverage.
8. Consume and share responsibly.

Fortunately, the web is full of useful resources to help with this. Virtually every library website has a page or pages dedicated to examining information, and plenty of other organizations and institutions have their own lesson plans and resources. Educators from elementary school through higher education have begun to introduce these lessons into their curricula. Another major boon for news literacy has been the rise of fact-checking websites such as Snopes.com, PolitiFact.com, and FactCheck.org. Unfortunately, these sites are often accused of having their own biases, and research suggests that users who are most in need of having their facts checked are also those least likely to visit a fact-checking site.[36] Regardless, these are great resources for analyzing content and seeking accuracy in information.

If other approaches to news literacy want you to think like a journalist, this book is about getting you to think more like a sociologist. Sociologists study the structure and functioning of human society with attention to the social problems that arise from living in groups. When applied to news, that means examining not just individual pieces of news content but the broader news media environment, including its structures and institutions, its professional norms and routines, its impact on citizens, and its potential for improving the conditions of democratic life and public welfare. And so again, the point of this book is simple. To truly be informed, self-governing citizens, we must have a holistic understanding of the news media that bring us the world. Although understanding individual news messages is important, it's not enough. Students and citizens alike need to know about the forces and influences that make news and information look the way it does and the implications for democratic life.

Perhaps this is a lot to ask of news literacy. Perhaps verifying claims and spotting hoaxes is enough for one educational task. Perhaps asking critical questions about the structure and function of news and information systems is too complex, too value laden, and too politically sensitive to gain traction in the polarized political and educational climates that have become commonplace in modern democracies. Perhaps. But that doesn't mean we can't try. Instead, we should invite the process of inquiry that is at the core of a critical contextual approach to news literacy, and we should welcome the opportunity provided by the messy digital landscape to examine the status quo, warts and all. If we take full advantage of this historic moment, we can shape the information environment going into the future and leave it better than we found it.

What exactly does it mean to gain a holistic understanding of news media structures and functions anyway? This can all sound pretty abstract and theoretical at this point. One major benefit to a content-based approach to news literacy with its focus on specific articles and videos is that it can provide a level of accessibility that is harder to achieve with a more sociological approach to news literacy. Examining individual trees is easier than comprehending an entire forest. There's no question that grasping the complexity of the news landscape is a difficult task, and this book won't even be able to cover all of it. However, the goal here is to introduce the reader to the major critical contexts of news and to provide enough examples and evidence that it becomes easier to see how these contexts influence our daily lives and the health of our societies.

How to Think Like a Sociologist

News literacy requires us to think not just like journalists but like sociologists. Thinking like a sociologist means taking nothing for granted. Instead, we must work to free ourselves from our preconceived notions about the world, to examine the way things are, to question social norms and practices. Sociologist C. Wright Mills called this the *sociological imagination*, or the ability to see the relationships between the daily lives of individuals and the historical and social contexts in which they live. As Mills famously put it in his 1959 book, "Neither the life of an individual nor the history of a society can be understood without understanding both."[37] Our difficulty in understanding the world comes from our often myopic focus on individual and personal experience without attempting to comprehend the systems where humans operate. The sociological imagination is that quality of mind, one that allows us to ask big questions and see larger connections. To really put our sociological imaginations to work, we have to take a step back from what we think we know and consider how larger forces shape our individual experiences. I like to think of the words of Yoda, the Jedi master: "You must unlearn what you have learned."[38]

Mills pointed out the need to differentiate between our "personal troubles," which are easier to see and to blame, and "public issues," which are often more hidden from view. For example, a person who is unable to find a job could be blamed for an individual failure to work hard enough or for being part of a family that wasn't supportive. That's a personal trouble. But there are a host of public issues that could also be relevant, such as general unemployment, a widespread economic downturn, a lack of jobs that pay a living wage, an absence of regulation in financial markets, the unaffordability of child care, the high cost of higher education, and so on. These are public issues that influence what individuals can and can't accomplish on their own. Not being able to get a date is a personal trouble, but it might also be related to broad social trends tied to changes in courtship and gender roles. It can be a personal trouble when someone trying to lose weight becomes anorexic, but it's also a public issue related to social expectations around body type and the mediated representations that reinforce them. Speaking of mediated representations, what we do and see on social media is shaped by laws and regulations about free speech and content restrictions, corporate policies of the companies that own social media platforms, web and app developers who design the sites, algorithms that determine what we are exposed to, social expectations about our presence and behavior online, and so on. Think for a minute about how your own individual experience is shaped by broader public issues like these.

Exercising our sociological imaginations requires us to realize that much of our reality is *socially constructed*, meaning it only comes into existence when we begin to interact with other humans and engage in collective decision making about how we will describe and discuss and structure the world around us. Money is an easy example. The piece of paper in your wallet has no intrinsic value. Its value only exists because a group of people in the form of a government say it does. Language is the product of a socially constructed reality. If we do not share it with others, it wouldn't be of much use. For example, the word "chair" is not the same as the thing you sit on; it is a symbol, a representation, that you and I can agree on (assuming you also speak English). The word "blue" is separate from the color it represents. It only has meaning because we have shared it. (In fact, what you perceive as "blue" might actually have nothing to do with what I see as "blue," but we both call it the same thing anyway.)

Here's a more abstract example that exemplifies the take-nothing-for-granted sociological approach we will eventually bring to news literacy. What makes music sound happy or sad? Tempo, lyrics, and instrumentation all contribute. But the defining trait is harmony—whether a key signature or interval is major or minor. Major chords are easily identifiable by the presence of a major third, which is four half-steps. Think of the pleasant "ding-dong" sound of a doorbell—that's a major third. Compare that to a minor third, which is three half-steps; think of the dark, ominous opening to Beethoven's Fifth: "duh-duh-duh-DUH." Have you ever heard this sound from a doorbell? Why do we prefer the chipper major third when a friend arrives at our door? Why does the difference between two piano keys (about 18 additional string vibrations per second) signify such different emotional connotations? Is there something innate in the music or in our brains that causes us to respond in this way? Hardly. This is what we hear because this is what we have learned.

Since the day we were born, we've been internalizing the message that the major third sounds happy and the minor third sounds sad or dark. Think of the lullabies sung to babies or the songs children grow up singing along with—overwhelmingly major. This is another example of a social construction, or an idea that has been created and accepted by people in a society. In fact, the whole idea of Western music is based on a system that goes back to (take a guess) the ancient Greeks, particularly Pythagoras (better known for his Pythagorean theorem—the one about triangles). There is a mathematical rationale for dividing octaves the way he did, but creating scales defined by 12 tones with specific intervals between each note is ultimately arbitrary and subjective. This is evident when listening to non-Western music such as ragas of India, which rely on different harmonic systems.

What does any of this have to do with news? Like music, money, and language, news is socially constructed. News is not the actual events of daily life but rather a representation of those events. Because news is one of the chief ways we learn about the world, it's important to realize that the world represented might or might not be the world as it is. As comedian Jerry Seinfeld once joked, "It's amazing that the amount of news that happens in the world every day always just exactly fits the newspaper." News is no longer confined to newspapers, but the joke is still relevant. Far more "news" happens each day than we end up hearing about, whether we're checking social media, listening to a podcast, watching television, or even just talking to friends and family. Jerry's joke helps illustrate a cornerstone principle for understanding news: news is a representation of reality. It is not a picture of reality itself but rather a selection of what happens every day in the world. And news media is one of those institutions of society that are constructed and shaped by powerful forces. Institutions are responsible for codifying and circulating these constructions, which only serves to reinforce them.

This is not a judgment, but it is a fact. News—however we define it—can do an excellent job of bringing us the accurate information we need, but it's important to realize that rather than being a complete picture of daily life, news is shaped by social structures and constructed by humans as they make decisions about what deserves to be news and what it should look like. Just as a photographer has to decide where to point her camera or a blogger has to select his topic, anyone who wants to share information has to decide what to focus on and how they will tell their story. Scholars call this *framing*, or the idea that news messages not only draw our attention to certain events and issues but also place them into a context that produces certain meanings.[39] For example, activists demonstrating on the steps of city hall could be described as passionate defenders of an important cause or as a nuisance that disrupted the day's business. When a country is engaged in military action overseas, news media can frame the story as a patriotic mission to bring democracy to the oppressed or as an undue interference in a sovereign nation's affairs. How a message is framed produces what most people think of as bias, or the tendency to prefer one viewpoint over another. But framing is also the chief way that news contributes to the social construction of reality. The way the world is presented to us shapes how we see the world.

The constructed nature of news was perhaps more evident decades ago when the only news available to most people came from a daily newspaper and a few broadcast television stations. If something didn't appear in one of those few outlets, it wasn't news. The explosion of information available in the digital age has vastly expanded the range of events and issues that qualify as news, and rather than news being the purview of a small group of elite gatekeepers, just about anyone can be a news producer. Today, it seems as if anything that could be considered remotely significant to us will make its way to our screen. While this revolution has given a voice to a wide range of viewpoints and offered many benefits, there's still a finite amount of news and information that appears in front of us on any given day, a fact that has significant implications. Figure 1.1 illustrates the general flow of news messages, from production to consumption. The process isn't always this linear, but it's a helpful way to think about how messages never exist in a vacuum—they are created in complex contexts, and they have complex effects.

News frames are put in place by a host of forces that influence what news ends up looking like, a process scholars refer to as *gatekeeping*. The news we receive gets filtered through a variety of gatekeepers—including ourselves—before it reaches us. Traditionally, gatekeepers have been the editors that made decisions about what becomes news and what gets left out. Today, individuals have far more power and influence over the news we consume and can act as our own gatekeeping force. But much remains out of our control as gatekeeping has changed and taken

FIGURE 1.1 How news messages are shaped, presented, and consumed.

new shapes. Whether a piece of information is created by a journalist at *The New York Times*, an opinion writer at *Teen Vogue*, an environmental activist promoting a cause on Facebook, or a friend posting to their Instagram account, they all will be influenced by their own personal goals, their own prior knowledge, their set of professional skills, the resources at their disposal, the expectations of their bosses and their audiences, and the economic and technological realities of digital media, where computer algorithms and profit motives play a major role in how messages get delivered.

After gatekeepers shape a message and frames are put in place, news plays a role in telling citizens what to think about in the first place, a process called *agenda-setting.*[40] If something appears in the news, that thing is now more likely to be on your radar, or more *salient* to you. A topic often doesn't enter the public agenda until it has entered the news agenda. For example, American news coverage of a 2014 outbreak of the Ebola virus contributed to public panic in the United States even though only five Americans were ever infected. Agenda-setting by news media is particularly strong in areas where Americans have little to no first-hand experience, such as national and international issues. In elections, voters are not likely to be concerned about an issue unless it gets significant media attention, as with, in 2016, Hillary Clinton's emails or Donald Trump's "locker room talk."

News not only draws our attention to certain issues and events but also shapes our beliefs and values related to ourselves and the world around us. That's called *socialization*, which is often defined as the process of internalizing the norms and ideologies of society. An *ideology* is a belief system that reflects how we see the world. Ideologies are usually thought of as political (e.g., liberal, conservative) or economic (e.g., capitalist, communist), but they can also reflect other ideas about how to organize society, such as racism or feminism. Many forces contribute to our socialization, ranging from family and friends to institutions such as school and church. News media is only one of these forces, but it does serve to help establish and reinforce our worldview.

One last sociological concept worth mentioning helps us examine the balance of power among the different layers of choice and influence in the information environment. *Structure* and *agency* are the yin and yang of our capacity to control our own lives. Structure refers to the organization of society and its influence on the range of options available to us. Agency is our ability to act independently and make our own choices. Individuals almost always have some agency to shape their own experience. For example, a journalist working for a news organization can usually select at least some of the stories she will cover and can decide whom to interview and what context to provide. At the same time, that journalist's agency can be influenced by resources such as time and money, professional expectations, the demands of her editor, the availability of sources, economic imperatives of media owners, and even the laws and policies that determine how she can legally operate. Often, these influences are limiting, as with time constraints or demands for profit, but structural influences also can enhance agency, as with the First Amendment's legal protection of press freedom.

The concepts described here are just a rough starting point, but these will help as we look deeper into the structures and institutions of the news and information environment. They will help you develop your sociological imagination and question some of the arrangements we take for granted in our daily lives.

Critical Contexts for News Literacy

If you read the headlines about news literacy, what I've described so far might sound far off. Particularly in the context of fake news and misinformation on the web, news literacy has often been framed in news media as the checking of facts and spotting of hoaxes. Even the idea of news literacy is socially constructed! I realize what I'm presenting here is something of a departure. However, 20 years of studying, teaching, and creating media have shown me how much more there is to know about our news media systems and their implications for democracy. It's my firm belief that, short of offering everyone a graduate education in journalism and media studies, it is possible to teach news literacy basics in terms of the critical contexts that shape the way we produce and consume information.

Is news literacy really just media literacy? What's the difference? I refer to both in this book even though my focus is certainly on news literacy. I'm sure some who read this will flatly disagree with my argument that news literacy should do all that I've described. It's true that the critical contexts approach has historically been part of the broader domain of media literacy—and sometimes even a contested one at that by educators who see it as "too political" or otherwise controversial. I'm sympathetic to these concerns since I know how difficult it can be to navigate certain topics even in my university classrooms, not to mention primary and secondary educational environments. But I also think we can do better. A failure to embrace these larger contextual issues only does a disservice to our students. It makes them more removed from the structures of society and the ways power is created and protected, and it makes students feel more powerless and helpless in the face of overwhelming odds.

I think if educators really care about education and about democratic life, they will see the importance of addressing critical contexts, and that's true whether their stated focus is news literacy specifically or media literacy more broadly. Although I do see news literacy as part of the broader domain of media literacy rather than a separate educational endeavor, I also see news literacy as distinct. Media literacy is often too broad in its focus and is forced to cover too much ground, especially when it comes to art and entertainment media, which can run far afield of news and information even if the critical contexts are related. So my approach to news literacy maintains a narrow focus on news and information content, and the critical contexts approach I've described encourages a broader understanding of the news media landscape and highlights the role of citizens and news in democratic life.

With this in mind, I present the *five stages of news literacy*, which roughly maps onto the content of this book (see Table 1.4). News literacy begins with the analysis of news content and the need to examine and verify claims. Next, we need to learn about the forces that influence news and information content, beginning with the routines and conventions of journalists and other information producers and ending with a broad understanding of news media systems. After that, we turn inward and examine the psychology of information production and consumption, and finally, we take responsibility for our news consumption and spread the word about news literacy in order to increase awareness and help others acquire the knowledge, skills, and attitudes of critical news literacy.

Going forward, the plan for this book is to establish the foundation of a contextual approach to news literacy and then to examine four specific contextual domains that form the core of news literacy in democratic life. The book wraps up by examining the challenges for news literacy and providing a path forward. We'll proceed as follows.

Chapter 2 examines what citizens know about the news and the theoretical foundations of news literacy. Although critical knowledge about news media structures is limited, research has found a variety of positive traits associated with news literacy including knowledge of current events, political participation, and political self-efficacy, or the belief that one's voice matters. This is significant because educating people about news media should be a lot easier than altering faulty beliefs and preconceptions.

Part II of the book dives into the critical contexts that are central to news literacy and its role in democratic life. Chapter 3 examines the dark and light sides of journalism including its normative goals and strengths as well as its structural limitations and weaknesses. Economic and technological changes have altered the

TABLE 1.4 The five stages of news literacy.

News Literacy Stage	Related Knowledge, Skills, and Attitudes
1. Fighting "fake news"	Spot hoaxes, verify claims, vet sources
2. Understanding news production	Identify news routines and conventions that influence content
3. Examining news media systems	Understand the role of political economic structures of news media and tensions between democracy and capitalism
4. Is it all in your head?	Understand the role of cognitive bias, motivated reasoning, and analytical thinking in personal news use
5. Spreading the word	Share information responsibly and help others acquire the knowledge, skills, and attitudes of critical news literacy

traditional news landscape, creating an opportunity for the spread of misinformation and "fake news." Chapter 4 looks at the structure of the news media system and the laws and policies that helped get us where we are today. Reviewing a brief history of legal and regulatory frameworks is important for understanding how news works. Broader economic trajectories around the globe such as neoliberalism also influence the current status quo.

Chapter 5 looks specifically at the political economy of the internet and how what was once a great opportunity for democracy and education has given way to commercialism and monopoly power. There is much we can do to alter this course and return to the original ideals of a networked society. Chapter 6 turns the focus to humans and the psychological processes that influence the creation and consumption of news. Evolutionary and political psychology can tell us a great deal about the limitations of human cognition in the face of digital technologies.

Part III turns to the future and considers ways news literacy can contribute to improving the conditions of democratic life. Chapter 7 discusses the many reasons to be hopeful even in this difficult environment and offers suggestions for taking our newfound news literacy and turning it into action. It also focuses on the critical perspective that is at the heart of news literacy and democratic society. To get to the truth, citizens must be encouraged to ask good questions and to engage with difficult issues rather than tune out. We must avoid a state of "critical apathy," where we spin our wheels analyzing content without ever making any changes to the structures that produce it.

The best thing about learning news literacy is getting to put it to use right away in your everyday life and being able to share it with others. As you continue your journey, I hope you will immediately see how knowledge about news can benefit you and those around you. News is so ingrained in our lives that it can be hard to take a step back and see it in a new light. I hope that by showing the complexity and messiness of our news media systems, this book helps you see the world a bit more clearly and, most importantly, makes you want to know more.

Questions for Discussion

1. What is the difference between "content" and "context" when it comes to news and information? Give examples of each.
2. Looking beyond "fake news," what challenges are presented by the modern news and information environment?
3. In what ways has misinformation been a problem prior to the digital age? What is similar and what is different when comparing past and present?
4. Does the surplus of news and information in the digital age make it easier or harder to be well informed? What is the impact of having access to so much content on democratic life?
5. Are you optimistic about our ability to improve the news and information environment and its role in democratic life? Why or why not?

Notes

1. Walter Lippmann, *Public Opinion* (New York: Harcourt, 1922), 3.
2. Lippmann, *Public Opinion*, 4.
3. David Foster Wallace and Robert Atwan, eds., *The Best American Essays 2007*, 2007 ed. edition (Boston: Mariner Books, 2007), xxiii.
4. "Word of the Year 2016 Is. . .," Oxford Dictionaries, accessed June 15, 2018, https://en.oxforddictionaries.com/word-of-the-year/word-of-the-year-2016.
5. See Daniel Kahneman, *Thinking, Fast and Slow* (New York: Farrar, Straus and Giroux, 2011).
6. Steven Erlanger, "'Fake News,' Trump's Obsession, Is Now a Cudgel for Strongmen," *The New York Times*, December 12, 2017, sec. World, https://www.nytimes.com/2017/12/12/world/europe/trump-fake-news-dictators.html.
7. Benedict Carey, "'Fake News': Wide Reach but Little Impact, Study Suggests," *The New York Times*, January 2, 2018, sec. Health, www.nytimes.com/2018/01/02/health/fake-news-conservative-liberal.html.
8. Margaret Leslie Davis, *The Lost Gutenberg: The Astounding Story of One Book's Five-Hundred-Year Odyssey* (Penguin, 2019), 212.
9. Jacob Soll, "The Long and Brutal History of Fake News," *Politico Magazine*, accessed June 7, 2018, http://politi.co/2FaV5W9.
10. Adrian Chen, "The Fake-News Fallacy," *The New Yorker*, August 28, 2017, www.newyorker.com/magazine/2017/09/04/the-fake-news-fallacy.
11. Chen, "The Fake-News Fallacy."
12. Soroush Vosoughi, Deb Roy, and Sinan Aral, "The Spread of True and False News Online," *Science* 359, no. 6380 (March 9, 2018): 1146–51, https://doi.org/10.1126/science.aap9559.
13. Kenneth Rapoza, "Can 'Fake News' Impact The Stock Market?," accessed June 7, 2018, www.forbes.com/sites/kenrapoza/2017/02/26/can-fake-news-impact-the-stock-market/#4ea9491c2fac.
14. Adam Goldman, "The Comet Ping Pong Gunman Answers Our Reporter's Questions," *The New York Times*, December 7, 2016, sec. U.S., www.nytimes.com/2016/12/07/us/edgar-welch-comet-pizza-fake-news.html.
15. Rebecca Hersher, "What Happened When Dylann Roof Asked Google For Information About Race?," *NPR.org*, accessed June 7, 2018, www.npr.org/sections/thetwo-way/2017/01/10/508363607/what-happened-when-dylann-roof-asked-google-for-information-about-race.
16. "Climate Change in the American Mind: March 2018" (Yale Program on Climate Change Communication, 2018), http://climatecommunication.yale.edu/publications/climate-change-american-mind-march-2018/.
17. Janna Anderson and Lee Rainie, "The Future of Truth and Misinformation Online," *Pew Research Center: Internet, Science & Tech* (blog), October 19, 2017, www.pewinternet.org/2017/10/19/the-future-of-truth-and-misinformation-online/.
18. Amy Mitchell, "Key Findings on the Traits and Habits of the Modern News Consumer," July 7, 2016, www.pewresearch.org/fact-tank/2016/07/07/modern-news-consumer/.
19. See Reuters Institute for the Study of Journalism, "Reuters Institute Digital News Report," 2018, www.digitalnewsreport.org/.
20. Clifford G. Christians et al., *Normative Theories of the Media: Journalism in Democratic Societies* (Urbana: University of Illinois Press, 2009), 91.
21. "Founders Online: From Thomas Jefferson to Edward Carrington, 16 January 1787," accessed June 15, 2018, http://founders.archives.gov/documents/Jefferson/01-11-02-0047.
22. "Image 2 of Thomas Jefferson to John Norvell, June 11, 1807," image, Library of Congress, Washington, D.C. 20540 USA, accessed June 15, 2018, www.loc.gov/resource/mtj1.038_0592_0594/?sp=2&st=text.

23. "Image 2 of Thomas Jefferson to John Norvell, June 11, 1807."
24. John Milton, *Areopagitica: A Speech of Mr. John Milton for the Liberty of Unlicensed Printing, to the Parliament of England* (Grolier club, 1890).
25. Burdette Kinne, "Voltaire Never Said It!," *Modern Language Notes* 58, no. 7 (1943): 534–35, https://doi.org/10.2307/2911066.
26. See Robert McChesney, *Telecommunications, Mass Media, and Democracy: The Battle for the Control of U.S. Broadcasting, 1928–1935* (New York: Oxford University Press, 1993).
27. Klint Finley, "What Is Net Neutrality? The Complete WIRED Guide | WIRED," *Wired*, May 9, 2018, www.wired.com/story/guide-net-neutrality/.
28. See Ben H. Bagdikian, *The New Media Monopoly* (Boston: Beacon Press, 2004).
29. Renee Hobbs and Amy Jensen, "The Past, Present, and Future of Media Literacy Education," *Journal of Media Literacy Education* 1, no. 1 (2009): 2–3.
30. Maddie Crum, "After Trump Was Elected, Librarians Had To Rethink Their System For Fact-Checking," *Huffington Post*, March 9, 2017, sec. Culture & Arts, www.huffingtonpost.com/entry/after-trump-librarians-develop-new-fact-checking-system_us_58c071d3e4b0ed7182699786.
31. Bill Kovach and Tom Rosenstiel, *Blur: How to Know What's True in the Age of Information Overload*, Reprint edition (New York: Bloomsbury USA, 2011), 202.
32. Kovach and Rosenstiel, *Blur*, 32.
33. James Klurfeld and Howard Schneider, "News Literacy: Teaching the Internet Generation to Make Reliable Information Choices" (Brookings Institute Center for Effective Public Management, June 2014), www.brookings.edu/wp-content/uploads/2016/06/Klurfeld-SchneiderNews-Literacyupdated-7814.pdf.
34. "Introducing IMVAIN," Stony Brook University Center for News Literacy, 2019, https://digitalresource.center/content/introducing-imvain.
35. "About," News Literacy Project, 2019, https://newslit.org/about/.
36. David C. Barker, "Distrust of Fact-Checking Is Not Restricted to the Right," *Vox*, July 3, 2017, www.vox.com/mischiefs-of-faction/2017/7/3/15893800/distrust-of-fact-checking-partisan.
37. C. Wright Mills and Todd Gitlin, *The Sociological Imagination*, 40th anniversary edition (Oxford, England and New York: Oxford University Press, 2000), 3.
38. *The Empire Strikes Back*, directed by Irvin Kershner (Los Angeles, CA: 20th Century Fox, 1980), film.
39. See Robert M. Entman, "Framing: Toward Clarification of a Fractured Paradigm," *Journal of Communication* 43, no. 4 (December 1, 1993): 51–58, https://doi.org/10.1111/j.1460-2466.1993.tb01304.x.
40. See Maxwell E. McCombs and Donald L. Shaw, "The Agenda-Setting Function of Mass Media," *The Public Opinion Quarterly* 36, no. 2 (1972): 176–87; Maxwell McCombs, *Setting the Agenda: Mass Media and Public Opinion* (Cambridge: Polity Press, 2014).

2

WHAT CITIZENS KNOW ABOUT NEWS AND WHY IT MATTERS

A primary stream of inquiry in political science works to understand and measure what citizens know about politics and governance. Pollsters gauge political knowledge by asking, for example, whether someone can correctly identify the sitting vice-president by name or say which branch of government determines the constitutionality of laws or tell which political party is more conservative.[1] These knowledge questions are different from the more familiar type of public opinion polling that asks about attitudes and opinions regarding specific political candidates or toward specific policies such as those related to immigration or health care or military action. The more foundational fact-based approach to political knowledge seeks to identify what people know about government and how it works. This kind of contextual knowledge, the thinking goes, is key to being able to navigate political affairs and contribute effectively to a self-governing society. Citizens with higher levels of political knowledge are more likely to be informed and engaged participants in democratic life and are more likely to feel like they have a say in what happens.

But what do citizens know about news media? What should they know? These are underappreciated questions, considering the central role news plays in democratic life. If the research on political knowledge tells us anything—that contextual knowledge about government and the political system is important to informed participation—then the same should hold true for knowledge about news media. Because news media is the chief method for citizens to learn about public affairs and democratic governance, it makes sense to suppose that people need to know factual information about how the system works beyond their general opinions about the best and worst sources of news or their vague notions about how journalists do their jobs. Knowing basic facts about the structures and institutions of the information environment should help citizens be more engaged and informed participants in democratic life and should feel like their voice matters.

The emerging research in news literacy is both disappointing and encouraging. Our levels of knowledge about news media—that is, our news literacy—are not great. For something that consumes so much of our time and attention, many of us know surprisingly little about the information environments we live in. At the same time, research suggests that, first of all, it is possible to increase people's levels of news literacy through a range of educational interventions (like this book and the class you might be reading it in). And, second, research has found that higher levels of news literacy correspond in general to the kinds of positive social outcomes we would hope to see: higher levels of political participation, greater knowledge of current events, lower endorsement of misinformation, and higher levels of *political self-efficacy*, or the idea that people can have a say in the world around them. Seeing this connection between news literacy and positive political engagement helps scholars identify and assess the goals and functions of news literacy education.

In this chapter, to learn more about news literacy and its role in democratic life, we'll first review the ways people access news and learn about the world. After that, we'll examine the theoretical and empirical foundations of news literacy and look at the research that measures various types of news knowledge and motivations as well as the connections between news literacy and political engagement. Although this literature reveals a significant lack of knowledge about the news media system and a general lack of engagement in the face of an overwhelming high-choice media environment, research also has found positive relationships between news literacy and participation in democratic life. The emerging evidence suggests that news literacy is important not just because it seems like stuff people should know but because it is positively linked to the goals most of us have for democratic society. In light of this, it can be seen as a major problem that only some citizens have access to news literacy education; a *news literacy gap* could leave some citizens behind when it comes to effective participation in democratic life. Finally, this chapter discusses how low levels of news literacy can be connected to an underperforming news media system that fails to provide information citizens really need; in other words, an insufficient supply of quality news and information can be linked to a lack of public demand for it.

What Is News Good For?

Before diving into research on news consumption and news literacy, it's useful to consider the role of news in society—not just the theoretical role it plays in democracy but the way people actually use news in day-to-day life. Why do we consume news in the first place, and what is it good for?

For starters, news is not necessarily the best place to look for an accurate portrayal of reality. Our perceptions of what is important or problematic or risky are easily skewed by the representations of reality that appear in the news and infor-mation environment. As cognitive psychologist Steven Pinker argues, "News is a misleading way to understand the world. It's always about events that happened and not about things that didn't happen."[2] The stuff that gets attention can make it seem like everything is constantly terrible. In his recent work on social progress, Pinker shows how the use of reason and evidence as ways of understanding the world has improved social conditions almost universally over past centuries and decades. Data suggest that life on planet Earth has generally gotten better based on major metrics of progress, such as levels of violence and poverty, which are down, and life expectancy and leisure time, which are up.[3] Some people have a hard time with these conclusions, noting that suffering still continues and progress is hardly inevitable. These points are true, of course; if they were not, there would be no need for this book because everything would be great and news would have nothing to report. I don't think Pinker aims to undermine or belittle the suffer-ing that goes on in the world, but his point is a good one. While there will always be work to do if we want to improve the human condition (and we should), it's important to note that if we really look back, we can see how humans have been pretty good at making things better overall. This is some helpful context we can bring to our news consumption in order to remember that news is not reality itself but only a representation of it.

Well, duh, you might say. Of course, news is about bad stuff—that's what makes it news! Well, yes, to some extent, but why? There are a number of reasons for this that we will explore in the chapters to come. But one reason is our own desire to know what's going on around us and to be attuned to any threats or dangers that might come our way. This is what has been called our "awareness instinct," which helps us stay safe and live life.[4] At one time, humans had an understandable need to know about things, like the proximity of a roving band of saber-toothed tigers or a rival tribe planning a village invasion. Today, our concerns are different, but we still have an instinct to be aware of threats in our environment, such as wildfires, toxic drinking water, child kidnappers, terrorism, corporate fraud, gov-ernment embezzlement, and other violations of legal and social contracts. Having an awareness of these threats is important, and we should be grateful to those who work to keep us informed. At the same time, it's good to remember to view threats in proportion to the danger they actually represent and to understand that this is not something news outlets are always interested in. For example, terrorism, because it is terrifying, gets loads of attention, but the actual risk it poses for most humans is insignificant compared to other issues we face.

Our instincts for awareness are part of our DNA as humans. To satisfy these instincts, news or something like it has been around as long as humans have lived. Most of human history has been dominated by an oral tradition of sharing knowledge and information through word of mouth, often by poets and story-tellers. Even as written language developed, literacy rates were extremely low as monks and scribes recorded religious texts and philosophical treatises. The first public message boards were used by ancient Romans more than 2,000 years ago, but the arrival of the printing press around 1450 is what allowed news media and mass communication to really take off. With what was essentially the world's first Xerox machine, sharers of information could now make mechanical copies of documents rather than having to copy by hand. The world's first newspaper came along in Germany in 1605, and newspapers spread rapidly after that.

The functions of early newspapers fluctuated based on the tensions posed by state control, commercial pressure, and the desire of publishers to provide a public forum free from outside influence. The early days of print media were marked by state and religious control of information and low levels of literacy. As Enlightenment ideals of liberty and reason arrived, many publishers were free and eager to engage in political discourse and to participate in what German scholar Jurgen Habermas calls the "bourgeois" *public sphere*, which flourished in the 17th century. For the first time, ordinary private citizens could discuss public life without fear of reprisal as public forums gained autonomy from state control and as literacy spread. Newspapers were often aligned with specific political candidates and parties and engaged in fierce ideological debates about social and economic policies. But conditions changed as industry and commerce began to take root in the 1800s, and the bourgeois public sphere floundered. By this time, according to Habermas, the press "could abandon its polemical stance and concentrate on the profit opportunities for a commercial business. In Great Britain, France, and the United States at about the same time (the 1830s) the way was paved for this sort of transition from a press that took ideological sides to one that was primarily a business."[5] Modern news media evolved only with the arrival of the 20th century, as pressures toward commercialization and professionalism gave rise to modern ideals of neutrality and objectivity.

Today's news media and our consumption of it reflects these contradictory origins. While commercial imperatives remain central, some news looks more like the partisan press of the early 1800s. We sense that news plays some central but undefined role in our shared civic life, so we choose our preferred outlets and passively consume what is presented as the news of the day. Some people have a sense that news is not supposed to be biased, so they are on guard against spin and propaganda. But just as many of us choose not to consume news at all, or we limit our consumption to a quick scan of headlines that appear in our newsfeeds or at the top of our homepages. There is no shortage of available information; indeed, the glut of news we are forced to contend with presents a paradox. We have access to more information than ever, but we hardly know what to do with it.

While our tools for representation have grown more sophisticated, our depictions and our perceptions have not. Our information environment certainly includes a broader range of subjects and voices, but we are collectively worse than ever at creating, consuming, and sharing accurate or reliable information. We are not growing more informed, and we are no more engaged.[6] You might think that the increase in news and information in the digital age would translate to an increase in democratic participation, but this is not the case. According to a report by Sweden's International Institute for Democracy and Electoral Assistance,

> global voter turnout was fairly stable between the 1940s and the 1980s, falling only slightly from 78 per cent to 76 per cent over the entire period. It then fell sharply in the 1990s to 70 percent, and continued its decline to reach 66 per cent in the period of 2011–15.[7]

In general, data show widespread low levels of and declines in knowledge and participation, which has major implications for democratic theory.[8] As political theory scholar Phil Parvin notes, "Empirical trends strongly suggest that any model of democratic decision-making and legitimacy needs to contend with the fact of widespread political disengagement and low levels of political knowledge."[9]

So what is news good for if it's not making us more informed or engaged? The fact that people continue to consume news in various forms suggests that, in some sense, the news media environment does an excellent job of satisfying our awareness instincts. But the fact that democratic outcomes related to knowledge and participation have not fared better suggests that something is wrong with news, or with us, or both. Our awareness instinct may be satisfied by learning about house fires and political scandals, but those stories aren't going to do much to make us better citizens. That's why the best news content often focuses on trends and patterns and puts seemingly random daily occurrences into larger contexts that provide meaning. Unfortunately, few news providers are set up to operate like this. When news outlets and web platforms depend on your attention for ratings and clicks, it's often easier and more important to produce results by publishing news that will accomplish these goals.

The basic question of the role of news media and its capacity to inform citizens is not a new one. As I mentioned at the outset, in his 1922 book, *Public Opinion*, journalist and political pundit Walter Lippmann pointed out the basic disconnect between the realities of the world and the representations that appear in news media. "The world outside and the pictures in our heads" is the phrase he used to describe the gap between empirical reality and what we conjure in our minds based on the information we have access to.[10] Lippmann was quite down on democracy and didn't hold much hope for informed citizen participation. Ultimately, he proposed that government be run primarily by experts who were best equipped to make informed decisions about difficult issues. Lippmann's prescription is not that far off from what we have today—limited participatory democracy with a heavy reliance on administrative agencies staffed by unknown bureaucrats who carry out the day-to-day affairs of government.

One of Lippmann's contemporaries was John Dewey, a philosopher and education reformer who also grappled with the difficult realities of democracy. The two are sometimes presented as having been engaged in a debate over the possibility of democracy, which isn't quite accurate, but they did offer divergent perspectives.[11]

Dewey agreed with Lippmann's concerns about the role of news media in democracy and called Lippmann's work "perhaps the most effective indictment of democracy as currently conceived ever penned."[12] Democracy was fundamentally flawed, as news—with its narrow focus on decontextualized events—could not accurately depict reality and citizens could not accurately perceive it. As a solution, Dewey suggested that news media should depict daily events "in the light of a continuing study and record of underlying conditions."[13] By putting daily life into broader social contexts, citizens could gain a more complete picture of reality. Dewey rejected Lippmann's vision of elite management of public affairs and instead called for "continuous reporting of the news as the truth, events signalized to be sure, but signals of hidden facts, of facts set in relation to one another, a picture of situations on which men can act intelligently."[14] In other words, news should truthfully present events in contexts that give meaning to daily occurrences so citizens are poised to make good decisions and act intelligently.

As we will see, the kind of reporting Dewey calls for is increasingly hard to come by. It is expensive and time-consuming, and when it is produced, it is not widely consumed. However, serious investigations boldly situated in meaningful contexts can end up having major effects on society. For example, reporting by the *Boston Globe* and others beginning in 2002 led to significant changes in the Catholic Church when patterns of sexual abuse by priests were brought to light. Similarly, many factors led to the resignation of President Richard Nixon in 1974, but years of reporting by the *Washington Post* and others brought attention to the abuses of power that led to his downfall. In the 1950s and 1960s, bold newspaper editors in the American South covered racial conflict and the Civil Rights movement in ways that influenced American attitudes and contributed to increased equality for African-Americans. These are just a few high-water marks in journalism history, moments where reporters, editors, and owners worked against difficult odds to ascertain and share the best available version of the truth.

On the other hand, when the press fails, the consequences can be just as significant. Reporting after the September 11, 2001, terrorist attack closely followed the narrative of the George W. Bush administration and failed to ask tough questions about how to respond. In the patriotic fervor that followed, the military response went unquestioned, and the role of Saudi Arabia, home to 15 of the 19 hijackers, received hardly any attention, partly because of the otherwise friendly relationship between the United States and the Saudi government. News media went on to provide overwhelming support for the 2003 invasion of Iraq, asking virtually no tough questions about the rationale for war or the evidence on which it was based.[15] Another missed story was the 2009 economic collapse and the recession that followed. Few saw the impending crisis coming despite reliable predictions, and the subsequent bailout of corporate giants received relatively little scrutiny. The causes of the crisis went largely unreported, and the markets remain relatively unregulated, paving the way for yet another collapse. The general trends toward deregulation of various industries across the developed world deserve more attention from news media because of the potential implications for the citizens they purport to serve. This is especially true as major issues such as climate change and global inequality loom large on the horizon.

These are extraordinary examples of the impact of news, both positive and negative. They are perhaps the stories that matter most—on abuses of institutional power, military intervention, economic stability—but they are not the day-to-day. Daily journalism is more likely to be centered on the diligent gathering of facts by hardworking reporters who, rather than hawking an agenda or grinding an axe, are most interested in collecting and sorting through mundane details in order to provide a comprehensive account of significant events and issues. They cover city council meetings, state government, court rulings, and so on. Reporters are constrained by many factors, as we will learn, but newsgatherers are more likely to be "biased" toward finishing their story by deadline and making it as complete as possible. As *Washington Post* columnist David Broder once put it,

> I would like us to say—over and over, until the point has been made—that the newspaper that drops on your doorstep is a partial, hasty, incomplete, inevitably somewhat flawed and inaccurate rendering of some of the things we have heard about in the past 24 hours—distorted, despite our best efforts to eliminate gross bias, by the very process of compression that makes it possible for you to lift it from the doorstep and read it in about an hour.[16]

News is never perfect, but when hardworking journalists do their jobs well, citizens benefit.

Now a key point: news that contains inaccuracies or omits a relevant source or neglects a perspective is not the same as "fake news." It's somewhat devastating that this needs to be explained, but this is the information environment we are in. "Fake news" is an oxymoron. "News" is never "fake." Real news—the kind that aims to faithfully represent major events and issues of the day—if nothing else, is truthful, at least to the best of human ability. It might contain errors, but that doesn't make it fake. For example, even when *The New York Times* failed to question some key pieces of evidence in the case for the 2003 invasion of Iraq, this omission—to which their editors later fessed up—did not make the reporting fake.[17] It was real reporting based on real newsgathering and real sources. It was certainly flawed, and the consequences were significant, but that doesn't discount the other high-quality journalism the organization has produced. To the contrary, the fact that the organization admitted their errors demonstrates accountability and transparency, which are hallmarks of trustworthy news organizations. In today's environment, it's more important than ever to learn the difference between organizations and individuals who have at least some public service objective—even if they are also commercially driven—and those who have no purpose other than to gain power or profit to serve their ideological and financial goals.

Where Do People Get News?

Believe it or not, most Americans still say television is their number one source for news, but the internet is catching up fast, especially for young people, and is likely to overtake television soon. A 2017 Pew report found 43 percent of Americans say they often get news online compared to 50 percent who say they often get news on television, including local, network, and cable television news. But strong trends show all demographics increasingly prefer online news. Among 18- to 29-year-olds, the internet is the preferred source at 50 percent, while television is a common source for only 27 percent. Radio remains a common news source for 25 percent and print newspapers for 18 percent.[18] Another 2017 report found Americans saying they turn to a variety of social media sites for news. Twenty percent said they "often" get news from social media, and another 27 percent said they "sometimes" do. Twitter, YouTube, and Snapchat are growing as news sources, while Facebook and Reddit remain popular favorites for news. Facebook is dominant, with 66 percent of American adults saying they use the site, and 45 percent of those say they get news there.[19] However, despite this heavy social media usage, people report extremely low trust in what they see there; only 5 percent of adults who use the web say they have a lot of trust in the information they get from social media.[20]

Globally, these trends are relatively consistent, although some differences appear from one country to the next. Around the world, large majorities say they closely follow national news (86 percent) and local news (78 percent).[21] The 2018 Digital News Report by the Reuters Institute for the Study of Journalism, which surveyed thousands of people from nearly 40 countries across 5 continents, found that 71 percent of people overall get news from television, but that ranges from 55 percent for 18- to 24-year-olds to 82 percent for those age 55 and up. The internet, including social media, is a news source for 82 percent of all people surveyed, while print comes in at 36 percent and radio at 33 percent. Reliance on social media for news has declined slightly from a 2013 peak at 51 percent to 45 percent in 2018. Nearly two-thirds of people access news through a "side door," meaning they are referred to news sites by social media, search engines, email, and alerts. Only 32 percent access news by visiting a news site directly. Messaging apps such as WhatsApp, which afford greater privacy, are on the rise in countries such as Malaysia and Brazil. When it comes to trust, 44 percent of people trust news overall, 51 percent trust the news that they themselves use, 34 percent trust search engine results, and only 23 percent trust news that appears on social media. More than half (54 percent) say they are concerned about sorting real from fake online, and the numbers are higher in more polarized countries such as Brazil (85 percent), Spain (69 percent), and the United States (64 percent).[22]

When looking at news use, all of these numbers are self-reported, so we have to take them with a grain of salt. Survey respondents can be inclined to inflate their reported news consumption because they want to see themselves as responsible, informed citizens even if they're not. Many people scan the headlines in their news feeds without clicking on or reading actual articles, so they might report this as news consumption even though it's really just a passive and superficial act. People routinely share articles they haven't even read. So the way people view their own news consumption can be quite subjective. Many social media users simply encounter news rather than seeking it out. Young people especially often say, "If something is important, it will find me." This is a form of *incidental exposure*, where people encounter news when they're doing or looking for something else. This is not strictly an online phenomenon; when people read a print newspaper, they often encounter front-page news they might not have been looking for on their way to the sports section or the crossword puzzle. Incidental exposure certainly affects how much news people end up seeing online, especially among 18- to 29-year-olds, of whom 88 percent say they use at least some form of social media.[23]

Critics have suggested that the online environment creates *filter bubbles*, where the computer algorithms behind Facebook and Google are customized so that users only see information that will interest and please them. Other evidence suggests that internet and social media users are actually exposed to a greater diversity of information, particularly when compared to someone who just watches cable television or sports all day. Most social media and search sites are *aggregators* that collect and display related items based on proprietary algorithms that change over time. (More on all of this in Chapters 5 and 6.) While users have some control over their news feeds, the behind-the-scenes calculations are generally hidden and are hard to know unless the companies who deploy them decide to reveal their secrets (which they typically don't). Facebook occasionally makes vague announcements about changes to their news feed algorithms, as when they announced in 2018 that they would begin showing more posts from friends and family, which meant less exposure for news outlets.

Like all social and search sites, Facebook is continually updating its algorithms to increase time spent on the site. Because "free" sites like Facebook and Google are funded primarily by advertising, they need to find ways to keep your eyeballs glued to the screen. Overall time spent on Facebook was down slightly in 2018, which means changes will continue to come. Facebook even began airing their own television ads to help convince users to keep coming back. Even with some decline in use, Facebook still has 1.4 billion *daily* users worldwide, so it's hard to underestimate the power of the company's influence and reach as well as its ability to collect and share data on its users. Together, Facebook and Google soak up two-thirds of all online advertising revenue and virtually all of the year-to-year growth in ad revenue, which means they have essentially monopolized the online environment. Of course, they produce no original content of their own; they merely aggregate. It's a valuable service, and it can even be good for incidental exposure, but it's been fairly bad news for news organizations who invest resources in original newsgathering only to have it monetized by others.

Even with customized news feeds and search results, many web users do not find the online experience entirely useful. Research and surveys demonstrate widespread confusion over the news media landscape. A 2017 Gallup survey found that 58 percent of Americans said the increase in available information makes it harder to be well-informed as opposed to the 38 percent who said it is easier.[24] That's a solid majority of people who find the glut of information out there to hurt more than it helps. The survey also found partisan differences. When asked if they felt enough information existed to sort out the facts, 72 percent of Democrats said "yes" as opposed to 46 percent of independents and only 31 percent of Republicans. So some people find the news landscape more manageable and reliable than others, and political affiliation is a big factor.

The glut of information alone is not the only problem. Knowing the contexts of what you're seeing or hearing is crucial to understanding the purpose of news content. For example, people have always had trouble separating news from opinion and fact from analysis, which can make it challenging to know the difference between straightforward reporting and spin and propaganda. As noted by Frank Sesno, a former CNN reporter and anchor who now runs George Washington University's School of Media and Public Affairs,

> One of the dangers is thinking that people know the difference between the editorial page and the front page, between a commentator or pundit commenting on something alongside a reporter who's supposed to be providing facts. In this environment, when you have news, talking points and opinions all colliding, it can be really disorienting to the audience.[25]

A basic component of news literacy is to know that these different information contexts exist and to be able to sort through them.

A Pew survey in 2018 found that Americans had difficulty with the relatively simple task of sorting fact-based statements from opinion-based statements.[26] Only 26 percent correctly identified five of five factual statements (e.g., "Spending on Social Security, Medicare, and Medicaid make up the largest portion of the U.S. federal budget") and 35 percent identified all five opinion statements (e.g., "Immigrants who are in the U.S. illegally are a very big problem for the country today"). Even with physical newspapers, which typically isolate and label opinion articles on specific pages inside the newspaper, readers are not sure about the difference. This is especially true online, where there is often no obvious differentiation and users also have to contend with blatant misinformation and propaganda. However, the Pew survey found that Americans with higher levels of political awareness or who consider themselves digitally savvy were around twice as likely to identify correct statements compared to those with low political awareness or digital savvy.

Young people, who are often thought to be among the most digitally savvy, actually have as hard a time as anyone in sorting through the glut of information out there. In a much-cited 2016 study of civic reasoning online by the Stanford History Education Group, researchers worked with more than 7,000 students from middle school to college and a range of demographic backgrounds across the United States. Students completed a variety of tasks, from identifying advertisements on a news website to deciding whether to trust the legitimacy of a photograph on a photo-sharing site to explaining why a given tweet might or might not provide useful information. The study's findings were stark:

> Overall, young people's ability to reason about the information on the Internet can be summed up in one word: *bleak*. Our "digital natives" may be able to flit between Facebook and Twitter while simultaneously uploading a selfie to Instagram and texting a friend. But when it comes to evaluating information that flows through social media channels, they are easily duped.[27]

The researchers provided a few suggestions for going forward, including designing new forms of classroom instruction and assessment to educate students to better evaluate information and spreading awareness of the problems they identified.

The challenges people face in navigating the news environment are reflected in their attitudes about news media. While most Americans say they believe news media are important to democracy, a majority say news media fail to perform this role well. Overall, trust in news media is at a historic low; only 33 percent have a positive view of news media according to Pew Research.[28] That's down from a 1976 high, when 72 percent of Americans said they trusted the media a "great deal" or a "fair amount," according to Gallup polling. When asked the same question in 2016, the number was 32 percent.[29] Today's low levels of trust depend dramatically on partisan affiliation. Republicans are much less likely than Democrats to say they trust news media or that news media are beneficial to the nation.[30] News consumption is also heavily influenced by partisan affiliation. People who report holding political views that are consistently liberal or conservative basically live in different information universes. Liberals consume a variety of mainstream sources such as *The New York Times*, CNN, NPR, and MSNBC, while conservatives are tightly clustered around a single source: Fox News.[31] What used to be a large mass audience for news has fragmented into partisan niches. This is part of a broader trend in American life as citizens and government have become more polarized and antagonistic.[32] As of 2018, a majority of Americans say the "fundamental design and structure" of government is in need of "significant changes" to make it work.[33]

Despite this rise in partisanship and concern about the function of government, extreme partisans and partisan news outlets are the exception, not the rule. More people report holding a moderate mix of political viewpoints or they simply do not know enough to take a position, and most news outlets still aim to provide nonpartisan content for large mass audiences. As political scientist Marcus Prior has found, the sense of widespread polarization does not reflect the population at large or the news media they consume. Highly partisan individuals may have a greater degree of influence and involvement in politics, but even these individuals, rather than being confined to strict partisan echo chambers, are exposed to a greater diversity of news content than other less partisan individuals.[34] As the authors of a Knight Foundation study put it,

> while digital media offer greater opportunity to construct echo chambers for a motivated few, the majority appears to continue to experience a largely mixed and centrist media environment. Even those who seek out and consume more ideologically extreme information sources seem to encounter cross-cutting content along the way.[35]

Despite the increase in polarization and the rise of fragmented niche audiences, it's possible that widespread consumption of the most popular mainstream sources will be the very thing that helps hold society together.[36]

The larger problem of today's news media environment may be the large numbers of citizens who can now easily avoid news altogether. Before the advent of digital media, citizens were fairly limited in their options, which made it harder to tune out. When the only channels on American television were the three major networks, if you wanted to watch TV at 6 p.m., you were watching the news. Today's *high-choice media environment* lets you pick from an array of non-news options. Instead of being confined to partisan echo chambers, more people are completely disconnected from the world of public affairs. Even the most popular cable news programs that draw audiences of two or three million viewers pale in comparison to popular prime time programming such as "The Good Doctor," "This Is Us," and "Young Sheldon," which routinely draw audiences of 10 to 20 million. The effect of this is to create a major gap in political engagement and civic participation, giving outsize influence over political life to extreme partisans who make the most noise while sidelining everyone else. As political science scholar Matt Levendusky has noted, "the growth of media choice strengthens the extremes while hollowing out the center, making the electorate more divided."[37]

How did we get here? A lack of knowledge about how the news media environment works is at least partly to blame for the fragmentation of audiences, along with heavy reliance on social media despite a lack of trust in it, frustration due to information overload, and the tendency to tune out altogether. A look at the research on what people know about news shows how a lack of knowledge makes a difficult task even harder.

The Theoretical and Empirical Foundations of News Literacy

As the news and information landscape has grown increasingly messy, a range of scholars, institutes, and others have produced a flurry of survey research, experiments, and reports trying to sort out not only the ongoing changes in news consumption, but also the kinds of knowledge citizens have about news today. But any time researchers attempt to measure and quantify something, it raises thorny questions about what we might expect or want people to know about news and how we might accurately assess that knowledge. Scholars call this "operationalizing" their variables, that is, turning an abstract concept into hard numbers. In these *quantitative* studies, researchers go to great lengths to design reliable surveys, but even the best of them are subject to interpretation and often rely on self-reporting. Quantitative researchers also conduct experiments in labs, which helps control outside influences but doesn't always reflect real-world conditions. A contrasting approach is *qualitative* research, where researchers conduct focus groups, interviews, and other methods to gather information and then attempt to explain what's happening, whereas quantitative researchers typically come up with a possible explanation first and then gather information to test the idea.

Either way, how do you define or quantify or measure ideas like "trust" or "skepticism" or "credibility" or "engagement"? A notoriously difficult concept to measure is "media consumption." What even counts as "media" these days? How might this differ from one person to the next? Do you even remember what media you consumed yesterday? What about "news literacy"? How would you define and measure that? As we have seen, there are many different approaches. The bottom line is that research is hard. It's difficult to get reliable measurements and explanations in the social sciences when dealing with such tricky subjects as humans and their often-inexplicable behavior. But that doesn't keep us from trying, and there is plenty of good scholarship out there—both *theoretical* (theory-based) and *empirical* (evidence-based)—that can inform our study of news literacy. So before we get into the actual findings from news literacy research, let's consider how this concept might be defined and measured in the first place.

Research focused specifically on news literacy is limited, but a handful of studies that do exist have my name on them. I began conducting and publishing research on news and media literacy in 2010, and, along with my excellent colleagues, I've worked to define and measure news literacy in a variety of settings. I bring this up not to toot my own horn but to begin to explain my particular approach to news literacy, which is different from some of the other approaches out there. My first published study found modest support for the idea that learning about the media system increased skepticism among news consumers.[38] In a simple experiment, college students either belonged to a test group that read a brief article about the pros and cons of corporate media ownership or belonged to a control group that read poetry. Afterwards, they all read news stories and assessed their credibility. Those who had learned about media ownership were more likely to say the news articles were less accurate or credible, which suggested they might view news through a more critical or skeptical lens when armed with a little contextual knowledge. This modest study conducted during my graduate education hardly produced definitive findings, but it was enough to suggest to me that the idea of teaching people about the news media system could help produce more savvy news consumers and, ultimately, provide a benefit to democratic society.

This idea was hardly mine. For decades, scholars, educators, activists, and others have been writing about different approaches to media literacy, which include a critical approach oriented toward broader contextual knowledge like the kind I advocate. The idea that media education should be rooted in an education in democracy, economics, history, and culture goes back to at least the 1970s, following the emergence of *critical pedagogy* and *critical and cultural media studies*, which emphasize the power relations that influence the production of media messages as well as the educational practices used to teach about the subject. Against this backdrop, modern media literacy emerged as a component of citizenship linked to inquiry-based learning about civics and social relations. In his 1985 book, *Teaching the Media*, Len Masterman suggested that media education include the study of the economics of the media and culture industries, and the power dynamics that influence media content. Masterman wrote that media education is

> an essential step in the long march towards a truly participatory democracy, and the democratization of our institutions. Widespread media literacy is essential if all citizens are to wield power, make rational decisions, become effective change-agents, and have an active involvement with the media.[39]

For Masterman and others, media literacy would give citizens the power to question and change their media environment and their society.

My approach to news literacy is rooted in the longstanding field of media literacy education and the critical tradition that is central to an effective examination of the broader news media environment and the forces that influence its content. But even among media literacy scholars, there is concern about the ideological implications of an explicitly critical approach to media literacy. As Renee Hobbs has noted,

> There is an obvious ideology that underlies even the most basic tenets of media literacy education—teaching students to question textual authority and to use reasoning to reach autonomous decisions. This agenda is radical enough, without adding additional baggage associated with other explicitly formulated political or social change objectives.[40]

However, media literacy scholars and educators have long agreed that media education should include these broad notions:

- media are constructed and construct reality
- the media have commercial implications
- media have ideological and political implications

- form and content are related in each medium, each of which has a unique aesthetic, codes and conventions
- receivers negotiate meaning in media[41]

These ideas emerged from the 1992 National Leadership Conference on Media Literacy, where prominent scholars and experts in the United States drew on models from other countries, especially the United Kingdom, Canada, and Australia, which proved to be ahead of the United States in developing media education. These five points show the consensus that media literacy is more than learning the techniques of media production or a narrow focus on the analysis of media texts. While these skills may be part of media education, students should also learn about the role of media in constructing social reality and the implications of media messages for democratic life.

The conference produced a now-widely embraced definition of *media literacy*: the ability to access, analyze, evaluate and communicate messages in a variety of forms. This broad definition intentionally covers a lot of territory in order to reflect and respect the diversity of approaches to media education. The conference report went on to note that the

> fundamental objective of media literacy is critical autonomy in relationship to all media. Emphases in media literacy training range widely, including informed citizenship, aesthetic appreciation and expression, social advocacy, self-esteem, and consumer competence. The range of emphases will expand with the growth of media literacy.[42]

In other words, media literacy is about fostering independent engagement and inquiry around media consumption whatever the educational focus may be.

The media literacy educators also agreed on a general pedagogical approach or a style of teaching that is typically embraced across the field. Like the ideas embedded in media education (i.e., construction, representation, ideology), the practice of teaching about media should reflect active, inquiry-based learning as opposed to being organized around teacher authority or rote memorization.

> No matter what the setting or project, but particularly for formal learning, media educators insist that the process of learning embody the concepts being taught. Thus, media literacy learning is hands-on and experiential, democratic (the teacher is researcher and facilitator), and process-driven.[43]

Many scholars and educators have emphasized the importance of student-centered learning in media education. The teacher is empowered to guide the process, but learning is more meaningful if meaning is established by the student, not the teacher. Renee Hobbs, a key leader in the field, has called for a "pedagogy of inquiry" at the center of media literacy: "The cultivation of an open, questioning, reflective, and critical stance towards symbolic texts should be the center pole of the media literacy umbrella, as it is the concept most likely to ensure its survival."[44] Hobbs has long sought to maintain a "big tent" for the field of media literacy, working to advance its acceptance by embracing the diversity of approaches.

Other scholars have been explicit about the need to focus on political and economic contexts of media production and consumption. The goal of media literacy, they say, is "to help people become sophisticated citizens rather than sophisticated consumers."[45] Media education should teach students to engage media texts, but it should also teach them to examine and challenge media institutions. As scholars Justin Lewis and Sut Jhally wrote in 1998,

> Media literacy, in short, is about more than the analysis of messages, it is about an awareness of why those messages are there. It is not enough to know that they are produced, or even how, in a technical sense, they are produced. To appreciate the significance of contemporary media, we need to know why they are produced, under what constraints and conditions, and by whom.[46]

Critics might say this type of conceptualization is too radical or ideological for media education. But Lewis and Jhally emphasize that this is not their aim. Rather, they propose only to demonstrate to students the factors that influence and control media content so that students can draw their own conclusions. Failing to do so is effectively an embrace of the status quo, which could be considered just as ideological as an attempt to challenge it. As Lewis and Jhally wrote, "We are advocating a view that recognizes that the world is always made by someone, and a decision to tolerate the status quo is as political as a more overtly radical act."[47]

Media literacy scholar James Potter helps to make this point that people should learn about media not merely to be inoculated against its evils or to automatically reject the status quo. Rather, media education should present a broad array of information and let learners draw their own conclusions. He writes:

> I argue that rejection of the ideology is not the goal; the goal, instead, should be to allow people to appreciate parts of the ideology that are functional for them and create new perspectives where the ideology is not functional for them. That is, the choice should be up to the individual. Mindlessly rejecting the media ideology *in toto* is not much better than mindlessly accepting it *in toto*.[48]

In other words, understanding the ideology or dominant systems of media is key to interpreting and decoding media messages, but it should be left up to individuals to decide for themselves what to do with this knowledge.

One way to think about media literacy comes from Potter's *cognitive model of media literacy*, which incorporates a variety of elements that influence a person's level of media literacy. Potter says his model requires more "conscious processing of information" and "preparation for exposures" than earlier conceptualizations of media literacy.[49] This model is useful because it breaks the broad concept of media literacy down into several important components. The foundation is five basic "knowledge structures," which include knowledge about media content, media industries, media effects, the real world, and the self. These interact with what Potter calls the "personal locus" or the combination of drives, needs, and intellectual abilities that influence how people construct meaning from the media they consume. The knowledge structures provide the basis on which people make decisions about media and process the information they consume. According to Potter:

> With knowledge in these five areas, people are much more aware during the information-processing tasks and are, therefore, more able to make better decisions about seeking out information, working with that information, and constructing meaning from it that will be useful to serve their own goals.[50]

In my own research with my colleagues Stephanie Craft and Adam Maksl, we adapted Potter's model to fit our approach to news literacy and constructed a way of measuring news literacy based on this theoretically informed definition.[51] Potter's first three "knowledge structures" include media content, industries, and effects. In our adaptation, knowledge about news content includes knowing about the values that underlie news and how it is constructed (for instance, knowing about the difference between journalism and public relations or knowing that news producers have influence over what gets aired on local television news). Knowledge about news industries refers to the impact of news media economics, ownership, and control of news organizations (that is, knowing that most media outlets are for-profit businesses and that concentration of media ownership has increased over the past few decades). Knowledge about news media effects includes knowing about the consequences of exposure to news (for example, knowing that most people think news affects other people more than it affects themselves and that people who watch a lot of television news tend to think the world is more violent and dangerous than it actually is).

The fourth knowledge structure of Potter's model is knowledge of the "real world," meaning a person's knowledge of the differences between reality and media depictions of it, and the fifth knowledge structure is "the self," which refers to awareness of our own motivations for seeking news content and whether we internalize news messages. In our adaptation, all five knowledge structures can play a role in assessing news literacy, but it's really the first three—content, industries, and effects—that seem most important. So far, the other components seem harder to assess and to connect to news literacy.

Potter's approach represents an attempt to pin down the necessary components of media literacy, and our adaptation of Potter's model to news literacy represents an attempt to turn each component into a set of real-life questions that we could use to begin to measure an individual's level of news literacy. (In our research, we called it "news media literacy" to show how our approach to news literacy was rooted in the already-established umbrella discipline of media literacy and to differentiate our approach from the content-oriented approach described in Chapter 1.) Our measure is an imperfect first-stab attempt at this, but it has been used in multiple studies by us and by other researchers as we all try to further develop this concept of news literacy and think of ways we might meaningfully describe and measure it.

It's worth noting that academics, administrators, policy makers, and others have become somewhat obsessed with measurement, particularly in the United States, sometimes to the detriment of actual learning. While assessment isn't inherently bad, the increase in standardized testing in the "No Child Left Behind" era since the early 2000s has sometimes led to a distortion of the goals of education as teachers "teach to the test" rather than being free to follow the curriculum that is best suited to their particular students. Similarly, communication and media research is heavily geared toward quantitative assessments of the subjects we study, which can certainly be useful but also can lead us to neglect the proverbial forest while we focus myopically on the trees. The scholarly journals that academics must publish in like to see original data of some kind, so there is a built-in bias toward measurement and quantification. This isn't all bad because research is meant to be slow and incremental, but it can also encourage us to obsess over minor or insignificant details and end up making minimal contributions to the critical issues we face in society. With news and media literacy, we certainly have a large enough body of existing evidence—about how the media system works, how content is produced, and how our personal psychology comes into play—to get a pretty good sense of what people should know in order to be news and media literate. However, empirical evidence plays an important role in policy making and school administration (as it should), so scholars do their best to find ways to produce data that will help us address the big questions around the connections between information, news, media, education, and democracy. Ultimately, we want to know two things: can you make someone more news literate, and what happens if you do?

What Does News Literacy Research Tell Us?

Among the variety of approaches that have emerged in the study of news literacy, many of the findings are disconcerting. Although many people demonstrate high levels of interest in news and heavy consumption of news on television and online, research and surveys generally find relatively low levels of knowledge about how news media work, how journalists do their jobs, how media ownership and control influences news content, and how the digital environment shapes their online experience.

In a massive study of 74,000 people around the world, the 2018 Digital News Report by the Reuters Institute for the Study of Journalism examined news literacy in 37 countries and measured people's knowledge about how news is made: who makes it, how it is selected, and how it is financed.[52] They asked three factual questions covering the role of advertising in providing financial support for public media, the difference between journalism and public relations, and how computer algorithms select content on Facebook. Notably, these issues reflect a contextual knowledge-based approach to news literacy rather than anything having to do with the analysis of specific pieces of content. (Also notably, this study relied on survey questions from my own past research with Craft and Maksl to inform the definition and measurement of news literacy.) In the Reuters survey, researchers found only 10 percent of respondents showed "very high" levels of news literacy, while 23 percent showed "high" levels, 34 percent showed "low," and 32 percent showed "very low" levels. Not terrible, but certainly not great.

Okay, but so what? Why does it matter whether people have any knowledge about where news comes from or how news is produced and consumed? Learning what people know about news media is one thing, but researchers also want to know what news knowledge will get you. For those who do have higher levels of news literacy, what other traits do they exhibit?

In the Reuters study, higher news literacy was associated with the use of newspapers and newspaper websites over television and with a very different approach to social media compared to the wider population. Those with higher literacy rely less on social media for news and seem to be more discerning when they do use it. They pay more attention to a range of credibility cues when deciding what to click on, including the headline or picture, the person who shared, and particularly the news brand that produced it. At the same time, highly news literate people pay the least amount of attention to the number of comments, likes, or shares on a social media post, which suggests a higher degree of savvy about the role of popularity as a governing principle in the online environment regardless of the quality of a given piece of content. Those with higher literacy levels also reported consuming news from a wider range of sources, and the idea of government interventions to deal with misinformation was viewed skeptically by this group. Finally, news literacy does not appear to have much of a link to trust in news, probably because higher news literacy is associated with greater skepticism. As the Reuters report notes, "the more people know about how the news is made, the more knowledgeable they will be about its limitations and imperfections. This may be why we see only a very small increase in trust levels as news literacy increases."[53] Overall, we can start to get a picture of the traits associated with being news literate, and they are generally welcome. Those with higher levels of news literacy appear to be more careful and deliberate about what they consume, which could help them be better informed and more engaged as citizens.

These findings are useful because, although we might assume that increasing news literacy is a good thing, without some kind of evidence, we don't know for sure. In fact, some scholars and educators worry that learning about news media can actually make people more likely to grow cynical and apathetic and distrusting and to disengage from public life. To the contrary, the good news from emerging research is that those with higher levels of news literacy generally show the kinds of positive traits we would expect and hope to see if we think responsible news use is vital to civic participation. In my own research with my colleagues, these positive traits include higher levels of current events knowledge, increased political activity, greater motivation to consume news, and lower endorsement of conspiracy theories.[54]

Possessing these traits is not necessarily *caused* by learning about news; you may have heard that "correlation does not equal causation." We can't say news literacy is responsible for producing these outcomes; we can only say that a positive relationship seems to exist. Identifying relationships between variables is often the best we can do when studying humans. It's hard to show that one thing definitively leads to another when there are so many variables that influence our attitudes and behavior. Still, it's useful to know where these sorts of connections exist. Having evidence about the relationships between news literacy and other variables can help us figure out what people need to know about news and can show why news literacy might be a good thing.

Some studies do get at the ability of news literacy to influence a person's knowledge, attitudes, and behaviors surrounding news media. These studies typically compare a group that received some kind of news media education with a group that didn't. If the two groups exhibit significantly different levels of news literacy and other traits, it can be said that the news or media literacy training and education are responsible for these changes. Broadly, these studies find that higher news literacy in individuals is connected to a variety of positive outcomes related to judgment, knowledge, and engagement. For example, news literacy researchers Emily Vraga and Melissa Tully have identified a reduction in perceptions of news bias following media literacy training and have found that exposure to a video about media literacy led to increased trust and perceptions of news credibility.[55]

A prominent news literacy class at Stony Brook University in New York has been the subject of several studies that wanted to examine its effects. One study found that students who took the class were highly engaged in the material, more knowledgeable about journalism, and more aware of current events, but at the same time, the students struggled to identify the commercial biases that influence news content or to reflect on news ownership or ideology.[56] A study I worked on used our news media literacy measurement to compare students who had taken the class to those who hadn't. Even though the class wasn't specifically geared toward the knowledge structures that informed our measurement, students who had taken the class still scored higher on the measure and demonstrated greater knowledge of current events and motivations to consume news.[57] This was true even when a year or more had passed after taking the class, which suggests that learning about news can have a lasting impact. And like other studies that compare groups that either received or didn't receive some kind of educational intervention, this study demonstrates that learning about news can have positive effects on people's knowledge, attitudes, and behaviors regarding news media.

Similar studies have found any exposure to media education can help produce more savvy news consumers. In a study of more than 2,000 youth ages 15 to 27, those who said they had some prior access to media literacy education (learning the importance of examining claims and evaluating evidence and learning skills to help judge the accuracy of information) were more likely to evaluate political information for its accuracy regardless of whether it fit with their preconceived notions about the issue. In psychological terms, they were more motivated by accuracy goals than by directional goals, which means they wanted to get at the truth instead of just being right.[58] This is an important finding, and it's one that also showed up in my research on news literacy and conspiracy theories. Psychologists say that rather than viewing the world in purely objective terms, we use a *motivated reasoning* process to make decisions and establish viewpoints. We can be motivated toward getting the answer we want or toward getting the best possible version of the truth even if it might challenge the way we prefer to see the world. So far, emerging evidence suggests news and media literacy might be connected to an increase in accuracy reasoning over directional reasoning. That's pretty great news because it's a lot easier to simply teach someone about how news is produced and consumed than it is to try to correct misperceptions they might hold about social or political issues that are important to them.

The bottom line is that most people do not appear to be well informed about how news works. And why would they be? It's something most people hardly ever discuss in any kind of nuanced way. It's a difficult topic that even most teachers aren't sure how to approach, and it's not really in the interests of most news organizations to raise these difficult questions. For many, there's really no incentive to shine a spotlight on news literacy, leaving most of us in the dark. At the same time, those who do demonstrate higher levels of news literacy do appear to also possess the traits we would hope to see among informed citizens who have a genuine interest in democratic life. Broadly speaking, they are more knowledgeable, engaged, skeptical, and discerning. If these connections tell us anything, it's that anyone who cares about improving both individual knowledge and the conditions of democracy should be devoted to increasing news literacy.

Why News Literacy Is and Isn't the Answer

Despite what the headlines might say about the role of news literacy in solving our problems with "fake news" and other misinformation, news literacy is no panacea no matter how you do it. As the following chapters will show, there are many problems with our news environment, and education alone is not the solution. As scholar danah boyd has pointed out, there is a great deal of "solutionism" around news and media literacy; indeed, the idea that there is any easy fix to complex problems should be viewed with skepticism. Boyd goes even further and suggests that media literacy might have "backfired" by leading people to question information to the degree that our common ways of knowing the world have begun to disintegrate. As boyd writes, "Media literacy asks people to raise questions and be wary of information that they're receiving. People are. Unfortunately, that's exactly why we're talking past one another."[59] Being skeptical and asking questions are undeniably good things when dealing with a messy information environment. But if the message goes too far and people stop believing anything they don't feel immediately comfortable with, it can undermine the foundations of the democratic process, as we have seen. So boyd has a point.

But that's why we need to do news literacy right. Any critical analysis of information will only succeed if it is grounded in the right kinds of contextual knowledge. Understanding the broader operations and implications of the news media environment can help people see individual pieces of content through a contextual lens that gives greater meaning to the information they are consuming and can help them distinguish quality from garbage. Furthermore, we need to examine actual evidence, not just anecdotes and hunches, to determine whether news literacy is effective and what it can do for people. So despite the valid concerns around news literacy and its limited capacity for solving the problems of information in democratic life, there are some reasons why education can play a key role in improving the news environment and the surrounding discourse.

First, there's the obvious point that news literacy education—even a variety of diverse approaches to it—has already been connected to several positive outcomes, as detailed in the studies reviewed previously. Evidence suggests that requiring formal education about news media could help broad swathes of citizens to become more savvy consumers of information, more engaged with reliable news sources, more motivated to consume news, more knowledgeable about public affairs, more politically active and involved, and more discerning when it comes to determining what's real and what's not. This appears to be true regardless of partisan affiliation, and the effects of educational interventions appear to be lasting.

A second consideration surrounding the importance of citizen knowledge about news is the role of the audience in determining what news looks like. News literacy has been called a "demand-side" solution to address the shortcomings of news media. Rather than (or perhaps in addition to) trying to change how news is created or produced (that is, the "supply side"), a more effective approach might be to work on the demand side—those who end up consuming news and information media (or ignoring it). In the *demand problem*, low levels of news literacy can be connected to an underperforming news media that fails to provide information citizens really need; in other words, an insufficient supply of quality news can be linked to a lack of public demand for it. If people are content with the constant bloviating that takes place on cable news or with the disproportionate amounts of attention paid by news media to sensational scandals and unimportant trivia, then this is what they will get. This is the basic logic of markets. If the demand is there, the supply will be ample; if demand dries up, the supply would wither as well. Defenders of the media marketplace often suggest that the media is simply giving people what they want. Well, yes, that's the problem. So if the demand side could be altered to reflect more of a dedication to a quality supply, the market could be forced to shift. This is not to say consumer preferences automatically dictate what a marketplace offers; that's not the case. But in a market where your eyeballs are being sold to advertisers, if the eyeballs go away, so does the advertising. Once financial support dries up, the market is ripe for change.

A third reason that news literacy education will be important in the years and decades to come is what I call the *news literacy gap*—the growing divide between those who are informed and empowered members of society and those who are not. Educating all individuals in society about news media will be essential to reducing economic and political disparities and to enhancing opportunity for all. In general, citizens across the developed world are being left out of the democratic process through sheer neglect by societies that were designed to promote equality and public welfare. As political scientist Phil Parvin writes,

> Democratic states no longer provide citizens at the bottom end of the wealth and income distribution with the ability to develop democratic capacity or political knowledge through participation in the civic and associational activities which play a central role in the development of these things. As a result, poorer citizens are losing both the desire to participate and the capacity for effective or informed political participation.[60]

Those with the proper skills and knowledge will be the ones to determine what the information landscape looks like and who is empowered to take part. Only citizens with sufficient news literacy will be able to make good decisions that serve the interests of themselves and of society. As Kovach and Rosenstiel write,

> The real information gap in the twenty-first century is not who has access to the Internet and who does not. It is the gap between people who have the skills to create knowledge and those who are simply in a process of affirming preconceptions without ever growing and learning. It is the new gap between reason and superstition.[61]

And actually, the *digital divide*—the socioeconomic gap between those who have access to the internet and other digital technologies and those who do not—remains a significant issue, as millions of Americans and other citizens still don't have reliable broadband connections, especially in rural areas.

A fourth but by no means final reason to promote news literacy is the public good that is provided by a well-informed citizenry. In economics, a *public good* is something that everyone benefits from regardless of how it is produced or consumed. In the strict economic sense, public goods are generally provided or regulated by governments because there is no commercial incentive to produce them. These include laws that preserve clean air and water, national defense systems, public service broadcasting, and public education. Compare these to a private good such as a box of chocolates—if the chocolates are mine, they can't also be yours, and once I've eaten them, they're gone. (The fancy terms here are "excludable"—mine not yours—and "rivalrous"—when they're gone, they're gone. Public goods are non-excludable and non-rivalrous.) Now think of a well-informed citizenry as a public good. If people are broadly knowledgeable enough to make decisions that benefit society, this is a good thing for everyone. Even information itself can be thought of as a public good. My consumption of it doesn't keep you from consuming it, and it still exists in the world even after I've consumed it. So news literacy, when shared widely, is a public good. Everyone benefits from having a citizenry that knows how to parse good information from bad based on a contextual understanding of the information environment. Dealing with complex problems like global warming and economic crises will require nothing less. And so whole societies could rise or fall depending on the ability of citizens to understand and evaluate their information environment. Although news literacy alone will not solve our many problems, it's in everyone's interest to create societies of news literate individuals.

Questions for Discussion

1. Why do people consume news? What needs does news help satisfy? How can news affect our perceptions of reality?
2. What is "political self-efficacy," and how is news connected to political and civic engagement?
3. How is news literacy rooted in the longstanding traditions of media education?
4. What is the "news literacy gap," and how should it be addressed?
5. How do news and news literacy function as public goods?

Notes

1. Michael X. Delli Carpini and Scott Keeter, *What Americans Know about Politics and Why It Matters* (New Haven: Yale University Press, 1996), 305–6.
2. Julia Belluz, "You May Think the World Is Falling Apart. Steven Pinker Is Here to Tell You It Isn't," *Vox*, August 16, 2016, www.vox.com/2016/8/16/12486586/2016-worst-year-ever-violence-trump-terrorism.
3. See Steven Pinker, *Enlightenment Now: The Case for Reason, Science, Humanism, and Progress* (New York: Viking, 2018).

4. Bill Kovach and Tom Rosenstiel, *The Elements of Journalism: What Newspeople Should Know and the Public Should Expect* (New York: Three Rivers Press, 2014), 1–2.
5. Jürgen Habermas, *The Structural Transformation of the Public Sphere: An Inquiry into a Category of Bourgeois Society*, Studies in Contemporary German Social Thought (Cambridge, MA: MIT Press, 1989), 184.
6. Pew Research Center, "Public Knowledge of Current Affairs Little Changed by News and Information Revolutions," April 15, 2007, www.people-press.org/2007/04/15/public-knowledge-of-current-affairs-little-changed-by-news-and-information-revolutions/.
7. Abdurashid Solijonov, "Voter Turnout Trends around the World" (International Institute for Democracy and Electoral Assistance, December 31, 2016), www.idea.int/publications/catalogue/voter-turnout-trends-around-world, 24.
8. Drew DeSilver, "U.S. Trails Most Developed Countries in Voter Turnout," *Pew Research Center*, May 21, 2018, www.pewresearch.org/fact-tank/2018/05/21/u-s-voter-turnout-trails-most-developed-countries/.
9. Phil Parvin, "Democracy Without Participation: A New Politics for a Disengaged Era," *Res Publica* 24, no. 1 (February 2018): 45.
10. Walter Lippmann, *Public Opinion* (New York: Harcourt, 1922), 3.
11. Michael Schudson, "The 'Lippmann-Dewey Debate' and the Invention of Walter Lippmann as an Anti-Democrat 1985–1996," *International Journal of Communication* 2, no. 0 (September 22, 2008): 12.
12. John Dewey, "'Public Opinion' (Review)," *The New Republic* (May 3, 1922), 286.
13. Dewey, "'Public Opinion' (Review)," 288.
14. Dewey, "'Public Opinion' (Review)," 288.
15. See W. Lance Bennett, Regina G. Lawrence, and Steven Livingston, *When the Press Fails: Political Power and the News Media from Iraq to Katrina* (Chicago, IL: University of Chicago Press, 2008).
16. David S. Broder, *Behind the Front Page* (New York: Simon & Schuster, 2000), 14. Quoted in Michael Schudson, *The Sociology of News* (New York: W.W. Norton & Company, 2012), 26.
17. "FROM THE EDITORS; The Times and Iraq," *The New York Times*, May 26, 2004, sec. World, www.nytimes.com/2004/05/26/world/from-the-editors-the-times-and-iraq.html.
18. Jeffrey Gottfried and Elisa Shearer, "Americans' Online News Use Is Closing in on TV News Use," September 7, 2017, www.pewresearch.org/fact-tank/2017/09/07/americans-online-news-use-vs-tv-news-use/.
19. Elisa Shearer and Jeffrey Gottfried, "News Use Across Social Media Platforms 2017," September 7, 2017, www.journalism.org/2017/09/07/news-use-across-social-media-platforms-2017/.
20. Michael Barthel and Amy Mitchell, "Americans' Attitudes About the News Media Deeply Divided Along Partisan Lines," May 10, 2017, www.journalism.org/2017/05/10/americans-attitudes-about-the-news-media-deeply-divided-along-partisan-lines/.
21. Amy Mitchell et al., "Publics Globally Want Unbiased News Coverage, but Are Divided on Whether Their News Media Deliver," *Pew Research Center's Global Attitudes Project*, January 11, 2018, www.pewglobal.org/2018/01/11/publics-globally-want-unbiased-news-coverage-but-are-divided-on-whether-their-news-media-deliver/.
22. "Reuters Institute Digital News Report" (Reuters Institute for the Study of Journalism, 2018), www.digitalnewsreport.org/.
23. Aaron Smith and Monica Anderson, "Social Media Use in 2018," March 1, 2018, www.pewinternet.org/2018/03/01/social-media-use-in-2018/.
24. Jeffery Jones and Zacc Ritter, "Americans Struggle to Navigate the Modern Media Landscape," accessed June 29, 2018, https://news.gallup.com/poll/226157/americans-struggle-navigate-modern-media-landscape.aspx.

25. Paul Farhi, "Sean Hannity Thinks Viewers Can Tell the Difference between News and Opinion. Hold on a Moment," *Washington Post*, March 28, 2017, www.washingtonpost. com/lifestyle/style/sean-hannity-thinks-viewers-can-tell-the-difference-between-news-and-opinion-hold-on-a-moment/2017/03/27/eb0c5870-1307-11e7-9e4f-09aa75d3ec57_story.html.

26. Amy Mitchell et al., "Distinguishing Between Factual and Opinion Statements in the News," June 18, 2018, www.journalism.org/2018/06/18/distinguishing-between-factual-and-opinion-statements-in-the-news/.

27. Sam Wineburg et al., "Evaluating Information: The Cornerstone of Civic Online Reasoning," accessed July 6, 2018, https://purl.stanford.edu/fv751yt5934, 4.

28. "American Views: Trust, Media and Democracy" (Knight Foundation, January 15, 2018), https://knightfoundation.org/reports/american-views-trust-media-and-democracy.

29. "Media Use and Evaluation" (Gallup), accessed July 6, 2018, https://news.gallup.com/poll/1663/Media-Use-Evaluation.aspx.

30. "American Views: Trust, Media and Democracy" (Knight Foundation, January 15, 2018), https://knightfoundation.org/reports/american-views-trust-media-and-democracy.

31. Amy Mitchell et al., "Political Polarization & Media Habits | Pew Research Center" (Pew Research Center, October 21, 2014), www.journalism.org/2014/10/21/political-polarization-media-habits/#.

32. "Political Polarization in the American Public" (Pew Research Center, June 12, 2014), www.people-press.org/2014/06/12/political-polarization-in-the-american-public/.

33. "The Public, the Political System and American Democracy" (Pew Research Center, April 26, 2018), www.people-press.org/2018/04/26/the-public-the-political-system-and-american-democracy/.

34. Markus Prior, "Media and Political Polarization," *Annual Review of Political Science* 16, no. 1 (2013): 101–27, https://doi.org/10.1146/annurev-polisci-100711-135242.

35. Andrew Guess and Brendan Nyhan, "Why Selective Exposure to Like-Minded Political News Is Less Prevalent than You Think" (Knight Foundation, n.d.), 12, https://kf-site-production.s3.amazonaws.com/media_elements/files/000/000/133/original/Topos_KF_White-Paper_Nyhan_V1.pdf.

36. James G. Webster and Thomas B. Ksiazek, "The Dynamics of Audience Fragmentation: Public Attention in an Age of Digital Media," *Journal of Communication* 62, no. 1 (February 1, 2012): 52–53, https://doi.org/10.1111/j.1460-2466.2011.01616.x.

37. Matt Levendusky, "Are Fox and MSNBC Polarizing America?—The Washington Post," February 3, 2014, www.washingtonpost.com/news/monkey-cage/wp/2014/02/03/are-fox-and-msnbc-polarizing-america/?utm_term=.a1dd09956ec4.

38. Seth Ashley, Mark Poepsel, and Erin Willis, "Media Literacy and News Credibility: Does Knowledge of Media Ownership Increase Skepticism in News Consumers?," *Journal of Media Literacy Education* 2, no. 1 (September 10, 2013): 37–46, https://digital-commons.uri.edu/jmle/vol2/iss1/3.

39. Len Masterman, *Teaching the Media* (London: Routledge, 1990), 13.

40. Renee Hobbs, "The Seven Great Debates in the Media Literacy Movement," *Journal of Communication* 48, no. 1 (1998): 23.

41. Patricia Aufderheide and Charles Firestone, "Media Literacy: A Report of the National Leadership Conference on Media Literacy" (Queenstown, MD: Aspen Institute, 1993), https://files.eric.ed.gov/fulltext/ED365294.pdf, 10.

42. Aufderheide and Firestone, "Media Literacy," 9.

43. Aufderheide and Firestone, "Media Literacy," 10.

44. Renee Hobbs, "The Seven Great Debates in the Media Literacy Movement," *Journal of Communication* 48, no. 1 (1998): 27.

45. Justin Lewis and Sut Jhally, "The Struggle over Media Literacy," *Journal of Communication* 48, no. 1 (1998): 109.

46. Lewis and Jhally, "The Struggle over Media Literacy," 111.

47. Lewis and Jhally, "The Struggle over Media Literacy," 119.

48. W. James Potter, *Theory of Media Literacy: A Cognitive Approach* (Sage Publications, 2004), 57.

49. Potter, *Theory of Media Literacy*, 68.

50. Potter, *Theory of Media Literacy*, 69.

51. Adam Maksl, Seth Ashley, and Stephanie Craft, "Measuring News Media Literacy," *Journal of Media Literacy Education* 6, no. 3 (March 15, 2015): 29–45.

52. "Reuters Institute Digital News Report" (Reuters Institute for the Study of Journalism, 2018), www.digitalnewsreport.org/, 10.

53. "Reuters Institute Digital News Report" (Reuters Institute for the Study of Journalism, 2018), www.digitalnewsreport.org/, 37.

54. See Adam Maksl, Seth Ashley, and Stephanie Craft, "Measuring News Media Literacy," *Journal of Media Literacy Education* 6, no. 3 (March 15, 2015): 29–45; Seth Ashley, Adam Maksl, and Stephanie Craft, "News Media Literacy and Political Engagement: What's the Connection?," *Journal of Media Literacy Education* 9, no. 1 (July 14, 2017): 79–98; Stephanie Craft, Seth Ashley, and Adam Maksl, "News Media Literacy and Conspiracy Theory Endorsement," *Communication and the Public* 2, no. 4 (December 1, 2017): 388–401, https://doi.org/10.1177/2057047317725539; Adam Maksl et al., "The Usefulness of a News Media Literacy Measure in Evaluating a News Literacy Curriculum," *Journalism & Mass Communication Educator* 72, no. 2 (June 1, 2017): 228–41, https://doi.org/10.1177/1077695816651970.

55. Emily K. Vraga, Melissa Tully, and Hernando Rojas, "Media Literacy Training Reduces Perception of Bias," *Newspaper Research Journal* 30, no. 4 (2009): 68–81; Emily K. Vraga et al., "Modifying Perceptions of Hostility and Credibility of News Coverage of an Environmental Controversy through Media Literacy," *Journalism* 13, no. 7 (October 1, 2012): 942–59, https://doi.org/10.1177/1464884912455906.

56. Jennifer Fleming, "Media Literacy, News Literacy, or News Appreciation? A Case Study of the News Literacy Program at Stony Brook University," *Journalism & Mass Communication Educator* 69, no. 2 (June 1, 2014): 146–65, https://doi.org/10.1177/1077695813517885.

57. Adam Maksl et al., "The Usefulness of a News Media Literacy Measure in Evaluating a News Literacy Curriculum," *Journalism & Mass Communication Educator* 72, no. 2 (June 1, 2017): 228–41, https://doi.org/10.1177/1077695816651970.

58. Joseph Kahne and Benjamin Bowyer, "Educating for Democracy in a Partisan Age: Confronting the Challenges of Motivated Reasoning and Misinformation," *American Educational Research Journal* 54, no. 1 (February 1, 2017): 3–34, https://doi.org/10.3102/0002831216679817.

59. Danah Boyd, "Did Media Literacy Backfire?," *Data & Society: Points*, January 5, 2017, https://points.datasociety.net/did-media-literacy-backfire-7418c084d88d.

60. Phil Parvin, "Democracy Without Participation: A New Politics for a Disengaged Era," *Res Publica* 24, no. 1 (February 2018): 31–52, https://doi.org/10.1007/s11158-017-9382-1, 36.

61. Bill Kovach and Tom Rosenstiel, *Blur: How to Know What's True in the Age of Information Overload*, Reprint edition (New York: Bloomsbury USA, 2011), 201.

PART II

Critical Contexts for Democratic Life

3

THE DECLINE OF JOURNALISM AND THE RISE OF "FAKE NEWS"

We can look to a host of examples to begin to understand the complexity of our information crisis, but the 2016 election in the United States remains the poster child for our dysfunctional news environment. Of course, there was the problem of rampant "fake news," but such misinformation is just a drop in the bucket of most people's news consumption. It's the mainstream news media outlets that get the most eyeballs that we should be most concerned with, and they delivered a particularly lackluster performance. A misguided approach to covering elections has long been central to American news media practices—mainly an obsession with polling and a near absence of any concrete information about policy issues—but 2016 really knocked it out of the park. There are plenty of reasons for this, but the appeal of the reality television star Donald Trump and his unprecedented antics made for such great television that it was hard to look away whether you liked him or not. The broadcast networks (ABC, CBS, and NBC) and the cable networks (CNN, Fox, MSNBC) alike just put him on television and watched the revenue stream in. As then CBS Chairman Les Moonves famously said of Trump's campaign to be president, "It may not be good for America, but it's damn good for CBS."[1]

Business boomed for the mainstream television news media, and it's easy to see why. "The money's rolling in and this is fun," Moonves went on to say. "I've never seen anything like this, and this is going to be a very good year for us. Sorry. It's a terrible thing to say. But, bring it on, Donald. Keep going." Even supposedly liberal CNN aired hours of raw footage from Trump's campaign rallies because network bosses knew people would tune in. Speaking at the Harvard Kennedy School of Government in October 2016, CNN President Jeffery Zucker reflected on the amount of airtime given to Trump since the beginning of the campaign in 2015. "If we made any mistake last year, it's that we probably did put on too many of his campaign rallies in those early months and let them run," Zucker said.

"Because you never knew what he would say, there was an attraction to put those on air." And Zucker would have known how strong the attraction would be—he happened to be president of NBC Entertainment when Trump's reality show *The Apprentice* first aired on the network.[2]

In the end, Trump benefited from a huge amount of *free media*, which is an industry term for the free airtime candidates get when they appear in regular news coverage (also called "earned media"). Contrast that with *paid media* or "bought media," which is the airtime candidates and their supporters must purchase when they want to run advertising messages. If news producers make their own independent decision to put a candidate on television, it can add up to a lot of exposure that costs the candidate nothing. According to industry estimates, throughout the entire campaign, Trump received the equivalent of more than $5 billion of free media exposure across media platforms, which was more than candidates Hillary Clinton, Bernie Sanders, Ted Cruz, Paul Ryan, and Marco Rubio combined.[3] Much of the coverage of Trump was negative—and the same was true for Clinton—but it didn't matter. The free airtime gave him plenty of carte blanche to get his message out, and he did just that.

This approach to campaign coverage is not terribly surprising given what we know about profit imperatives for commercial media, especially when combined with what we know about human audiences and how we make decisions, that is, based largely on emotions and mental shortcuts rather than rationality and analytical thinking. Reaching people in the rational parts of their brains is much harder than tickling their emotional centers, which respond strongly to fear, anger, desire, and other ancient human responses to the world around us. But that's exactly the problem. When guided by profit motives over public service, it's not surprising that this type of coverage is typical of what many news outlets produce. If news media wanted to serve the interests of the voting public, they could do so by giving preference to substance over flash and original reporting over commentary. This is not to say that all news media are always guilty of falling down on the job. Quite to the contrary, there is plenty of quality, substantive journalism out there, and we should give major applause (and dollars) to that labor and its fruits. But that material is simply not what most people end up consuming on a regular basis.

How can we do better? First, we have to understand the problems. The rest of this chapter is focused on the myriad reasons for our current crisis. It's hard to grasp the complexity of the confluence of political, economic, technological, historical, and cultural forces that have given rise to the information environment of the digital age. Gaining a better understanding of this interplay is the first step to increasing our news literacy and improving our comprehension of the world around us.

How Did We Get Here?

When news media are oriented toward selling airtime to advertisers or increasing quarterly profits for their corporate owners or maximizing the number of clicks, likes, and shares they get online, there is one main overriding concern: popularity. What's popular is what sells. Now put this basic fact into the context of our information revolution and we can start to see why things are so messy. The bottom line is that economic imperatives often rule the day. As a result, news organizations often turn to cheap and easy bottom-of-the-barrel programming to generate the most revenue for the lowest cost. This is particularly true for television, which has come out on the other side of the digital transformation with huge profits. At the same time, new online-only digital outlets have emerged to fill the gap in original news reporting, and a few major national newspapers that have gone online such as *The New York Times*, which has been around since the 1800s, have found ways to weather the digital storm and maintain both quality and profitability. The *Times* added 500,000 new digital subscriptions in 2016, and the *Wall Street Journal* added 150,000. And public media such as PBS and NPR remain popular and maintain high standards.

It's the local metropolitan newspapers—so important to covering local communities and keeping citizens tethered to a common, shared reality—that have suffered the most. Overall, daily newspaper circulation in 1950 was 53 million, or more than 100 percent of households (because some households subscribed to more than one paper). In 2010, that number was around 43 million, or 37 percent of households, and that includes print and digital circulation. In 2017, the number dropped to 31 million, the lowest rate since 1945.[4] The local newspaper business has been in decline for more than a decade due largely to the internet, as advertisers found other ways to reach the public and as classified advertising went online. This has left news organizations scrambling for what remains of the economic pie. But there's another reason the news business has been in decline, and that's due to the rise of debt-financed corporate mergers and acquisitions that date back to the 1990s when business was booming and no one foresaw the coming technological revolution. As newspapers began to collapse and lay off working journalists, the amount of real journalism being produced declined, especially locally. As a result of the decline of original reporting and quality journalism in traditional print news organizations, many people dropped their subscriptions. That meant less revenue from subscriptions but also from advertising, which is worth less when there are fewer eyeballs being reached.

The point is that the picture of success or decline of traditional journalism varies depending on where you look and how you measure it—a stark reminder that it is rarely useful to speak of a single monolithic entity such as "the news media" or especially "the media." Journalism jobs and ad revenue are down, but paid circulation for newspapers (print and digital) is actually up as more news outlets rely on their readers to pay the bills. And interest in news remains high. One industry study in 2016 found that 169 million American adults read a newspaper in a month, including print and digital.[5] That's 69 percent of the U.S. population that engages with news at least once a month (a low bar for sure, but still something). Surprisingly, half of readers remain committed exclusively to the print product, while 30 percent read some combination of print and digital news. Millennials, which make up a quarter of the U.S. population, are 24 percent of the newspaper-reading audience. Newspaper audiences have always trended older, more educated, and more affluent than non-readers, but digital news products have made news more accessible to younger audiences. Online, there is a proliferation of national and niche outlets, but these are often devoted to commentary and analysis, and they are rarely oriented toward local communities. Television remains the most popular medium for news (for now), but it is often dominated by sports, weather, soft news, commentary, and advertising, as opposed to substantive public affairs reporting. Overall, bright spots certainly exist across the news landscape, but the general picture is one of ongoing challenges and uncertainty as outlets of all kinds work to find a recipe for both vitality and profitability.

What other forces have affected news outlets as they work through the digital transition? For one, massive growth among public relations and information officials has meant tighter control over the kinds of information reporters can gather.[6] And along with tighter control has come an increase in the amount of one-sided persuasive messaging being produced by information officials (including those working for government and for private companies and non-profits) who can now get their message out to the public without having to deal with pesky journalists. Throw in the 2009 recession that led to more layoffs and closures at newspapers, and add in the rise of Google and Facebook (and a few other digital giants), which now dominate the web in terms of users and soak up almost all growth in digital ad revenue. Don't forget the growing distrust among the public toward institutions in general but especially the news media, which is only made worse by constant hostile references to the press as an "enemy of the people" by none other than the president of the United States. And finally, with all of these other influences in mind, we can start to factor in the role of "fake news." Intentionally producing false information in order to gain profit or power, or simply to confuse and mislead, is nothing new, but the means and motivations for doing it are unprecedented. Misinformation of any kind poses a major threat, but as we can see, fake news is only a small part of the problem, and it certainly doesn't match the proportion of time and attention we've given it compared to the other problems before us.

To see how we really got here, we need to go back a lot further than the 21st century; exploring that history is the focus of Chapter 4. For now, we need to see how many different moving and intersecting parts affect our information environment. The rise of fake news can only be understood in the context of the decline of journalism and the vacuum it has left behind. I define *journalism* as "the process of representing reality in a way that aims to inform and empower citizens with a truthful account of important issues and events."[7] The practice of journalism produces news as an outcome, but they are not necessarily the same. Journalism is certainly an embattled component of democratic life, and today's news environment is plagued by the loss of vibrant public service journalism that historically played a key role in a well-functioning democracy. This is not to say that such reporting is dead. Even in recent years, news media have brought light and clarity to many important events and topics, ranging from human rights abuses to corporate malfeasance to political wrongdoing to global conflict, demonstrating the need for a vibrant public service journalism that measures itself by more than clicks, likes, and advertising dollars.

However, it's not enough to fondly recall the glory days of Watergate and other high-water marks. Journalism also has historically tended to reproduce and reinforce social inequalities and marginalize minority voices. (See, for example, the frequent negative representations of the Black Lives Matter movement and the absence of critical reporting on the financial industry and its hold over politics and the economy.) To be news literate, we need to examine both the strengths and weaknesses of modern journalism and the influences that affect news content rather than simply celebrating or glorifying news media without a broader examination of the nuances of journalism's role in society and its patterns of news coverage. News literacy requires an understanding of the normative goals for journalism (that is, the idealized version of the practice) as well as the structural obstacles and empirical realities that sometimes stand in the way.

For starters, we must consider the problem of markets and profit margins, the role advertising plays in determining what news is covered and what news is omitted, and the turn toward opinion and punditry. This also includes an examination of the misunderstood notions of objectivity and bias as well as the journalistic routines and organizations that influence content. Critical news literacy also includes an understanding of the economic and technological forces that have led to the decline of traditional journalism and what that means for the news media environment. This decline left a vacuum that needed filling, but the new arrivals have not lived up to the promise of traditional journalism. The resulting information vacuum has contributed to the rise of "fake news" and misinformation.

To begin to add some nuance to this discussion, this chapter proceeds with a careful definition of the different kinds of fake news as well as the different kinds of journalism. It's too easy to view either of these categories—or even "the media" as a whole—as a single monolithic entity. Afterwards, the rest of the chapter covers the influences that affect the news and information environment, paying attention to the contexts of framing, gatekeeping, indexing, and other major media theories. This connects the critical, contextual approach to news literacy to the contemporary news media environment, which will only grow increasingly messy as journalism continues to decline, digital manipulation grows, and a multitude of voices continue to flood the internet. To sum up, "fake news" is a red herring that distracts from the real challenges citizens face. Understanding the complex contemporary environment is not possible without knowledge of critical news contexts.

Fake News and Its Rise

Let's start with *fake news*, which is a term many would prefer to banish from the language. As I mentioned earlier, the term is an oxymoron because news is, by definition, real and true, not fake. More importantly, the term has been used by different people to mean so many different things that it hardly has any meaning. But because the term is certainly not going away, here is my working definition that should capture what most people mean by *fake news*—false or fabricated information created and disseminated by human actors with the intention to mislead or deceive in order to gain power or profit. This covers a wide spectrum of media content, but it definitely does not include the real reporting of actual journalists and other independent news producers.

Let's first recall what fake news *is not*. It's possible for news content to be incomplete or to be framed a certain way or even to contain errors without being "fake." For example, even the reporting by *The New York Times* that helped make the case for the 2003 invasion of Iraq—flawed as it was—was certainly not fake. The stakes were high, and the outcome was costly in terms of human lives and financial resources. But the reporting was not fake. Furthermore, the *Times* exhibited transparency and accountability when they later took ownership of their flawed reports and parted ways with reporter Judith Miller, who played a major role in the flawed coverage. One hallmark of real news producers is their ability to fess up when they've made an honest mistake. Fake news, which intends to mislead, distort, fabricate, and lie, has no interest in holding itself accountable.

Understanding the difference is important because some people have been misled into thinking that fake news is the same as critical or negative coverage, a pathology heralded particularly by U.S. President Donald Trump. Trump is notorious for his attacks on a range of longstanding, traditional news organizations, ranging from *The New York Times* to NBC to CNN. He has repeatedly referred to the news media in general as "the enemy of the people," a phrase that has been used for centuries and across cultures from the French revolution to Nazi Germany to the Soviet Union to criticize and ostracize political opponents, whose crime of opposition was often punishable by death. From the Roman Senate to Donald Trump, politicians have used the rhetorical device as a political strategy to bolster populist and nationalist agendas and to help divide citizens and electorates into warring camps.

With this in mind, it is easy to see that "fake news" is just another way for Trump to attempt to isolate and delegitimize the work of journalists when he perceives their coverage to be negative. He made this clear when he used Twitter on May 9, 2018, to declare

> The Fake News is working overtime. Just reported that, despite the tremendous success we are having with the economy & all things else, 91% of the Network News about me is negative (Fake). Why do we work so hard in working with the media when it is corrupt? Take away credentials?

Finally he had clarified that, to him, "negative" coverage is what he really means when he says "fake." For example, Trump often refers to reporting about Russian interference in the 2016 election as "fake" even when it is based on easily verifiable facts and evidence. In this case, reporters have not necessarily set out to make Trump look bad; it's simply the reality that the findings so far and the ongoing investigation remain a dark cloud over his presidency, so any reporting about it is bound to appear "negative" to Trump and his supporters.

Attacks on the press have been at the center of Trump's campaign and presidency. He has called journalists "very dangerous and sick" and said he is "providing a great service by explaining this to the American People." At his rallies, he encourages his supporters to attack the press verbally and has even been accused of inciting violence against reporters. The political strategy of attacking the news media is nothing new and was certainly much worse when it was commonplace to intimidate, imprison, and even kill those who spoke ill of a malevolent ruler. These practices still occur in parts of the world; keep in mind that most people on planet Earth live in countries that do not enjoy freedoms of the press, speech, or expression. In the Western world, verbal attacks on the press and accusations of bias have been widespread for decades, particularly on the political right. In the United States, talk of "liberal media bias" grew in the context of the Cold War and the McCarthy era, but it was really conservative talk radio host Rush Limbaugh and others like him who popularized the tactic. Limbaugh's show became nationally syndicated in 1988, and he was free to launch a one-sided attack on the political left after the repeal a year earlier of the Fairness Doctrine, a 1949 FCC rule that required a "reasonable" balance of competing views. The rise of conservative talk radio showed the popularity and profitability of the format, which set the stage for the emergence in the 1990s of Fox News, which positioned itself as a conservative alternative to the mainstream liberal media. From this lineage emerged Sarah Palin, the governor of Alaska who became a vice presidential candidate when she was selected as Senator John McCain's running mate in 2008. Her populist bravado was celebrated as she critiqued the "lamestream media" for their liberal bias. From there, it was not a far distance to Trump's overt attacks.

There is nothing wrong with critiquing news media. The practice can even be healthy, and it's good to root out political bias and unfairness where it occurs. But that's distinctly different from tossing news out as "fake." So now that we've determined what "fake news" is not, how can we better understand what it is? Because the term has been used in so many different ways, it can be helpful to think of fake news as a spectrum of true or false information that intersects with the benign or harmful intention of the message producer. That is, is the creator using true or false information, and are they trying to be funny, to provide social commentary, or to intentionally deceive and mislead? Also, how transparent are the producer's aims? In Table 3.1, you can see the differences and where trouble arises.[8]

Let's start with the left column, "low intent to mislead or deceive." Whether the content is true or not, if the producer's intentions were not malicious, it's

TABLE 3.1 Truth versus intention in "fake news."

	Low intent to mislead or deceive	*High intent to mislead or deceive*
High truth	Satire, commentary, or simply being right	Propaganda, some advertising
Low truth	Parody, joke, or simply being wrong	Disinformation, hoax, fake news

not "fake news" in the contemporary sense. It's simply right or wrong, often for the purpose of making a joke or providing some kind of commentary. If the content is high in truth, it can fall in the category of satire (defined as the use of humor, irony, exaggeration, or ridicule to expose and criticize), such as *The Daily Show* on Comedy Central, which often uses facts about politics and politicians to provide a humorous critique. When intent to mislead is low and truth is high, we can also think of this as simply being right (which does occasionally happen on the internet). If the content is low in truth, this could be a parody (defined as an imitation of the style of a particular writer, artist, or genre with deliberate exaggeration for comic effect), such as *The Onion*, which combines the format of traditional news outlets with false information to make jokes. Also, if intent to mislead is low and truth is also low, you can think of this as simply being wrong, which happens to most of us from time to time (not me). (That was an example of low truth but also low intent to mislead because it was a joke.) There can be overlap between these categories depending on the content at hand—*The Daily Show* can be thought of as a parody of a typical broadcast news program, and *The Onion* produces satire as part of its parody of a real news outlet. In any case, these categories should be easily identifiable as long as we know a little something about the source of the information and its goals. Media producers and outlets that are truly producing satire or parody (with no intent to deceive) should be easily identified by their content, their ownership structure, their employees, and their general reputation, which can usually be gleaned from a quick online search. With this in mind, let's go back to our earlier definition of "fake news" and see if either of these categories fit the bill: false or fabricated information created and disseminated by human actors with the intention to mislead or deceive in order to gain power or profit. As long as intent to mislead is low, it is not fake news.

The other side of the graph is a little trickier. Here, we are always dealing with a high intent to mislead or deceive, but does it matter whether truth is high or low? According to our definition, yes, it matters. Fake news must be "false or fabricated," so if truth is high, it is not fake news. It could be some other kind of malicious or nefarious content, which is usually the case with propaganda, which relies on truthful but incomplete information to persuade and influence (as when governments work to establish citizen support for a war effort). This is also the case with some kinds of advertising that try to trick the viewer into thinking the message is something other than what it is. For example, *sponsored content* is advertising that takes on the appearance of a news message. Even when labeled correctly, these types of messages are confusing and misleading to news consumers, but this still is not what is meant by fake news. Fake news can be identified by a low level of truthfulness and a high intent to mislead or deceive. This was certainly the case with the messages produced by a variety of actors surrounding the 2016 U.S. election and the Brexit campaign, who used false information to mislead voters to make a certain political choice or to deceive media consumers into clicking on non-news websites in order to make a profit from digital advertising. This is also the case with ongoing disinformation campaigns by certain foreign actors, hackers, and others who seek to undermine and destabilize democratic societies by spreading false information. In this case, the goal might not be to influence a specific vote but rather to delegitimize the information environment broadly and make it harder for citizens to know who or what to believe at all. The slippery concept of "fake news" has been so used and abused that it is nearly meaningless. But if we commit to a clear definition like the one provided here, it is fairly easy to see what qualifies.

Whose Problem Is Fake News?

The next question is, whose problem is fake news and what should we do about it? Other than offering widespread education in news literacy, how can the problem be addressed? Is it up to Facebook, Google, and others to monitor the content on their sites and banish the purveyors of fake news? Would the digital media giants be willing to commit the necessary resources to this task anyway? How will they decide exactly what should be removed? Should governments intervene? How should they go about censoring content, particularly in light of the existing legal protections for free speech and press? While we are busy trying to figure out who should do it, the problem will almost certainly get much worse before it has any chance of getting better. The future of fake news is the "deep fake," or fabricated images, videos, or audio recordings created through the use of machine learning that synthesize preexisting content with false or fabricated content.[9] Of course, the motion picture industry has been using fake computer-generated imagery for years to create entertainment, but what happens when ordinary people can abuse the same technologies for their own dark reasons? The consumer technology needed to produce deep fakes is already here, as seen in the celebrity pornography that already exists online. Today, the results often are passable at best, but in just a few more years, anyone on the internet will likely be able to easily and cheaply produce and distribute all kinds of fabricated media content that looks no different from content that is 100 percent real. The problem is so serious that the U.S. Department of Defense, recognizing the potential threats posed to national security, is working to develop its own advanced detection technology.[10] Somewhat ironically, the tools are being created by the Defense Advanced Research Projects

Agency (DARPA), the same group that in the 1960s supported the development of the original networking technology that made today's internet possible.

Assuming the problem is going to get worse before it gets better, who falls for fake news, and what is its impact? It's still hard to say, but plenty of researchers are trying to find out. One evidence-based theme is that fake news appears to have a wide reach but a shallow impact. The reach is certainly wide. As one prominent fact-checker found, in the months before the 2016 U.S. election, fake news stories garnered more engagement on Facebook than stories from 19 major mainstream outlets combined.[11] An MIT study found that false information easily outperforms real news on Twitter, and the culprit is primarily humans, mostly from retweeting fake news, rather than being the work of fake robot accounts as you might assume.[12] The depth of the impact is less clear. One study that analyzed the browsing histories of a representative sample of 2,525 Americans found that fake news made up only a small part of their news consumption. As *The New York Times* summarized, "One in four Americans saw at least one false story, but even the most eager fake-news readers—deeply conservative supporters of President Trump—consumed far more of the real kind, from newspaper and network websites and other digital sources."[13] Most fake news sites they identified— 80 percent—supported Trump, and Trump supporters were much more likely to visit pro-Trump fake news sites than Clinton supporters were to visit pro-Clinton fake sites. But overall, consumption of fake news was low in comparison to other non-fake news—only 6 percent for Trump supporters and just 1 percent for Clinton supporters. This doesn't tell us who believed what they saw or what effect it had on their behavior. And actually, individuals over age 60 were much more likely than younger people to visit fake news sites, which could be reflected in the votes of those who switched from voting for Obama in 2012 to Trump in 2016. That study also noted that consumers of fake news are not visiting fact-checking sites. So for all the efforts of diligent fact-checkers at Snopes, PolitiFact, and FactCheck.org, they do not seem to be reaching those who need them most. Researchers also have noted that fake news is only a small part of most people's information consumption and doesn't have much effect because people are more influenced by the "real news" they consume.[14] On some level, this makes sense— if you mainly consume Fox and supported Trump, a fake story about how terrible Hilary Clinton was will probably not have much effect on you. The same is true if you're a fan of MSNBC and were a Clinton supporter. Many of our views are informed by the mainstream media we consume, and a few fake stories are not necessarily going to change that.

On the other hand, other recent research points more directly to the idea that the influence of fake news may have been strong enough to tip the election in favor of Donald Trump. One study by researchers at The Ohio State University sought to understand what caused defections by supporters of President Barack Obama in 2012 who became Trump voters in 2016. Using three sample fake news items in a large, nationwide survey, researchers linked belief in fake news stories to defection by Obama voters. Of those who didn't believe any of the fake news items, 89 percent voted for Clinton in 2016. Of those who believed two or all three fake stories, only 17 percent supported Clinton. After accounting for many other relevant variables, the researchers concluded that belief in fake news was enough of a factor to account for Trump's narrow win. They write:

> Though our evidence does not "prove" that belief in fake news "caused" these former Obama voters to defect from the Democratic candidate in 2016, our study results suggest that it is highly likely that the pernicious pollution of our political discourse by fake news was sufficient to influence the outcome of what was a very close election.[15]

It wouldn't take much to tip the scales one way or the other.

Then there's the Russia connection. In January 2017, the U.S. intelligence community, including the CIA, FBI, and Office of the Director of National Intelligence, concluded with confidence that Russia meddled in the 2016 election. As Director of National Intelligence Dan Coats said, "Russia conducted an unprecedented influence campaign to interfere in the U.S. electoral and political process."[16] Of course, Trump has repeatedly sought to cast doubt on the claim, calling it "fake news" and a "hoax," but the evidence increasingly speaks for itself. We now know that the Russian influence campaign wasn't limited to fake news and social media, but that was a key part of it. One recent, extensive study concludes that, indeed, Russian influence "likely" changed the outcome of the 2016 election. In her book *Cyberwar: How Russian Hackers and Trolls Helped Elect a President— What We Don't, Can't, and Do Know*, veteran political communication scholar and expert Kathleen Hall Jamieson describes the ways in which "the Russians were able to exploit the dispositions of reporters, the capacities of the social media platforms, and our nation's respect for a free market and championing of freedom of speech and of the press."[17] Like terrorists who exploit open societies in order to commit atrocities, Russian operatives took advantage of the open communication systems and values of the West to infiltrate elections and the democratic process. The spreading of fake news and disinformation was and will continue to be at the center of these attacks.

Some remain skeptical that fake news influenced the election outcome, largely because it's generally hard to change people's minds. Scholar Brendan Nyhan has pointed out that even time-tested persuasion efforts such as television advertising and campaign mailers have a small to negligible effect on average. As Nyhan writes, "Much more remains to be learned about the effects of these types of online activities, but people should not assume they had huge effects."[18] To be sure, we will never know exactly why people vote the way they do or how much consumption of and belief in fake news might have something to do with it. But as emerging research continues to explore the role of fake news and how it is spread through social media, it's increasingly hard to imagine that the tools and tactics available in the online environment cannot give a significant nudge in a close election. The 2016 election saw 136 million ballots cast, and despite losing the popular vote by nearly 3 million votes, Trump won the Electoral College thanks to fewer than 80,000 votes in Wisconsin, Michigan, and Pennsylvania.[19] Now think about the data-driven voter targeting available particularly through Facebook, which made possible the Cambridge Analytica scandal, where the political consulting firm working with the Trump campaign gathered and exploited data from more than 50 million Facebook profiles.[20] That's just one instance we know of where attempts to influence voters may have contributed to the election outcome. It seems increasingly probable that digital influence efforts can help pick a winner.

There's one more thing to consider when it comes to the question of who believes fake news and why. Recent research points to the role of cognition and analytical thinking in the tendency to believe false information. Studies have shown that a lack of reasoning or "lazy thinking," as one study calls it, might have more to do with susceptibility to partisan fake news than confirmation bias or individual ideology.[21] Analytical thinking as a basic component of individual psychology can tell us a fair amount about how a person operates, ranging from their skepticism toward religion to how they make moral judgments to whether they are more cooperative or more self-interested.[22] We'll return to this topic later, but, in short, the good news from these findings is that analytical thinking can be taught. As one study notes, "interventions that increase analytic and actively open-minded thinking might be leveraged to help reduce belief in fake news."[23] That's a significant possible path forward, as we work to help people escape the morass of the digital age.

Further research will bring clarity to these questions in time. For now, let's remember that fake news—regardless of its effects—is a relatively small component of the information environment. While it's possible that fake news could tip the scales in a narrow contest, the broader election coverage offered by traditional mainstream news outlets is where we really should look to understand the influence of news media on election outcomes.

Real News and Its Decline

If fake news shows us what news is *not*, what is news? In some sense, *news* is simply new information about noteworthy events and issues. But that's a broad definition, and it doesn't capture what most of us think of as news. Above all, news should be truthful. When news is the output of a journalistic process, it should be accurate, honest, verified, and independent, meaning it is not beholden to any other interest than the truth. Truth can be tricky, of course, particularly in the face of legitimate competing points of view, but good journalists manage this problem by seeking independent, empirical verification of the information at hand. While journalists themselves are not expected to be objective (because no human is ever objective), professional journalists (i.e., salaried employees of established news organizations) who make a serious claim to report news adhere to these values and standards. Even many non-professional journalists such as those reporting independently online have shown themselves to basically subscribe to the same norms and standards as traditional journalists.[24]

There is no one way to define or practice journalism, but good journalism delivers accurate and impartial news and information based on the ideals of accuracy and fairness. Journalists provide a valuable public service when they uncover previously unknown information and put facts in context. News should help people make informed decisions and provide a public forum for community members to talk to each other. News can be both entertaining and informative, and it can be designed to reach large mass audiences or smaller niche groups. It can be distributed through all kinds of media formats, from newspapers and magazines to radio and television to the internet and digital devices. Whatever form it takes, news producers strive to provide a truthful account of important issues and events.

As a result of this time-tested approach to reporting news, some news outlets today are doing some of their best work ever. Consumption of news among the public is up, more people are paying for news, and generally, if you really want to be a well-informed citizen and you have the time, skills, knowledge, and resources to do it, there has never been a better time to be alive. At the national level, competition has increased as some outlets have intensified their focus on national politics and social issues. For example, the rivalry between *The New York Times* and the *Washington Post* has helped generate some of the best political coverage to date, and nonprofits and other digital-only news organizations are providing the journalism people need while exploring new ways of getting the job done. And many journalists today are doing their jobs in spite of relentless attacks and major opposition, primarily from one side of the political spectrum.

Let's also acknowledge the lofty ideals serious journalists often subscribe to and the important role they play in society when they do their jobs well. As veteran journalists Bill Kovach and Tom Rosenstiel tell us in their seminal book, *The Elements of Journalism: What Newspeople Should Know and the Public Should Expect,* "the primary purpose of journalism is to provide citizens with the information they need to be free and self-governing."[25] And in order to accomplish this, journalists must adhere to certain principles, first and foremost among them, that *journalism's first obligation is to the truth* and *its first loyalty is to citizens.* These normative goals began to take shape near the start of the 20th century as journalism emerged as a serious profession, and news organizations began to take seriously their important role in democratic life. Similar ideals have appeared in mission statements and editorial declarations in the ensuing decades, and the history of modern journalism is full of examples of journalists seeking truth and transparency, holding powerful people and institutions accountable to the rule of law and norms of society, and representing the voices of voiceless citizens who otherwise might have had no one to speak on their behalf.

If news is so great, why is it declining? The information revolution of the 21st century certainly provided enormous economic and technological challenges to traditional news media. But throughout the history of modern journalism, the lofty norms of an idealized profession have run up against the stubborn realities of a mixed enterprise. For decades, media scholars have explored the empirical realities that often interfere with an otherwise high-minded mission. While these challenges are nothing new, the economic, technological, and political challenges of the digital age have served to accentuate the longstanding problems with news media, and the explosion of alternative voices and distractions have made negative influences on news production and consumption more powerful than ever. Let's explore some reasons for this, which can help us understand and explain the patterns of news coverage we see and dispel some of the myths and misunderstandings that surround the production of news.

Objectivity and Bias

Common critiques of news typically center on the idea that news content is politically biased in favor of liberals or conservatives and that this can be explained by the simple fact that individual journalists are biased. They peddle their own personal views as fact and try to advance a certain narrative. While it's true that partisan bias can sometimes be found, news literacy requires a more nuanced understanding of bias. Subjectivity in news does not come so much from personal opinion being injected into news content but rather from journalistic norms and routines and from outside influences that affect news content.[26] Partisan bias is relatively easy to identify, and it often exists primarily in the eye of the beholder. Partisans on both ends of the political spectrum can look at the same piece of news content and conclude that it's biased against their own point of view—scholars call this the *hostile media effect*. Also, bias can be relative. For example, the political "center" in Europe tends to be more left than the American "center," so these labels can have limited usefulness due to their lack of specificity. The reality is that most news products, like most news consumers, are not highly partisan. But what's harder to identify are the structural biases and frames that appear in news content.

Bias is a tendency or inclination to prefer one thing over another, which is a pretty benign phenomenon in general. Having preferences is part of being human, and sometimes a bias can be an extremely good thing. For example, most people are happy to be "biased" against slavery and human trafficking and to be "biased" in favor of surgeons who wash their hands before going into the operating room. So sometimes "bias" actually represents the stuff of social and cultural progress, including civil and human rights. Sometimes having a bias is just the equivalent of having good judgment, being humane, or relying on the best available evidence.

Good journalism is often "biased" in favor of broadly shared social goals like equal rights and the protection of children, as evidenced by concern over migrant detention centers or increasing awareness around sexual assault allegations. Sometimes journalists are accused of bias simply for seeking out evidence and verification. In the case of the 2003 U.S.-led invasion of Iraq, many news outlets failed to challenge the Bush administration's case for war, which was based on flawed evidence.[27] But the few journalists who did approach the rationale skeptically faced harsh criticism and were ignored by their own newspaper chains.[28] Did they exhibit a "bias" against the Bush administration, or did they simply get the story right? Thousands of American soldiers and Iraqi citizens died in a war based on what is now a well-documented false pretext. The outcome might have been different if more journalists had been biased in favor of good evidence.

The alternative to bias is thought to be objectivity, but this widely known journalistic ideal is also widely misunderstood, sometimes even by journalists themselves. *Objectivity* is a method used by journalists to independently examine the quality of claims and evidence given to support a position or point of view. The goal is to recognize the built-in personal and cultural biases held by all humans and to provide a method for gathering and evaluating information in impartial ways. The method of objectivity is modeled after the scientific method, which is based on dispassionate observation and experimentation. Objectivity in journalism is very much a 20th-century invention in the United States.[29] Before that, there was no such thing as objectivity. From early colonial America up through the Civil War in the 1860s, it was expected that newspapers would express partisan viewpoints based on their ties to political parties and organizations. Many factors contributed to the rise of objectivity. First of all, journalism wasn't considered a "profession" in the modern sense until the early 1900s. Before that, journalists often aimed primarily to tell a good story without regard for independence from influence. They weren't expected to follow professional norms or ethics because those didn't yet exist. This sensationalistic *yellow journalism*—named after the "Yellow Kid" comic that ran in newspapers of the time—appeared in the late 1800s and focused on scandal and intrigue. At the same time, this period produced some of the earliest investigative reporting, exposing corruption in business and in government. Around the 1920s, journalism schools were created, which contributed to the emergence of professional journalism. The job of a journalist was no longer the purview of anyone with a notebook but rather became the province of a more elite set. Only then did it become common to examine the subjectivity of perception and its effects on the newsgathering process.

Two other factors—one technological, one economic—also contributed to the rise of objectivity. Technologically, the invention of the telegraph in 1844 changed the way news and information were distributed, by separating communication from transportation.[30] Imagine having to get on a horse and ride for days to spread news of anything from an election outcome to a military invasion. The arrival of the wired—and later the wireless—telegraph made it possible to spread news quickly. The Associated Press was the leading "wire" service, established in 1846, and the organization realized they could increase the value of their product by minimizing partisanship and standardizing their output to make it more accessible to the widest possible range of subscribers. The other major social change in the late 1800s was economic. As advertising became the main source of revenue for newspapers, publishers realized they could appeal to more advertisers by reaching larger audiences, particularly those audiences with the resources to go out and purchase the goods and services advertisers wanted to publicize. Striving for impartiality over partisanship became the best way to reach larger audiences and make more money.

Today, although the prevalence of partisan media has increased, the objective method remains central to professional newsgathering. Some journalists are so fiercely dedicated to the idea of neutrality, both in reality and in perception, that they abstain from voting in elections. Among these individuals, not voting is thought to be both a public demonstration of a commitment to objectivity and a private way of preserving impartiality in one's own mind. The idea of not voting may come from a good place but is ultimately unnecessary and misguided because this is not what objectivity is really about. Casting a private vote is a civic duty that journalists can take part in without compromising their independence. Most journalists do, however, follow the standards of their organizations and the ethics of the profession that recommend or even require the avoidance of overt political activity. Professional journalists typically do not display yard signs or bumper stickers that support political candidates, parties, or organizations. They typically do not contribute money to candidates or campaign on their behalf. Expressing such an allegiance would create a *conflict of interest*, where the reporter would appear to be—or would actually be—beholden to particular expectations. If a journalist does have an unavoidable conflict of interest, such as writing about a civic or community group they belong to, or a topic in which they have a vested financial interest, professional codes call for them to demonstrate transparency by disclosing the conflict publicly.

Another view of objectivity—even as a method—suggests that the ideal is nothing but a sham. According to some, it's actually harmful for journalists to suggest to the public that they are somehow capable of suppressing their own viewpoints and maintaining an impartial approach to the topics they cover. In this view, journalists should dispense with the pretense and be open and honest about their personal beliefs and preferences. Journalists who emerge from this mold typically do not work—and would not want to work—for organizations that expect an adherence to some version of objectivity. This kind of reporting can be seen in outlets that do not profess an allegiance to objectivity and are open about their point of view, such as the political commentary that appears in magazines and on cable news. It's worth noting that news audiences are at least partly responsible for the rise in popularity of commentary and opinion reporting, having expressed a preference for "voice" in news content, particularly when that voice aligns with their own. This is evident from looking at the top "trending" stories that appear even on mainstream news sites such as *The New York Times*, which are often more likely to be opinion and analysis than traditional front-page "objective" hard news reporting.

This demonstrated preference for opinion runs contrary to what people actually say they want from their news. People often say what they want from news media is accurate, unbiased reporting that eschews opinions and emotions. A 2017 Pew Research study in 38 countries found that 75 percent of respondents said it is never acceptable for a news organization to favor one political party over others, and only 52 percent said their country's news organizations do a good job of fairly reporting different political positions.[31] The desire for impartiality certainly sounds good, and it warms the hearts of traditional journalists and educators who want people to focus on facts first and opinions second, but there are reasons to be skeptical of these claims, as people's behaviors often suggest otherwise. On the other hand, while impartial news remains the gold standard for many in journalism, there can actually be good reasons to favor analysis and commentary over traditional reporting. Sometimes "the facts" alone do not provide the needed context and meaning for news consumers to make sense of what they read and see. So opinionated reporting—as long as it is based in solid facts and evidence—can actually serve a valuable purpose. The problem is that so much opinion reporting is really just propaganda masquerading as news.

It's easy to see how the idea of objectivity has become associated with concepts of "fairness" and "balance," which can be useful. Legislators and other officials often have legitimate opposing views about important issues, such as tax structures, health care, and how to address the problem of climate change. That's why it's common for journalists to take a "both sides" approach to reporting news. For some news producers, this is good enough. A Republican says one thing, a Democrat says another, and the story is complete. But others criticize this approach, saying it reduces the journalist's role to that of a mere court stenographer, who simply records what people say in a courtroom, even when some of those statements might be demonstrably false. One media theory known as *indexing* describes this approach, noting that news reporting on political and policy issues typically adheres to the parameters of debate set by political elites. In other words, news is simply an "index" of what government officials say. And when there is little dissent, the news can become dominated by a singular point of view, as with the 2003 invasion of Iraq, when few politicians dared question the case for war.

Rather, good journalism should work to verify claims made and examine relevant evidence. Reporters need to be skeptical of the information their sources provide, and they need to help citizens understand which points of view most closely align with the truth on an issue. This method is a valuable approach to public affairs reporting, but it can sometimes put journalists in the uncomfortable position of being an arbiter of truth and can lead to accusations of bias when a reporter appears to be "taking sides." But simply presenting two competing sides of an issue often does not reflect reality, and it can easily omit other legitimate points of view. More importantly, the "both sides" approach often leads to the problem of *false equivalence*, where competing positions are given equal weight even though only one is supported by actual evidence. Taken to its extreme, the idea of balance becomes absurd. For example, the conspiracy theory that the Earth is flat has gained traction in some contrarian corners of society. Should reporters qualify references to the planet by highlighting the ongoing "debate" about its roundness? Most would say "no." Similarly, news content has typically represented the social consensus around issues of overt racism and white supremacy—thankfully, most people don't feel like the Ku Klux Klan needs to be consulted to bring "balance" to every story involving race.

On the other hand, reporting on the issue of climate change shows where the problem arises. For years, the "both sides" approach has given many the impression that scientists still debate whether the earth is getting hotter due to human activity. In reality, the science on this is long settled, and any attempt to provide balance between those who accept the scientific reality and those who reject it provides a tremendous disservice. In this case, balanced reporting has misled the public and made it harder to consider and implement effective public policy solutions to mitigate the problem. The October 2018 report from the United Nations Intergovernmental Panel on Climate Change shows the clear urgency of the problem, yet in the United States only 70 percent of people say they believe global warming is happening, and only 57 percent believe it is caused mostly by human activity.[32] These numbers represent significant increases in recent years as the reporting has improved, but the problem remains. The "both sides" approach is certainly safer and easier for journalists who want to avoid accusations of bias and are reluctant to concern themselves with the truth of a matter. But it's important to highlight the inaccuracy of invalid claims. Even the simple act of reporting on misinformation—even when it is described as such—can confuse news consumers about the actual veracity of the information merely by planting the seed of an idea.

Structural Bias and News Frames

Comparing the typical conservative and liberal criticism of biased news can help us further unpack the idea of media bias.[33] The conservative critique often focuses on the liberal bias of individual journalists and their organizations. It's true that professional journalists are more likely to identify as Democrats than as Republicans, although the majority describe themselves as political independents. According to the typical conservative critique, the political biases of liberal journalists means that their work is inevitably biased in favor of liberal positions. This critique focuses heavily on the agency or independence of individual journalists and downplays the influence of professional norms and external forces, such as markets, audiences, sources, and owners. But judging news based on the personal preferences of individuals says little about the actual content of the work they produce. Even a dedicated communist can write flattering portrayals of conservatives if that's what they have to do to get a paycheck. So rather than obsessing over individual preferences, it's more useful to look at the actual content produced, which can even veer to the right if liberal journalists end up overcompensating for their own biases.

If the conservative critique emphasizes agency, the liberal critique emphasizes structure. In the liberal critique, most media outlets are owned by large profit-seeking corporations, which means news content will typically reflect the interests of capitalist owners and advertisers. In this view, organizational goals take priority over individual ones, so it doesn't matter what preferences are held by individual journalists. Through a process of self-selection, journalists either accept and internalize the expectations of their employer or go work elsewhere. Scholars have often criticized the U.S. media system for being controlled by nondemocratic forces. In their 1988 book, *Manufacturing Consent: The Political Economy of the Mass Media*, Edward Herman and Noam Chomsky go so far as to describe news media as "effective and powerful ideological institutions that carry out a system-supportive propaganda function by reliance on market forces, internalized assumptions, and self-censorship, and without significant overt coercion."[34] Specifically, they point to five "filters" that influence news content: ownership, advertising, sourcing, negative responses by establishment power, and fear of imagined threats. Although some critique these scholars for over-emphasizing the influence of structural forces over individual agency, plenty of evidence supports their conclusions.

Which critique is correct? It's possible that both views describe different types of news coverage. If journalists highlight inequality or injustice surrounding civil rights or public welfare, news can appear to take a liberal tone. On the other hand, if news promotes the importance of economic growth and offers only positive coverage of the financial industry, conservative positions can dominate. Both critiques can appear to be true, depending on your perspective. We can learn more by looking deeper into how news is actually made. Neither the liberal nor the conservative critique tells much about the professional routines, norms, and values that influence news coverage. A range of research has worked to document these forces. Sociologists such as Gaye Tuchman and Herbert Gans were among the first in the 1970s to conduct newsroom ethnographies—studies of the inner workings of newsroom practices and operations—in order to identify values that guide news producers.[35]

In his 1979 book, *Deciding What's News: A Study of CBS Evening News, NBC Nightly News, Newsweek, and Time*, Gans identified several of these values that frame news content. "Ethnocentrism and nationalism" are prominent approaches to covering foreign affairs. The United States appears as a global force for good, operating in the best interest of all involved. Anytime the United States is engaged in military conflict, such as the 1991 Gulf War or the 2003 Iraq invasion, the nationalist frame is evident. The purpose of a conflict is presented as making the world more free and spreading democracy even when there is more to the story. "Altruistic democracy" is the idea that democracy is the best form of government and always operates in the best interest of citizens. The "responsible capitalism" value suggests that free enterprise and economic growth are always positive forces, and government regulation is a negative interference. "Small-town pastoralism" suggests that news gives preference to rural communities and "Main Street" values. "Individualism" is the value of individual liberty over social cohesion, and "moderatism" limits coverage of excess or extremism. Gans's study suggests that bias in mainstream news content is more likely to be oriented around values such as these rather than overt political partisanship.

Other scholars have identified a range of structural biases that are built into the news media system and that influence the content produced.[36] As media scholar Andrew Cline has pointed out, highlighting various examples of liberal or conservative bias might feel good, but it doesn't actually help us understand or explain news content in a meaningful way.[37] It's more helpful to examine different types of *structural bias*, or preferences that are built into the way news is produced and that shape what news looks like. News obviously has a preference for timeliness, which might seem like a silly thing to point out, but it reminds us that news is always looking for something new and fresh, which often means neglecting meaningful contexts that could bring light to an issue. For instance, you might read or hear about today's legislative vote on a health care bill without ever learning much about how it came to be, whose interests it serves, or what impact it might have. Similarly, it's difficult to develop a holistic understanding of issues around racial inequality and segregation without knowing something about historic and discriminatory practices—such as the "redlining" that allowed banks to deny loans to people based on demographics, which made it harder for minorities to buy homes and build equity. Offering history lessons isn't necessarily the job of the news, but if we are mainly learning about social problems from news, we are definitely seeing only part of the picture.

Another seemingly obvious structural bias is a preference for visuals, especially on television. If a story cannot be well told visually, it is less likely to get coverage. That can mean a disproportionate focus on sensational events such as car accidents, house fires, terrorist attacks, natural disasters, protests, rallies, and inflammatory stump speeches. It's not that these are insignificant, but it's cheap and easy to endlessly repeat footage of eye-catching visuals, while it's expensive and challenging to dig through government documents to examine tax policy or agricultural subsidies and to tell those stories that don't come pre-packaged with an obvious visual component. Along with the visual bias comes the narrative bias, where good stories need a strong narrative arc with a clear beginning, middle, and end. Election campaigns have a near-perfect three-act structure, from the declaration of candidacy to the campaigning and debating to the election night outcome, which all provides excellent fodder for a good story. They have protagonists and antagonists, and they are full of drama. Again, that's not necessarily bad, but it does mean other less compelling stories can be neglected. Good narratives typically include some kind of conflict, which is another bias. News is often negative and highlights disagreement among adversaries, which is not surprising, but it does paint a skewed picture of the world and gives the impression that policy making is always about competition, and never about cooperation.

A preference for the status quo is another built-in structural bias. News rarely challenges conventional wisdom about economic growth or commercialism or social class or the American two-party political system. This can be explained, in part, by the winner-take-all nature of two-party governance, but it certainly makes it harder for a third party to ever become viable or compete on a level playing field. Another type of bias—a "fairness bias"—reflects the "both sides" approach to newsgathering discussed earlier, which can generate a false equivalence between unequal positions. All of these structural biases can often be wrapped up into the one bias that rules them all, which is a commercial bias. Profit imperatives often demand that news be profitable, which creates incentives to prefer what's popular over what's important. Furthermore, when news is supported by advertising, news producers have an incentive to make sure the advertising content is unchallenged by the news content. This is not to say that advertising automatically dictates news content; that kind of outright influence would be too easy to spot and too hard to digest. It's a softer influence that makes its way into the news. Think of enthusiastic television reporters who go live on Black Friday inside big box retail stores where there are great deals to be had. Have you ever heard the message that we already have plenty of stuff and we should think about reducing our levels of consumption?

Framing, discussed briefly in Chapter 1, is another way to think about bias. Scholar Todd Gitlin defined framing as "principles of selection, emphasis, and presentation composed of little tacit theories about what exists, what happens, and what matters."[38] Imagine taking a picture with your camera—you have to point the camera somewhere and decide what to include and what to ignore. How do you decide? The general idea of framing is often traced to sociologist Erving Goffman's 1959 book, *The Presentation of Self in Everyday Life*, which treats face-to-face interactions as a sort of performance where individuals select what sort of "self" they will put forward.[39] When applied to news, framing is about the many subtle and often unconscious choices that are made when presenting a story. *Media frames*, according to Gitlin, are "persistent patterns of cognition, interpretation, and presentation, of selection, emphasis, and exclusion, by which symbol-handlers routinely organize discourse, whether verbal or visual."[40] "Symbol-handlers" are the message creators, whether traditional journalists or others, who decide where to direct attention and how to present their selections. According to scholar Robert Entman, framing is a mix of "selection" and "salience."[41] Reporters select events and actions for coverage based on their own perceived reality and then make them *salient*, or prominent, in their reporting based on their own subjective analysis and interpretation. Because of their orientation toward certain news frames, reports often focus on conflict, winners and losers, and wrongdoing. As a result, certain sources such as government officials, experts, and industry leaders often have a major advantage when it comes to setting the terms of a debate.

While framing is an inevitable outcome of the process of selectively representing reality, good journalists strive to take a "wide angle" approach to a story and to consider as many different perspectives as possible. Sometimes, this requires producing multiple stories on a topic. Such thorough reporting is time consuming and expensive, which helps explain why news producers often omit important contexts from the issues and events they cover. Shanto Iyengar helps explain this by differentiating between "episodic" and "thematic" frames.[42] *Episodic frames* focus on specific individuals and events, which can lead news consumers to view social problems in terms of the personal failures of individuals rather than seeing large social or economic contexts that affect daily life. For example, news stories about homelessness and poverty often focus on individuals and their struggle to survive, which makes news consumers more likely to blame the individual for their own laziness and ineptitude. At the same time, when stories emphasize personal success over broader social forces, it's easy to think individuals have the power to determine their own fate when the reality is that some individuals benefit from socioeconomic and cultural privileges more than others. Compare this with *thematic frames*, which provide context about larger social and national issues that contribute to social problems. In this case, forces such as high unemployment, widespread poverty, and government policy making become the focus of a story, which helps illustrate that success or failure is often not about the personal triumph or shortcomings of individuals but rather depends on how the fabric of society is woven. (This might remind you of the "sociological imagination" from Chapter 1—recall the difference between "personal troubles" and "public issues.") News is often dominated by episodic frames, which tend to display a bias toward personal stories and anecdotes, which often simplify complex issues and ignore important social contexts. As a result, news consumers are left with a poor understanding of the broader forces and influences that affect how the world really works.

To sum up, our common notions of objectivity and bias are often misguided and unhelpful. While it's good to be able to highlight partisan bias in news and to identify individuals and their organizations for their patterns of partisanship, news consumers would benefit from an expanded view of the broader forces that influence news production. We should first examine our preconceived notions, and then examine the structural factors at play as well as the values and frames that appear. Who is featured in a story and who is left out? What perspectives are present? Is the story complete and accurate? Has the information been verified by independent experts or witnesses? Ultimately, what is the meaning being conveyed and whose interests does it serve?[43]

Questions for Discussion

1. What are the differences between journalism and other kinds of news and information?
2. Looking beyond news content, what are the structural contexts that influence how and why news is produced and consumed?
3. What types of bias can be found in news media beyond the overt forms of political bias people often talk about?
4. How does a misunderstood notion of objectivity contribute to the problem of false equivalence? How can a news consumer identify and avoid such reporting?
5. What kinds of frames tend to dominate most news content? Analyze the framing at work in different types of news media. What frames tend to prevail and why?

Notes

1. Eliza Collins, "Les Moonves: Trump's Run Is 'Damn Good for CBS,'" *Politico Magazine*, February 29, 2016, www.politico.com/blogs/on-media/2016/02/les-moonves-trump-cbs-220001.
2. Mary Ann Georgantopoulos, "CNN's President Says It Was A Mistake to Air So Many Trump Rallies And 'Let Them Run,'" *BuzzFeed News*, October 14, 2016, www.buzzfeednews.com/article/maryanngeorgantopoulos/cnn-president-mistake-to-air-so-many-trump-rallies.
3. Emily Stewart, "Donald Trump Rode $5 Billion in Free Media to the White House," TheStreet, November 20, 2016, www.thestreet.com/story/13896916/1/donald-trump-rode-5-billion-in-free-media-to-the-white-house.html.
4. Michael Barthel, "Despite Subscription Surges for Largest U.S. Newspapers, Circulation and Revenue Fall for Industry Overall," *Pew Research Center*, June 1, 2017. www.pewresearch.org/fact-tank/2017/06/01/circulation-and-revenue-fall-for-newspaper-industry/.
5. "Newspapers Deliver Across the Ages," *Nielsen*, December 15, 2016. www.nielsen.com/us/en/insights/news/2016/newspapers-deliver-across-the-ages.
6. Al Tompkins, "SPJ Research Suggests That a Surge in PIOs Negatively Impacts Journalism," *Poynter*, September 5, 2018. www.poynter.org/news/spj-research-suggests-surge-pios-negatively-impacts-journalism.
7. Seth Ashley, Jessica Roberts, and Adam Maksl, *American Journalism and "Fake News": Examining the Facts* (Santa Barbara, CA: ABC-CLIO, 2018), xi.
8. See also Edson C. Tandoc, Zheng Wei Lim, and Richard Ling, "Defining 'Fake News,'" *Digital Journalism* 6, no. 2 (February 7, 2018): 137–53, https://doi.org/10.1080/21670811.2017.1360143.
9. Thomas Kent, "Fake News Is about to Get so Much More Dangerous," *Washington Post*, September 6, 2018. www.washingtonpost.com/opinions/fake-news-is-about-to-get-so-much-more-dangerous/2018/09/06/3d7e4194-a1a6-11e8-83d2-70203b8d7b44_story.html.
10. Will Knight, "The Defense Department Has Produced the First Tools for Catching Deepfakes," *MIT Technology Review*, August 7, 2018. www.technologyreview.com/s/611726/the-defense-department-has-produced-the-first-tools-for-catching-deepfakes/.
11. Craig Silverman, "This Analysis Shows How Viral Fake Election News Stories Outperformed Real News On Facebook," *BuzzFeed News*, November 16, 2016.

www.buzzfeednews.com/article/craigsilverman/viral-fake-election-news-outperformed-real-news-on-facebook.

12. Peter Dizikes, "Study: On Twitter, False News Travels Faster than True Stories," *MIT News*, March 8, 2018. http://news.mit.edu/2018/study-twitter-false-news-travels-faster-true-stories-0308.

13. Benedict Carey, "'Fake News': Wide Reach but Little Impact, Study Suggests," *The New York Times*, August 9, 2018, sec. Health. www.nytimes.com/2018/01/02/health/fake-news-conservative-liberal.html.

14. Ibid.

15. Erik C. Nisbet, Paul Beck, and Richard Gunther, "Trump May Owe His 2016 Victory to 'fake News,' New Study Suggests," *The Conversation*, February 15, 2018, http://theconversation.com/trump-may-owe-his-2016-victory-to-fake-news-new-study-suggests-91538.

16. Karen Yourish and Troy Griggs, "8 U.S. Intelligence Groups Blame Russia for Meddling, but Trump Keeps Clouding the Picture," *The New York Times*, July 16, 2018, sec. U.S., www.nytimes.com/interactive/2018/07/16/us/elections/russian-interference-statements-comments.html, www.nytimes.com/interactive/2018/07/16/us/elections/russian-interference-statements-comments.html.

17. Kathleen Hall Jamieson, *Cyberwar: How Russian Hackers and Trolls Helped Elect a President—What We Don't, Can't, and Do Know* (Oxford: Oxford University Press, 2018), 16.

18. Brendan Nyhan, "Fake News and Bots May Be Worrisome, but Their Political Power Is Overblown," *The New York Times*, February 16, 2018, sec. The Upshot, www.nytimes.com/2018/02/13/upshot/fake-news-and-bots-may-be-worrisome-but-their-political-power-is-overblown.html.

19. John McCormack, "The Election Came Down to 77,744 Votes in Pennsylvania, Wisconsin, and Michigan (Updated)," *The Weekly Standard*, November 10, 2016, www.weeklystandard.com/john-mccormack/the-election-came-down-to-77-744-votes-in-pennsylvania-wisconsin-and-michigan-updated.

20. Kevin Granville, "Facebook and Cambridge Analytica: What You Need to Know as Fallout Widens," *The New York Times*, May 14, 2018, sec. Technology, www.nytimes.com/2018/03/19/technology/facebook-cambridge-analytica-explained.html.

21. Gordon Pennycook and David G. Rand. "Lazy, Not Biased: Susceptibility to Partisan Fake News Is Better Explained by Lack of Reasoning Than by Motivated Reasoning." *SSRN Scholarly Paper*. (Rochester, NY: Social Science Research Network, 2018). https://papers.ssrn.com/abstract=3165567.

22. See Gordon Pennycook, Jonathan A. Fugelsang, and Derek J. Koehler, "Everyday Consequences of Analytic Thinking," *Current Directions in Psychological Science* 24, no. 6 (December 1, 2015): 425–32, https://doi.org/10.1177/0963721415604610.

23. Michael Bronstein et al., "Belief in Fake News Is Associated with Delusionality, Dogmatism, Religious Fundamentalism, and Reduced Analytic Thinking," *SSRN Scholarly Paper* (Rochester, NY: Social Science Research Network, September 14, 2018), 2, https://papers.ssrn.com/abstract=3172140.

24. See Tim P Vos, Stephanie Craft, and Seth Ashley, "New Media, Old Criticism: Bloggers' Press Criticism and the Journalistic Field," *Journalism* 13, no. 7 (October 1, 2012): 850–68, https://doi.org/10.1177/1464884911421705.

25. Bill Kovach and Tom Rosenstiel, *The Elements of Journalism: What Newspeople Should Know and the Public Should Expect*, 1st rev. (New York: Three Rivers Press, 2007), 12.

26. See Michael Schudson, *The Sociology of News* (New York: W.W. Norton & Company, 2012).

27. See Oliver Boyd-Barrett, "Judith Miller, The New York Times, and the Propaganda Model," *Journalism Studies* 5, no. 4 (2004): 435–49.

28. Max Follmer, "The Reporting Team That Got Iraq Right," *Huffington Post*, March 28, 2008, sec. Politics, www.huffingtonpost.com/2008/03/17/the-reporting-team-that-g_n_91981.html.

29. See Michael Schudson, *Discovering the News: A Social History of American Newspapers* (New York: Basic Books, 1978).

30. James W. Carey, *Communication as Culture: Essays on Media and Society* (Boston: Unwin Hyman, 1989), 11–28.

31. Amy Mitchell et al., "Publics Globally Want Unbiased News Coverage, but Are Divided on Whether Their News Media Deliver," *Pew Research Center's Global Attitudes Project* (blog), January 11, 2018, www.pewglobal.org/2018/01/11/publics-globally-want-unbiased-news-coverage-but-are-divided-on-whether-their-news-media-deliver/.

32. "Yale Climate Opinion Maps 2018." *Yale Program on Climate Change Communication* (blog), accessed October 16, 2018, http://climatecommunication.yale.edu/visualiza tions-data/ycom-us-2018/.

33. Pamela J. Shoemaker and Stephen D. Reese, *Mediating the Message in the 21st Century: A Media Sociology Perspective*, 3rd edition (New York: Routledge/Taylor & Francis Group, 2014), 9.

34. Edward S. Herman and Noam Chomsky, *Manufacturing Consent: The Political Economy of the Mass Media* (New York: Pantheon Books, 2002), 306.

35. See Herbert J. Gans, *Deciding What's News: A Study of CBS Evening News, NBC Nightly News, Newsweek, and Time* (Evanston, IL: Northwestern University Press, 2004); Gaye Tuchman, *Making News: A Study in the Construction of Reality* (New York: Free Press, 1978).

36. See Shoemaker and Reese, *Mediating the Message in the 21st Century: A Media Sociology Perspective*; Pamela J. Shoemaker and Tim P. Vos, *Gatekeeping Theory* (New York: Routledge, 2009).

37. Andrew Cline, "Bias," in *21st Century Communication: A Reference Handbook*, 2 vols. (Thousand Oaks: SAGE Publications, Inc., 2009), 479–88, https://doi.org/10.4135/9781412964005.

38. Todd Gitlin, *The Whole World Is Watching: Mass Media in the Making and Unmaking of the New Left* (Berkeley: University of California Press, 2003), 6.

39. Erving Goffman, *The Presentation of Self in Everyday Life* (London: Penguin, 1990).

40. Gitlin, *The Whole World Is Watching*, 7.

41. Robert M. Entman, "Framing: Toward Clarification of a Fractured Paradigm," *Journal of Communication* 43, no. 4 (December 1, 1993): 52, https://doi.org/10.1111/j.1460-2466.1993.tb01304.x.

42. Shanto Iyengar, *Media Politics: A Citizen's Guide*, 3rd edition (New York: W. W. Norton & Company, 2015), 255.

43. I asked a similar set of questions in Ashley, Roberts, and Maksl, *American Journalism and "Fake News,"* 108.

4

THE STRUCTURE OF NEWS MEDIA SYSTEMS

What do you know about "net neutrality"? It's the idea that the internet should be treated as a level playing field, which means internet service providers (like Comcast and Verizon) don't get to pick and choose what kind of content makes its way to your laptop or smartphone. It's not a controversial proposition for most people; there is widespread support for the idea. The main opposition has come from those associated with—surprise—internet and wireless service providers, who would like to reserve the right to control access to content even if they profess never to place limits on what you can or can't see. If the internet is to be a truly democratic medium where participation is open to all, it might make sense to want to protect a diverse, competitive marketplace by implementing laws and policies that do so. But does this represent unnecessary government intervention in the marketplace, or is this exactly what government is for—to promote competition and innovation by preventing the powerful few from exerting their will over society at large?

Whether you are for or against net neutrality, it could have major implications for how you access all types of media content, from sports and entertainment to news and information. Without a policy of net neutrality in place, it could allow an internet service provider like Comcast to create different levels or types of access to different types of content, and it could give priority to the content it already owns and profits from, such as NBC and Universal. And it can make (and has made) services like Netflix pay extra to send video over the web, which is one thing for a giant like Netflix, but it makes it virtually impossible for a competitor to enter the video streaming marketplace.[1] This is where structure and content collide, so it is policy decisions like this one that create the news media system for the rest of us.

Historically, the design of news media systems has not been a democratic process or a question of popular preferences or needs. Rather, it's generally a matter of technical details that are left to experts and administrators to work out. That's because policy making is often a highly tedious, highly boring process, and most of us would rather eat raw beets than wade through the details of federal rulemaking. But media laws and policies create the context for our mediated interaction, and they have a major effect on the content we see. That's why news literacy requires an understanding of that context, so we need to step back and take a broad look at how the system works and see what kinds of content are privileged by the structural arrangements that surround us.

This chapter shows how competition among elite interests has driven the creation of news media systems through complex legal and regulatory structures, and we'll see how those structures affect what kind of content gets produced and how it gets distributed. Exploring some basic concepts such as gatekeeping and positive liberty helps us understand the power of the First Amendment to protect the rights of individual citizens (not just media corporations), the role of statutory law in establishing libel and ownership rules, the role of the courts in interpreting those rules, and the process of administrative rulemaking (or lack thereof) related to news content. And knowing about possible alternatives to the status quo illustrates the possibilities of policy making in the public interest.

Finally, by comparing international news media systems, it becomes easier to see and understand different approaches, such as the hybrid systems of Europe, which often have strong commitments to public media versus the highly commercial approach in the United States. Global trends indicate an increase in privatization and commercialization of news media, leading to predictable patterns of news coverage in line with elite interests and profit-making. Understanding the rise of neoliberalism and deregulation since the 1980s helps explain the decline of public service journalism during that period. To show how we arrived at this moment, a little history is in order, and we'll see how history matters in our effort to understand the structure and function of news media today.

All of this can be a lot to take in, especially for news literacy beginners. But knowing more about the structure of the news media system is key to gaining a holistic view of the news and information environment. To help us understand these different layers of influence and their effects, we need a model that can help us break it all down.

Gatekeeping and the Hierarchy of Influences

Let's start by viewing the news production process through the lens of gatekeeping, and we'll work our way up to the more abstract and invisible layers of influence at the structural level. As we established in Chapter 3, even the best and most legitimate journalists and news organizations are subject to a host of internal and external forces that influence their output. This is described by the concept of *gatekeeping*, which shows how routines and structures encourage news media to select and emphasize certain aspects of reality. Scholars Pamela Shoemaker and Tim Vos have defined gatekeeping as "the process of culling and crafting countless bits of information into the limited number of messages that reach people every day, and it is at the center of the media's role in modern public life."[2] The general idea of gatekeeping originated with Kurt Lewin, who developed the metaphor in 1947 to examine how food makes its way from store and garden to the kitchen table. The first application to news production appeared in David Manning White's 1950 study of the story selection process used by one newspaper editor who was charged with deciding which wire stories to include and which ones to exclude.[3] White called the editor "Mr. Gates" and concluded that his individual subjectivity was the most significant factor in the news selection process. More recent research has challenged this finding because we now know much more about other forms of influence that shape the process.

A central goal of media sociology research is to find explanations for why news content turns out the way it does. Scholars who have studied the range of influences on news media have synthesized wide bodies of literature on the different forces that affect news content. In their seminal book, *Mediating the Message in the 21st Century: A Media Sociology Perspective*, Shoemaker and Stephen Reese describe the process in terms of five levels, which they term the "hierarchy of influences."[4] The levels are as follows:

1. Individuals
2. Routine practices
3. Media organizations
4. Social institutions
5. Social systems

Shoemaker and Reese suggest that it is helpful to visualize the five levels in the form of a fancy wedding cake, with individuals at the top, where they seemingly have all the freedom in the world to do as they wish. In reality, they are held up by a variety of other sources of influence including the less obvious social systems in which they must operate (see Figure 4.1). Recall the sociological concept of structure and agency, where individuals often exist in tension (and occasionally in harmony) with the broader social structures that influence the ranges of available options.

While the *individual level* is only one of the five, it tops the cake and remains significant. This is not mainly because of an individual's personal partisan affiliation or their agenda-driven news coverage. Rather, the level covers the more subtle personal characteristics that make up an individual's background, such as age, gender, ethnicity, education, and class status. Because journalists self-select into the profession, part of the individual level seeks to examine who becomes a journalist in the first place and why. That can include an individual's own self-conception as a professional, which could influence their adherence to professional codes of ethics and other content guidelines. Individuals can view themselves as scrappy

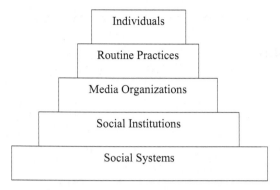

FIGURE 4.1   Hierarchy of Influences Model.

Source: Pamela J. Shoemaker and Stephen D. Reese, *Mediating the Message in the 21st Century: A Media Sociology Perspective*, Third edition. New York: Routledge/Taylor & Francis Group, 2014.

muckrakers or social misfits who answer to no one or they can self-identify as social or cultural elites, such as those who cozy up to government officials and dress up for the annual White House Correspondents' Dinner. Even more subtly, journalists can also be influenced their own *implicit biases*, which are the stereotypes held by individuals based on their own personal experience and their socialization to the world around them. A range of social and cultural biases are pervasive throughout society related to traits including race, religion, gender, age, and others. No one likes to think they are influenced by these unconscious thoughts, but plenty of research has emerged to support this reality.[5] Like anyone, journalists can be influenced by their own implicit biases when they cover women and minority populations, who are often treated differently than males. Female politicians, for example, are often scrutinized for their appearance and their role as caregiver while men rarely face such questions. Ultimately, it is one thing to have a clear partisan agenda, but it is quite another to be influenced by a particular background, identity, and culture. The latter is much more significant for a holistic examination of news content. Good journalism is marked by the rejection of stereotypes of all kinds, especially when the practice flies in the face of pervasive cultural norms.

The next level of the hierarchical model "cake" covers the *communication routines* of news producers, that is, how they do their jobs on a day-to-day basis. For starters, journalists do not start every day with a blank slate. Rather, they bring to their work a set of professional norms and values that direct their attention. This is perfectly understandable; trying to tell the news of the day with no parameters would be an impossible task. News judgment is the process of selecting stories based on generally accepted values, which include prominence and importance, conflict and controversy, the unusual, human interest, timeliness, and proximity. These are news values because they are things that audiences find interesting and important, and they also reflect the collective priorities of individuals and organizations. Routines encourage journalists to follow each other rather than breaking away from the pack. It is routine to rely heavily on official and expert sources as well as public relations practitioners and information specialists. Routines require journalists to conform to certain expectations, such as producing a certain number of stories of prescribed lengths by preset deadlines. Stories must fit the space available in print and on television. Some of this differs in the digital environment, but that adds different requirements such as engagement on social media and multimedia production. Many journalists routinely follow "beats," or topic areas they focus on, such as local or state government, "cops and courts," and education. (A dedicated "labor beat" that covered the working class used to be common at newspapers but has virtually disappeared today.) Routines also include some of the behaviors discussed earlier, such as an adherence to an objective method and to an avoidance of conflicts of interest. These routines do not reflect individual preferences; instead, they are embedded in the process of producing news, and they have a major influence on the outcome.

Beyond routines, news media *organizations* are the third level of influence in the hierarchy. An organization has a collective identity and is governed by policies and structures that have an often unseen influence on news content. Profitability is a leading goal for most commercial news outlets, which means news producers and their content must support this goal. When news outlets are only small parts of much larger corporations, ownership of the organization can have a major effect on content. Stories that get more attention generate more revenue, so these often get priority. And in the digital age, metrics and analytics make it easier than ever to see exactly what's popular and therefore successful. News producers can be encouraged to avoid risky behavior that might upset advertisers and owners. Along with a focus on economic gain comes a focus on reduction of costs. This can mean reducing expenses by cutting staff, decreasing pay, and reducing the amount of work produced. The physical size of newspapers has shrunk significantly in the 21st century, and some have reduced the number of days they publish. The organizational structure of a news outlet influences how decisions are made and who gets hired and fired. Finally, in the age of the much-maligned news media, an organization as a whole must decide whether and how they will respond to extreme criticism and pressure from government and the public. Sometimes, organizations have responded to criticism collectively, as when the *Boston Globe* led the nation's news outlets to respond defensively to President Donald Trump's sharp critiques.[6]

The fourth and fifth levels of the hierarchy of influences consist of forces that lie beyond the boundaries of news producers and their organizations, and this is where we really begin to explore the structure of news media systems. The fourth level covers the *social institutions* that influence news production. In his book *Public Policymaking*, James Anderson defines an institution as "a set of regularized patterns of human behavior that persist over time and perform some significant social function or activity."[7] Rules and structures are the manifestations of these behavior patterns in political life, but as Anderson points out, these arrangements "are usually not neutral in their effects; rather, they tend to favor some interests in society over others and some policy results over others."[8] The social institutions that influence news media include government, markets, advertisers, audiences, technology, law and policy, social movements, nongovernmental organizations, education, and so on. Each of these can exert various kinds of pressure on news producers, which is often reflected in news content. Sources of news have significant influence over what gets covered and how news is framed. Official government sources, such as presidents and prime ministers, have an outsize influence, as pretty much everything they do and say becomes news. Other officials such as spokespeople for city halls and police departments appear routinely in news content, which affords them the opportunity to make sure their point of view is expressed. Interest groups such as the National Rifle Association or National Right to Life or the National Organization for Women or the Sierra Club all work to get their messages out, often by holding events and demonstrations specifically designed to draw media attention and coverage. (Daniel Boorstin in his 1961 book, *The Image*, famously labeled such happenings "pseudo-events" or a "new kind of synthetic novelty which has flooded our experience."[9]) News makers also are influenced by other news makers. News organizations keep close eyes on each other, often in an effort to stay ahead of the competition—but not too far ahead. Advertising exerts indirect influence on news content by financing much of it, and pressure can also be direct, as when news outlets are occasionally "punished" by advertisers such as powerful tobacco companies who have sometimes pulled or threatened to pull their lucrative ads when news outlets covered smoking's adverse health effects.[10] Media markets and policies as well as technology and digital platforms can also affect news production and content, as we will explore in the following paragraphs.

At the bottom layer of the cake of influences sits the *social systems* that influence news. This level is the most abstract and hard to grasp, but it is arguably the most important because of its broad power over society and also because it is generally hidden from view. The broad ideological and cultural foundations of society are typically so ingrained in our lives that it is nearly impossible to see them as anything but natural and inevitable outcomes of modern life. The concept of *hegemony* describes a condition where a dominant group holds power over others and exerts its ideological influence accordingly. Taken one step further, the idea of *cultural hegemony*, as advanced by Antonio Gramsci and other critical theorists, suggests that the ruling class in a society actually works to manipulate the values and norms of the broader population so that the dominant ideology becomes accepted and internalized by all.

The implications for news media include the tendency to adopt and perpetuate the dominant ideology because it seems so embedded in the fabric of society that it is hardly worth questioning or challenging. Any nation with a capitalist economic system values private ownership and free markets, and any democratic political system has some interest in promoting individualism and autonomy through responsible self-governance. In news, these values are often taken for granted as natural, positive social forces, and that's not necessarily a bad thing, nor is it reasonable to expect news content to regularly question broad social structures that often seem far removed from reporting the details of daily life. But these values inform certain news reporting, as when business profiles often focus on the success of individuals (often in the face of difficult odds) rather than framing entrepreneurialism in the context of the legal system that makes it possible or the down sides of narrow self-interest. Those who make the news always operate within the bounds of the broader social structures, and it's no surprise that they would be influenced accordingly.

Scholar Daniel Hallin can help us understand the influence of dominant norms with his concept of the *sphere of legitimate controversy*, a realm where agreed-upon ideas are acceptable subjects of debate, which contributes to the marginalization of views outside the mainstream.[11] (Hallin's idea is similar to what's called the Overton window—the range of policy topics that are acceptable for debate at any given moment.) Topics such as health care and immigration policy are the subject of legitimate debate, but other ideas are broadly settled, such as the ideas that American-style democracy is the superior system of government or that private enterprise and a growing economy are always good things. For Hallin, these ideas lie within a sphere of consensus, where there is thought to be broad agreement and no challenge is necessary. On the other hand, there are also unworthy ideas and values that are largely rejected by news media, such as those held by certain social protesters, dissenters, and political actors who lie outside the mainstream. In this sense, the dominant or "legitimate" thinking in a society operates as a kind of social control and tells news producers and citizens alike what is acceptable and what is not.

I hope this brief tour of the hierarchy of influences model helps show the different forces that influence news content and helps situate the power of individuals and organizations within broader social structures that shape news. To proceed, let's get into the nitty gritty of some of the social institutions and systems that affect news and then consider how different structures can lead to different outcomes.

Media Law and Policy

News media systems do not just appear out of nowhere. Nothing about their structures or operations is natural or inevitable or immutable. Rather, they are created by human actors who make deliberate and accidental decisions, often acting with incomplete or inaccurate information, sometimes with the best of intentions, but other times in attempts to protect and consolidate power. The result is a set of legal and political arrangements that shape the news production process and indirectly influence the content that gets produced. Let's take a look at how the process works and see how it has unfolded over time.

To begin, one of the most important institutions in society is the *market*, where people engage in the economic activity of selling and purchasing goods and services. In a "free market," these exchanges are theoretically unencumbered by rules and regulations, but as we will see, laws and policies always shape markets and give advantages to certain participants. There's really no such thing as a "free" market because buyers and sellers need certain rules of the road to guide their enterprise, and external costs to society are often parts of market exchanges that do not get accounted for between buyers and sellers. (Think of the pollution that results from burning fossil fuels; these are spewed in the atmosphere and written off as an external cost.) These issues certainly apply to the news media marketplace, but there's more. The news media marketplace for the exchange of news and information is an especially complex one for several reasons: one, news media receive unique legal protections in most developed countries, such as the constitutional protection provided by the First Amendment in the United States; two, news media ownership is highly concentrated and barriers to entry are high, which reduces competition and limits the range of options available for consumers of news; three, profitmaking often provides an incentive to cater to the needs of shareholders and advertisers first, and citizens second; four, news often operates on a "dual product model," where the real product is the audience, which is sold to advertisers; and five, news media play a unique role in democratic society as the main source of ongoing education for self-governing citizens. These and other factors make the market for news unusually complex and in need of special oversight. However, markets for news are often subject to a hands-off regulatory approach regarding the content they produce even as laws and policies create structures that are designed to favor certain speech and press interests over others.

Legal protections for news media industries can make it difficult for governments to regulate content except in a few cases such as obscenity and defamation (a.k.a. publishing false information). Instead, the effect of media law and policy often means the creation of regulatory structures that favor the interests of big businesses who own news organizations. In the U.S. context, the First Amendment clearly says "Congress shall make no law" that would limit speech or press freedom. Pretty clear, right? It doesn't get much more straightforward than "*make no law*." Of course, that's never been the case. The First Amendment was signed into law in 1791 as part of the Bill of Rights, and, along with speech and press freedom, it protects religious freedom, the right to free assembly, and the right to petition the government. But only a few years later, Congress passed the Alien and Sedition Acts of 1798, which included the criminalization of "false, scandalous, and malicious writings against the government." The act had its critics who claimed it violated the First Amendment, but many of the founding fathers who wrote the Constitution and Bill of Rights didn't see a contradiction. This was partly because the Federalists had an interest in protecting what was then a fragile republic, but it also shows that even as the law was written, not everyone was clear on its meaning and intent. This means it's up to the courts and regulatory agencies such as the FCC to figure out how to interpret and apply constitutional law.

Also keep in mind that the First Amendment was originally a reaction by early American colonists against the censorship and licensing of the press that took place in Britain, and it was mainly designed to protect the rights of individual citizens who had something to say. There was no such thing as CNN back then, so the idea that these legal protections could be claimed by large corporations wasn't even a possibility. Today, these protections often get reinterpreted as existing for the benefit of news and media industries. In general, this is a good thing because a free press is obviously vital to society, and much of today's news is produced by news organizations that are often part of large corporations. But at the same time, the use of the First Amendment as a shield against any kind of intervention on behalf of citizens or the public interest is what allows media companies to get away with ignoring their responsibility to society, and the effects are significant. Media companies provide increasingly limited amounts of substantive news coverage. They can adopt hyper-partisan outlooks that spread propaganda and misinformation. They can operate under a commercial business model that allows for enormous profits and leaves out speakers who can't afford to participate, which is particularly problematic when it comes to politics. And media companies can even use the First Amendment to protect their rights to exclude diverse voices. In short, although legal protections are designed to benefit society, news media businesses have co-opted the laws to protect their own desires for profit and power.

How did we get here? To get a complete picture of how law and policy affect the news media environment, we need to take a historical look at the evolution of media regulation. Taking a long historical view rather than simply looking at a snapshot of our current moment is important because history matters. It helps us see that nothing in our modern societies is natural or inevitable; rather, the world as it is has been constructed by humans and the decisions they made that got us here. Some decisions were deliberate and some accidental, some made with the best intentions and others without much consideration for where they might take us. And some decisions are made specifically to consolidate power and profits in the hands of those who get to determine or at least influence the outcomes.

The moments when significant decisions get made—scholars call them "critical junctures" or "policy windows"—are important because of their lasting effects. Once a major policy decision is made, a path is created, and it becomes difficult to stray. The fancy term for this is *path dependence*, and a famous example is the invention of the QWERTY keyboard used by English speakers throughout the world today. Designed in part to keep mechanical typewriter keys from jamming, the QWERTY keyboard became standard after its adoption by the five major typewriter manufacturers, which merged to become the Union Typewriter Company in 1893. Even though other keyboard layout options were available, the QWERTY path was laid down long ago, and "exit costs," or the difficulties of changing to a new system (i.e., replacing every keyboard in the English-speaking world and requiring everyone to learn to type all over again), are too great to allow for a change. The rest, as they say, is history—at least for now. Perhaps a new window will open as new forms of digital communication emerge and typing as we know it gets replaced by something else.

Many have argued that we have already reached a new critical juncture in communication with the arrival of digital technologies and the legal, political, and economic questions they bring. For instance, how can we best preserve the internet as a positive force for democracy? Looking back through time at moments where some paths were chosen and others were rejected can help us recognize what a critical juncture looks like and see what alternatives might have been available and considered even if they were ultimately rejected. Learning about this history drives home the point that our current news media systems are not natural or inevitable but only emerged as a result of debates and deliberations.

For starters, while it's easy to take free expression for granted, most of history and most of the planet shows that free expression is an exception, not a rule. For centuries, speech and press rights were limited or nonexistent, and state censorship was common. It didn't matter much because most people couldn't read and were excluded from participation in public life anyway, but it had devastating consequences for anyone who dared speak out against those in power. Ideals of free expression only emerged during the Enlightenment era in the 1700s. In the American colonies, the famous John Peter Zenger trial of 1735 established the idea that a democratic press should be free to criticize public officials. The First Amendment, adopted in 1791, enshrined the concept of press freedom and its importance to democratic self-governance. These ideals are now widespread in the developed world and also in the developing world, but they are also increasingly under siege as authoritarianism has spread in the 21st century. Press and news media are often the first targets of authoritarian rulers who know their power will remain limited unless they can control the sources and spread of information.

While the First Amendment created protections for speech and press freedom, the emergence of new technologies starting in the 1800s presented new challenges. First, the arrival of the wired telegraph in the mid-1800s required difficult decisions over who would be in control. In the United States, the telegraph was quickly monopolized by Western Union and operated as a private business, but in Britain, the government allotted control to the post office, which operated the service as a public utility. Later, around the start of the twentieth century, the original "wireless" technology offered the ability to send signals over the airwaves and was used by amateur radio operators and inventors, but was especially important to ships at sea, who needed to communicate with each other and with shore stations. An absence of regulations caused the airwaves to become cluttered with competing signals and limited the usefulness of wireless for emergency communication. The scope of the problem became clear in 1912 when an ocean liner struck an iceberg and sunk to the bottom of the sea. The ship—RMS

Titanic—sent distress signals over the airwaves, but these were unheard by nearby ships whose radio operators had turned off their equipment for the night and gone to bed. As the rescue efforts mounted, interference from competing signals made it harder to help the survivors. The tragedy of the *Titanic* made it clear that a hands-off, "free market" approach was not working.

Regulating the Air

In the United States, Congress had already begun to develop a plan to regulate the airwaves, but the disaster in the North Atlantic made it clear that some kind of regulatory framework was needed. The result was the Radio Act of 1912, which adopted international standards for emergency communication and required for the first time that all broadcasters be licensed by the federal government's Department of Commerce. Meanwhile, in Europe, most nations had already adopted international standards as early as 1903 and were already moving toward government-operated broadcasting systems. As World War I broke out in 1914, European governments had a sense of urgency to take control of their broadcasting systems. As the United States entered the war, the navy came to dominate the airwaves, which led some to advocate for a full government takeover of broadcasting in the United States. While some favored control by the navy, others proposed control by the Post Office Department. And amateur operators wanted to preserve their own access to the airwaves, as did others with a stake in radio, including political parties, universities, newspapers, churches, and department stores. In other words, plenty of different individuals and organizations had an interest in radio, and their competing visions for the technology would eventually have to be managed with a policy solution.[12]

Before the 1920s, wireless technology was mainly used for point-to-point communication, as between ships at sea, and the idea of "broadcasting" to a large mass audience didn't even exist. Only in the 1920s did it occur to some that this new technology could be a useful way to reach many people at once. In the United States, the commercial broadcasting industry began to emerge as the major radio equipment manufacturers realized the enormous potential. The big four companies that emerged would have a lasting presence: the Radio Corporation of America (RCA), General Electric (GE), Atlantic Telephone and Telegraph (AT&T), and Westinghouse. The lack of a clear regulatory framework for who could broadcast and on what frequencies led to the passage of the Radio Act of 1927, which created the Federal Radio Commission and empowered it to grant licenses to operate in the "public interest, convenience and necessity." There would be no government takeover of the airwaves, nor would there be any attempt to sell licenses to the highest bidder. Rather, licenses were granted for free to the established commercial broadcasters while others were excluded from the airwaves. The licenses were awarded to those with the best technology, the clearest signals, and the most "neutral" programming. This gave a decided advantage to the established commercial broadcasters.

Compare this to the approach in most European nations, notably Britain, where the British Broadcasting Company was formed in 1922 as a government-controlled consortium of radio manufacturers, a heavily regulated private monopoly. By 1927, the company had shifted to a publicly owned corporation operating under a royal charter from the monarchy. Financed by licensing fees paid by citizens and largely protected from political influence, the British Broadcasting Company (BBC) model served as the world's primary alternative to a commercial approach to broadcasting. By explicitly avoiding private ownership of the airwaves, the new BBC was designed to provide a public service, to avoid commercialism, and to promote equal access to culture and knowledge.

To some in Britain, the American approach represented the way *not* to do broadcasting due to their concern that the American design was based on commercial rather than democratic impulses. The creators of the BBC were motivated by the notion of "public service," which placed broadcasting in the context of a public utility that aimed to bring culture to the masses and maintain broad access to privilege and opportunity. By contrast, the U.S. approach and the concept of the "public interest" ultimately gave preference to industry and economic concerns. Thanks to path dependence, these early designs have endured through time, and even though both systems have changed since their origins, these different policy solutions dating back to the early 1900s still provide the foundation for broadcasting in each country today. In the United States, a small handful of large corporations continue to control most of the major news media; meanwhile, the BBC is the largest broadcasting service in the world and maintains its public service mission.

As the British and other broadcasting systems solidified in the 1930s, the outcome for the American system remained unsettled. Ongoing debate surrounded the issue of control of the airwaves, with many firmly opposed to advertising of any kind. One amendment debated in Congress would have allocated one-fourth of the available spectrum to noncommercial and educational entities, but this failed to gain traction. With the Communications Act of 1934, the commercial broadcasting system was fully realized as the newly created Federal Communication Commission (FCC) was tasked with the regulation of all wired and wireless communication, which cemented the existing licensing system into place. The 1934 law still provides the framework for American communication policy today, including the regulatory approach to the internet and the policy of net neutrality. These early policy decisions about who gets to speak and who does not have had a lasting effect. The commercial system does not restrict content per se, but, by creating the system as it is, the result has certainly been to privilege some speakers over others.

It's important to view this outcome in the context of the growth of market society in general in early 20th-century America.[13] As American culture merged with corporate power, the idea of a "public interest" was increasingly viewed as the ability to participate in consumer society, and the regulation of broadcasting was designed for just that purpose. As sociologist Paul Starr has written, "Commercial radio did not merely become entrenched as an interest group; it became embedded in culture and consciousness, and it gathered legitimacy until it seemed impossible that it could be any other way."[14] The idea of a *laissez faire*, or "hands off," approach to licensing broadcasters actually had the effect of concentrating a large amount of influence in the hands of a powerful few. This sort of lack of regulatory intervention is often heralded as a democratic solution, but it often has the backwards effect of encouraging and facilitating concentrations of power, which generally has led to various kinds of inequality, marginalization, and homogenization of American life. It is decidedly undemocratic.

By the end of the 1930s, radio had exploded in American life, and despite the commercial domination of the airwaves, the FCC took seriously its mission of regulating radio (and later television) in the public interest, especially as critics became increasingly vocal about problems of commercialization and the effects of concentrated ownership.[15] In 1940, the FCC issued its "Report on Chain Broadcasting," which addressed concerns over monopoly practices among radio networks. The FCC created new standards that were meant to address—among other things—anticompetitive practices by the National Broadcasting Corporation (NBC). As a result, the NBC Blue network was sold to become the American Broadcasting Corporation (ABC). In the same era, the FCC created rules designed to increase competition by limiting ownership over multiple stations and networks. The Supreme Court and Department of Justice occasionally stepped in as well, using antitrust law to challenge concentrated ownership. For example, General Electric was forced to divest its ownership of the Radio Corporation of America in 1930 (although GE reacquired RCA in 1986 only to liquidate it in the following years), and in 1945, the Supreme Court ruled against the Associated Press for anticompetitive practices in news distribution.

In addition to regulating the structure of the broadcasting industry, the FCC took steps to improve the quality of content. In 1941, the Mayflower Doctrine required radio stations to remain neutral in news and politics and refrain from editorializing. In 1949, it was replaced by the Fairness Doctrine, which required that broadcasters meet their public interest obligations by providing significant coverage of public affairs and providing a "reasonable, although not necessarily equal" representation of competing viewpoints. This was one of the few regulations in the history of American media policy to ever place restrictions on news content itself. Enforcement was sometimes lax and uneven, but the rule did discourage broadcasters from offering blatantly one-sided commentary; the repeal of the doctrine in the 1980s helped make it possible for highly lucrative talk radio, including such giants as Rush Limbaugh, to emerge and dominate the airwaves.[16] Until the 1987 repeal of the Fairness Doctrine, some complained that it violated the First Amendment because of its content requirements, but it was deemed constitutional by the Supreme Court in 1969 in a ruling stipulating that broadcasters must uphold their obligation to serve the public interest as stewards of the public airwaves. The same logic did not apply to newspapers because of the theoretically unlimited nature of print publications, but newspapers did face ownership restrictions during this period as well as the occasional antitrust charge.

The unevenness of regulatory interventions was also evident in the late 1940s, when the FCC attempted to spell out specific public service requirements for broadcasters in the FCC "Blue Book," but commercial broadcasters were fiercely opposed, leading to the Blue Book's defeat and demise.[17] As of the 1950s, as television exploded into American homes, a surge of new programming was dominated by commercial entertainment as opposed to airing the kinds of cultural or education programming many had hoped for.[18] In 1961, the chairman of the FCC, Newton Minnow, labeled the commercial television landscape a "vast wasteland" and called for greater programming in the public interest. However, commercial broadcasters faced few challenges and easily renewed their licenses to the public airwaves.

Eventually, a lack of educational programming led to the creation of public media in the United States. Congress passed the Public Broadcasting Act of 1967, which created the Corporation for Public Broadcasting to support noncommercial and educational programming on television and radio. For the first time, the United States had two noncommercial alternatives on the mainstream airwaves: the Public Broadcasting Service (PBS)—known for such childhood staples as *Sesame Street* and *Mr. Rogers' Neighborhood*—on television and National Public Radio (NPR). These outlets remain important American institutions and receive broad public support, but their funding is paltry compared to that of public media systems in other developed nations. Rather than being well supported by public funding, PBS and NPR receive most of their funding from grants and small donations—from viewers like you.[19]

Despite its commercial structure and its considerable flaws, from the 1950s through the 1970s, American news media in print and on television was overwhelmingly trusted by Americans. From Walter Cronkite to Watergate, news media cemented their place as a major institution in American life. After coverage of the Watergate scandal in the 1970s helped bring down a corrupt president, journalists were celebrated in popular culture as noble defenders of democracy. Network news divisions generally were not expected to be profitable, and news media owners for broadcast and print outlets devoted considerable resources to original newsgathering both at home and abroad. For many, these high-water marks represent the pinnacle of American news media in terms of quality, trust, accuracy, and overall reliability.

The Rise of Market Fundamentalism

Enter *neoliberalism*, or the idea that if something doesn't have market value, it simply doesn't have value. This leaves governments to promote pro-corporate policies that often benefit the powerful few rather than helping ordinary citizens when markets fail. Beginning in the late 1970s, this new regulatory philosophy began to take hold in the developed world, particularly in the United States and Britain, bringing profound changes to business, markets, governments, labor, and public service. Before that, *liberalism*—a philosophy of liberty and equality born from the Age of Enlightenment—guided government policies to promote and protect freedom and openness but also sought to balance the centrality of markets with the needs of citizens, bringing a sense of public responsibility to the organization of society. The rise of liberalism followed the disasters of the Great Depression and World War II, which showed the need for strong government intervention in society. This meant progressive taxation and distributed wealth were used to support government investments in education, health care, and infrastructure and to provide protections for workers, children, the poor, and even the environment.

Neoliberalism brought a reversal of these trends and a massive expansion of the centrality of markets—not governments—in society. As George Monbiot has written, "Neoliberalism sees competition as the defining characteristic of human relations. It redefines citizens as consumers, whose democratic choices are best exercised by buying and selling, a process that rewards merit and punishes inefficiency."[20] To this end, governments turned toward "deregulation" and a hands-off approach to policy making. In theory, this approach was the best and even most democratic way to ensure the individual freedom necessary to pursue life, liberty, and happiness. But the reality of this approach was to create new policies that favored market exchanges and powerful interests. The fallout has produced extreme inequality and created perverse incentives by the wealthy few to pursue blatant self-interest despite the costs to society.

As Monbiot has documented, neoliberalism has helped produce unnecessary violence, financial catastrophes, and ecological collapse, where social and environmental costs are mere *externalities*, or the unaccounted for side effects of market exchanges. Often decried as "market fundamentalism," neoliberalism is designed to bring economic growth at any cost and to ensure that any gains that result go primarily to the wealthy few, who regard their success as the result of smart entrepreneurialism when the reality is that they have benefitted from status and privilege and control. While this state of affairs has brought widespread discontent to much of the public, the philosophy has thrived through its invisibility. To ordinary citizens, at this point, this is just the way things are.

News media and communication generally were among those industries most affected by the rise of neoliberalism. Through the 1980s, the widespread "deregulation" across American industries led communication policy makers to take an even stronger market-oriented view and eliminate virtually all remaining public interest requirements for media producers and owners. To policy makers, media came to be viewed as merely another product to be bought and sold. This idea is best summed up by the regulatory philosophy of then FCC chairman Mark Fowler, who famously told *Reason* magazine in 1981, "television is just another appliance—it's a toaster with pictures."[21] In other words, media content is just another consumer product requiring no special treatment or restrictions despite long-held public interest obligations. The 1980s saw the elimination of the long-standing Fairness Doctrine, the loosening of ownership restrictions, the relaxation of programming guidelines and limitations of advertising, and the extension of broadcast licensing periods. In some ways, these deregulatory moves could be justified by a newly competitive market created by cable and satellite technology, but they also were certainly brought about by pressure from industry groups seeking to solidify their dominant positions in media.

The deregulatory trend continued into the 1990s, culminating in the sweeping Telecommunications Act of 1996, which amended the original Communications Act of 1934. The law was heralded for its ability to remove regulatory hurdles and help media grow in a newly converged landscape and a competitive economic environment. But as journalist and scholar Ben Bagdikian documented in his 2004 book, *The New Media Monopoly*, the new law was the "major accomplishment" of the "big five" media conglomerates at the time—Time Warner, Disney, News Corporation, Viacomm, and Bertelsmann—which engaged in "cartel-like relations" to preserve their dominant market positions, resulting in a narrowing of choices and limiting of voices. As Bagdikian famously concluded, "This gives each of the five corporations and their leaders more communications power than was exercised by any despot or dictatorship in history."[22]

As this overview shows, the structure of a news media system has a significant effect on the content it produces. American media regulation has always consisted of a contradictory mix of strong speech protections combined with a *laissez faire* approach to ownership and public service requirements. While the "hands off" approach is often thought to be the best way to ensure political and economic freedom and growth, the reality is that government has an important role to play in promoting free speech and expression and in limiting the concentrations of power that dominate media industries. Ultimately, any regulatory framework— even one that claims not to exist—will have an effect on news media content. The point of all of this is to help us remember that the structure of the news media system—and the content it produces—is not natural or inevitable, nor is it set in stone. As we will see later, a more democratic news media is not only possible but perhaps even preferable if we care about ensuring and protecting high-quality news and information that can serve the needs of democratic life.

Profit and Power

The idea of regulating news media might seem outdated in an age of infinite content. But there's a big difference between drowning in a sea of information and having easy access to an abundance of reliable journalism. And despite the advent of digital technology and the internet, since the arrival of neoliberalism and market fundamentalism, trends in news media ownership have led to news media markets that are highly concentrated with high barriers to entry, which means less competition and less choice for consumers and citizens. Diversity of ownership across news media has always been limited, but concentration of ownership has increased drastically since the 1980s, giving tremendous power to a small hand-ful of actors that are able to dictate the national conversation. A small handful of big corporations dominate the newspaper, magazine, radio, television, and digital industries. The internet makes it appear that anyone can participate, but the real-ity is most page views and most advertising revenue go to the same small handful of corporate-owned websites. There's no question that new voices have emerged online, and entertainment options have exploded. But concentrated ownership and reduced competition in news media affects the content available and ensures that the messages that get produced and the issues that get attention will often be supportive of the interests of corporate owners. Concentration of ownership also makes it harder for new entrants into the market to get a foothold to offer alternatives and increase consumer choice. While capitalism is theoretically based on competitive markets and low barriers to entry, the reality of the news media marketplace is quite different.

The result of all of this is a mainstream news media market that is dangerously homogenized (that is, mostly the same), even as it exercises an enormous amount of power over the public mind. This is not necessarily new because, historically, the opportunity to create media products has always been limited. In the 500-or-so years between the invention of the printing press and the internet, a printing press was required if you wanted to print and distribute news and information. Similarly, recall how the telegraph was dominated in the United States by the monopoly power of Western Union. As radio broadcasting emerged, the makers of radio equipment—RCA, AT&T, GE, and Westinghouse—saw the opportunity at hand and soon dominated the market. Television was similarly dominated by established radio broadcasters. In the 1980s, cable and satellite technology began to introduce competition to the broadcasting industry, but the deregulation that took place in the 1980s and 1990s made it easier than ever for large corpora-tions to consolidate their holdings, thereby reducing competition. Media com-panies that once focused entirely on producing news and other media products were bought up by much larger corporations, such as the acquisition of NBC by General Electric in 1986. Think about it—what does a company like GE, which makes home appliances and jet engines and provides global financial services, have to do with news and media production? For these large conglomerates, news media outlets are just another subsidiary, an opportunity for increased revenue with little regard for public service imperatives.

Today, NBC has since merged with the parent company of Universal Studios to create a new conglomerate, NBC Universal, which is owned by the even larger global telecommunications conglomerate, Comcast, which has an obvious interest in producing its own content to distribute through its networks. This strategy, known as *vertical integration* in the business world, is a smart way to diver-sify holdings and control multiple parts of the supply chain, from production to distribution. But it has obvious downsides for consumers and citizens, who typically end up with fewer options and lower-quality news and information. A similar trend has played out in the newspaper business, which began the 20th century with local ownership and diverse competition. In the United States, at least 500 cities had two or more competing daily newspapers. But as group ownership increased and circulation began to decline, metropolitan areas saw less competition and less local control. Today, only around ten U.S. cities have two or more competing dailies, and 85 percent of newspapers are under group ownership.[23] When new technologies emerge, there is no reason they must be subsumed in the hands of a powerful few. A more democratic news media system would help protect and preserve a more open and inclusive democracy.

It might seem like diversity of ownership and control has exploded in the digital age, but the trends toward consolidation and commercialism have only accelerated. Even though many citizens have access to hundreds of channels, endless streaming video, multiple social media platforms, and a billion websites, there has been a reduction in the amount of quality journalism produced, especially at the local level. A few major companies dominate today's media landscape, including Comcast, Disney, Time Warner, 21st Century Fox, and National Amusements, all of which generate annual revenues in the tens of billions of dollars. For them, news is only a small part of their operations and not one they need to be terribly concerned with except to the extent that it generates revenue, which is accomplished by cutting staff and reducing resources. Real reporting is not only expensive, but it's also not especially popular compared to sports and entertainment. This creates little incentive to invest in serious public service news content.

In the digital environment, the picture is equally dim and perhaps more so. The web is dominated by a small handful of companies, mainly Google, Facebook, and Amazon, which consume the majority of digital ad revenue. Most page views go to the same top ten sites, and access to the web is limited to a small number of internet service providers, namely Comcast, Charter, AT&T, and Verizon.[24] The real problem is that the companies that dominate the web make virtually no investment in the production of original journalism; instead, they simply aggregate and distribute the work of others, which means big profits for them while the real news producers are left with mere scraps. More on all of this in the next chapter.

Like the rest of the news media business, local newspapers and television outlets have followed a similar pattern. Even as local television remains the primary source of news for a majority of adults, it is dominated by a few major companies including Sinclair, Nexstar, Gray, Tegna, and Tribune. These companies controlled 179 broadcast outlets in 2004 and 443 outlets in 2016.[25] News broadcasts often are dominated by commercials, soft features, weather, and sports, and little investment is made toward coverage of original news content related to public affairs. With the rise of the internet, broadcast audiences have declined, but revenues have increased, with many television owners reporting 30 to 40 percent profit margins.[26] Compare that to many other industries, where profit margins are more likely to be in the single digits. Broadcast companies often own newspapers as well, but many have separated their newspaper divisions into new companies in order to protect their more successful television outlets. Newspapers still provide the bulk of serious, original reporting, but they have been hardest hit by technological and economic transformations. Unfortunately, it is democracy that suffers.

Advertising and the Audience Commodity

One thing that hasn't changed much over the past 100 years is the basic business model of much of the news media industry. Throughout the 20th century, advertising has served as the primary source of revenue for most news outlets. What's weird about this is the strange dynamic it creates between news producers, consumers, and advertisers. If advertisers are the ones paying the bills, the customers of news producers are not primarily the audience members consuming the news but rather the advertisers who cover most of the costs. In other words, the audience is the product being sold to advertisers. This is known as a *dual product model*, where the media product appears to be "free," but the real product is the consumer's attention, which is being sold to advertisers. As the saying goes, if you're not paying for it, you're not the customer—you're the product being sold. Scholars call this the *audience commodity*, noting that consuming advertising is the "work" audiences must perform to receive "free" media content.[27]

This model has pros and cons. On the pro side, relying on advertisers to pay for news production helps make news available for all citizens even if they can't afford it. Second, it provides a funding model that prevents news outlets from having to rely on government subsidies or other sources that could potentially exert a negative influence over the content being produced. And third, it also gives the producers of goods and services an easy way to reach a large audience and inform them about products for sale. These are useful traits, particularly in a vast consumer economy where news is often something many people are reluctant to pay for directly.

Then there are cons, some of which are obvious and some more subtle. Let's explore three main problems. First, if advertisers are footing the bill, they might have an interest in controlling the content that gets produced. For some reason, many people have no problem imagining that government funding for news media inevitably leads to authoritarian control in the style of Orwell's *1984*, but they can't imagine the controlling influence of advertising. That's partly because the influence is not direct; that is, advertisers typically do not call up a news outlet, tell them what to do, and threaten to pull the advertising if they don't comply (although this does occasionally happen). Instead, it is a largely unspoken influence where news producers often exert their own self-censorship and avoid publishing or airing material that would upset their funders. This could mean certain companies or industries go unexamined, and it certainly means no critical words should be said about commercialism, corporate consolidation, economic growth, and advertising itself.

Second, to generate sufficient advertising revenue, news outlets are encouraged to cater to audiences that are attractive to advertisers, that is, those with money to spend, especially discretionary money and lots of it. This is why news content often centers on uncritical business and financial news, and often caters to older news consumers. There are few consumers who can afford to buy luxury cars, for example, so if a news audience does not include plenty of those potential buyers, there is no reason to advertise to them. This means news is more likely to represent the interests of middle and upper classes with no serious attention to the needs of poor and working classes, especially the structures and institutions that often advantage the wealthy and disadvantage the poor such as public education, the courts, and health care. Little constructive or critical attention is paid to labor issues, homelessness, rising wealth inequality, stagnating wages, declining median net worth, and rising levels of debt of various kinds. Also consider that only around half of Americans are invested in the stock market, and the richest 10 percent of Americans own 84 percent of all stocks.[28] And certain populations are even less likely to own stocks, including those without a college education, young people, unmarried people, and minority groups including African-Americans and Hispanics. So when you see the nightly news obsessing about the daily fluctuations of the stock market and what it means for investors, you know whom they're talking to.

The third and perhaps biggest problem is that the entire commercial media system is built on one central message: consume, consume, consume. The message of advertising is that you are not okay the way you are, but fortunately there is a world of goods and services that can make you whole again. Advertising often generates the appearance of a need where none exists, a practice called *need creation*. That's why ads often make no attempt to provide factual information. What claim could one make regarding the merits of brown sugar water? That's why you see a polar bear open a bottle of soda followed by a nonsensical slogan, and now your life is 30 seconds shorter. Instead of making factual claims, ads often employ a variety of persuasive techniques designed to turn off your thinking brain and engage your emotions. Ads prey on our deeply held values to create positive associations with consumer goods. We see these ads as stupid or funny but mostly trivial; they don't really affect us. But the underlying message of all advertising is that we must buy things, and the effects are cumulative. We come to see ourselves as consumers first and citizens second, and people often experience feelings of anxiety and emptiness when they are presented with idealized and romantic notions of the "good life." By contrast, one message you never hear is that you're fine the way you are; you don't need anything. Just be who you are.

Understanding advertising requires its own set of literacies and knowledge structures, but at the very least, it's important to see how central advertising is to the news media system and to understand the effects of this influence. To see this influence at its most extreme, just watch or read news around Thanksgiving. Not only do you find endless ads about great deals from Black Friday to Cyber Monday, but news delivers the same message! You can't miss the breathless local television anchor reporting live from the local department store, excitedly showing you where to shop and what to buy. Sure, everyone likes to find a good deal, but is it really the role of news media to help you shop? Or at the least, shouldn't they give an equal amount of attention to the downsides of endless, wasteful holiday consumption? Where's objectivity when you need it! What appears on the surface to be harmless fun is actually a serious indictment of the structure of news media systems that rely in whole or in part on a message about the desirability of consumption. In this commercial system, the news content must support the needs of advertisers whether the public is served or not.

Comparing Media Systems Around the World

Is there any alternative to a commercial news media system dominated by a market orientation, saturated with advertising, and marked by a failure to serve democratic needs? I'm glad you asked. To see the range of available alternatives, all we have to do is take a look at media systems around the world. Because many democratic nations recognize the vital role news media plays in democratic society, many of these nations have chosen to make strong commitments to public, nonprofit, and noncommercial news media, which can operate independent of political or economic pressures. Research supports the idea that those who consume nonprofit and noncommercial news media tend to be better informed and engaged than those who consume commercial news media, so it makes some sense for governments to play a role in promoting the kind of information that will lead to more democratic outcomes. The American system, which is almost entirely commercial and for-profit, actually stands alone among developed nations, which often have hybrid systems that provide a mix of robust public service broadcasting along with other publicly funded news options.[29]

Let's first note that news media systems around the world vary significantly, and most people on the planet actually live in countries with little to no press freedom.[30] That includes countries such as North Korea and Iran, where the government owns and controls the news media, which always represents the perspective of the government. Countries such as Brazil and India have some press freedom, including legal protections for the press, but journalists can still face direct government censorship as well as obstacles stemming from political pressure, concentrated ownership, and even violence and intimidation. The gold standard for press freedom is found in countries like Denmark and Finland, which have hybrid media systems with a diverse mix of public and private ownership, significant subsidies for non-commercial media, and regulations that increase the diversity of information available as well as access to it.

On the press freedom spectrum, the United States falls in the "most free" category according to independent, non-governmental observers such as Freedom House and Reporters Without Borders, but it's far from the top of the list, and its rank has declined over the past decade. In Freedom House's 2017 Press Freedom report, the United States is tied for 33rd place out of 199, coming in behind Iceland, Costa Rica, and Estonia.[31] Similarly, Reporters Without Borders ranks the United States at number 43 out of 180, coming in after the Czech Republic, Ghana, and South Africa.[32] Most of the other developed, industrialized countries of the West rank more highly than the United States, including Austria, New Zealand, Australia, Germany, Spain, France, and the United Kingdom. The top-ranked countries are routinely those of northern Europe and Scandinavia, including Norway, Sweden, Denmark, Finland, and the Netherlands.

While the United States has strong legal protections for the press thanks largely to the First Amendment, its media system is not as economically diverse as the top-ranked countries, and it can be subject to undue political interference that inhibits the ability of the press to report independently and without fear of consequence. Economically, the U.S. system offers limited support for publicly funded noncommercial media, namely PBS and NPR. The deregulated media landscape limits access to diverse information compared to other developed nations, and the news industry has faced major economic obstacles that have challenged its ability to remain viable in the digital age. And while American news producers experience relatively little direct censorship, journalists today work in a highly charged political landscape where they often face harassment and intimidation, or they are forced to align with the partisan interests of corporate owners. This is especially true during the Trump era; starting with his primary campaign, Trump commonly disparaged and harassed journalists and news outlets and threatened to revoke the press credentials of those he didn't agree with. Trump has regularly referred to their work as "fake news" and declared the news media an "enemy of the people." "I have a running war with the media," Trump has boasted. "They are among the most dishonest human beings on earth."[33] Disparaging the press is not exactly a new political tactic, but Trump's approach is unprecedented in the modern era (at least since the Nixon administration) and only serves to undermine the important role a free and independent press plays in democratic life. After the Cold War ended in the 1980s, press freedom around the world trended upward, but in recent years the trend has reversed. An increasing number of journalists have been subject to threats, intimidation, and even murder, which is concerning not only for the press as an institution but for other political and social institutions as well. Authoritarians often target the press before going after other institutions such as courts and elections, which help to prevent authoritarian power grabs. So any crackdown on press freedom should serve as an early warning system for other attacks on democratic society.

Nations with the historically freest and most vibrant press systems stand apart for a few reasons. They feature less private ownership and greater commitments to funding public, noncommercial media. Countries with mixed systems offer substantial public subsidies for broadcasters, in order to increase the amount of public affairs news content available and to reduce the influence of market forces. And people actually tune in. Public television channels throughout Europe routinely rank at the top of audience share, including a high of 67 percent for Denmark.[34] In the United States, news programming on public media reaches a limited audience and has limited funding. In 2017, the Corporation for Public Broadcasting, which distributes most of its funding to public media outlets around the country, received $445 million in federal appropriations.[35] That's around $1.35 per American. In other developed nations, spending on public media can range from $30 per person in Canada and $34 in Australia to $90 in the United Kingdom and $133 in Norway.[36] Some of these subsidies go to commercial news outlets, which must meet requirements for the distribution of public affairs programming to large national audiences.

And some of this money helps support a level playing field for political candidates. In many developed countries, political candidates and parties tend to receive free access to the airwaves to make sure the playing field is level and that everyone has a chance to be heard. In the United States, candidates need to raise huge sums of money to buy access to the airwaves and get their message out.[37] In theory, this means anyone can participate in the political process, but in reality, participation is generally limited to the wealthy few. This approach is representative of the typically American "negative" approach to protecting freedom; in this view, the best way to ensure freedom is through the absence of government involvement, which avoids the necessity of any messy decision-making related to who gets what. Compare this with the more typical approach in other developed nations, especially in Europe, where "positive" protections for liberty allow governments to play more active roles in increasing equality of opportunity. (More on this in Chapter 5.) Looking at the rankings, organizations like Freedom House and Reporters Without Borders appear to value these positive commitments to press freedom. If a free press is one that delivers quality independent journalism without political or economic constraints, it makes sense that enlisting the power of government to work to promote this kind of activity actually improves the press system and makes it more "free." And the results aren't limited to the activities of journalists and news outlets; rather, the benefits ultimately go to the public. Scholars have shown that hybrid media systems with positive commitments to press freedom and public media yield citizens who are both informed and engaged.[38]

Some readers might say: "That's all well and good for those European socialists, but it's simply not the American way." But actually, it is. The United States has a long history of public support for the press system. History shows a significant precedent for public subsidies for journalism in the United States. Public spending on news production and distribution goes back to nation's founding, when postal subsidies and government printing contracts made it possible for the emerging press system to thrive. Subsidies for printers and the press in the 1800s amounted to the equivalent of billions of dollars in today's money.[39]

Comparing media systems—and comparing systems across time—helps us see that no media system is natural or inevitable. Rather, media systems are constructed by human actors over time and as a result of the accidental and deliberate creation of policies and practices shaped by political struggles. Thus, it's important to consider who benefits from the arrangements that emerge and to ask whether public resources are being marshaled to serve public benefits. As scholars Rodney Benson and Matthew Powers noted in their review of public media systems around the world,

> In fact, government has always and will always influence how our media system functions, from the early newspaper postal subsidies to handing out broadcast licenses and subsidizing broadband deployment. The question is not if government should be involved, but how, and that is a question that demands an in-depth conversation, not a shouting match.[40]

Finally, let's be clear about one thing. A system of government control certainly is not preferable. No democratic society wants to go down the road of George Orwell's *1984* or anything like it. We are all on guard against it, and it's relatively easy to spot the kind of overt government control that Orwell depicted. But the reality we increasingly face is the one depicted in Aldous Huxley's *Brave New World*. As Neil Postman explained in his 1985 book, *Amusing Ourselves to Death*, in Huxley's vision, there is no need to ban or censor critical information because no one wants to consume it in the first place.[41] Instead, we are all hopelessly lost in a world of earthly delights, ignorant to our domination by a powerful few. That's why we have to be vigilant not only against government power but also against the powers of commercial markets and their decidedly undemocratic impulses.

Markets Versus Publics

Learning about the structure of the news media system over time and across borders is a critical context for news literacy because it shows us how the news environment is constructed and how different approaches have different outcomes. Comparing market orientations versus a public sphere model can also help explain the content we see and hear, as described by sociologists David Croteau and William Hoynes in their book, *The Business of Media: Corporate Media and the Public Interest*.[42] In a *market model*, media businesses compete in a marketplace for consumer dollars, whether direct or indirect. A market-oriented approach can have benefits in meeting the needs of democratic societies as long as competitive markets encourage innovation and experimentation and news providers are able to easily adapt to changing needs and desires of news consumers. Proponents of free markets suggest that this is the best way to maximize personal and political freedom—by letting consumer demand dictate what the supply should look like without undue interference from government. This sounds attractive, especially for its theoretical consistency and simplicity.

In reality, a market approach doesn't account for how the world really works. First, people often can't say what they want because they don't know what they want in advance of being given a narrowly defined set of options. Reality TV? Football night? Action movie? Thoughtful political discourse? It's no coincidence that companies spend huge amounts of money marketing their products to influence consumer tastes and preferences—and that includes news media companies. Second, the tastes and preferences of citizens often don't have anything to do with the information they need to be well-informed citizens. No one wants to tell people they have to consume their information vegetables along with their entertainment desserts, but for democratic life to work, that's the reality. And because every citizen's vote counts equally—whether they are informed or not—it's in everyone's interest to make sure we are all informed and empowered to make good decisions. It's a basic problem of democracy that everyone's vote counts equally whether they are informed or not. That problem is not likely to be reconciled, so the answer is to do what it takes to increase citizen knowledge and informed participation.

A third problem results from the concentration of ownership in news media markets. This results in a lack of competition and no real incentive to be innovative with the creation of new products and services or to provide the "information vegetables" necessary for an informed citizenry. Fourth, markets lack a morality of their own—call it "amorality"—which means products and producers can be beneficial or harmful provided they create revenue for their owners. Fifth, markets have no inclination toward democracy and thus have no incentive or desire to represent society as a whole but rather to focus on the segments that are most commercially useful. Overall, markets are not great at meeting social or democratic needs not associated with profitability. Scholars use the term *market failure* to describe what happens when market activity does not provide what society needs. Market failure requires government intervention, usually in the form of regulation or subsidies, to make corrections.

Compare this to the *public sphere model*, which draws on the work of German scholar Jürgen Habermas, who defined the public sphere as a space in civic life, distinct from markets and governments, that allows for critical discourse and debate. In *The Structural Transformation of the Public Sphere*, Habermas maps out the decline of the civic space starting as consumer capitalism and mass media took hold of public life beginning in the 20th century.[43] Under a public sphere model, news media are valued for their ability to provide an important public service without the constraints imposed by economic imperatives of growth and profit. In this sense, news media are not required to cater to the whims of popular demand and can instead strive to provide substantive content that will be supportive of democratic needs. Not surprisingly, the public sphere model is most closely associated with public media systems and outlets, and with independent journalists, that are most likely to be insulated from the need to generate profits for owners and shareholders and to be immune from political pressure and influence. By contrast, the market model is associated with commercial interests, and the content produced is what is most popular and profitable. Rather than viewing the two approaches as black and white, it can help to imagine a spectrum where even commercial outlets sometimes put public service over profits. And even the most service-oriented public outlets still face pressures and obstacles at times. The important thing is to provide citizens with a robust mix of content and even for commercial outlets to strike the right balance between profits and public service.

To this end, a modern media reform movement has created an agenda for a more democratic media system that's more responsive to the needs of citizens and society. This can include reforming the corporate media model, providing subsidies for quality journalism, strengthening public service broadcasting, increasing opportunities for citizen engagement and participation, and using media to promote democratic ideals including the values of diversity and pluralism. It will take a lot to overcome the market-oriented values and commercial impulses of neoliberalism as well as the basic rejection of the role of governments in providing widespread public benefits that has taken hold in much of the Western world. The structures of news media systems and institutions are not likely to grow more democratic as long as those who make the policies benefit from concentrated power and profit. But the kinds of structural changes needed to address these problems will not come without widespread awareness of the problems we face. That's why learning about these political, economic, historical, and societal contexts is so important to news literacy.

It's worth noting that the whole project of news literacy and media literacy is a challenge to power and thus represents, at least to some degree, a threat to the status quo. It's not like we're calling for revolution here, but even a modest request for critical awareness and regulatory reform is not one that's generally well received in the halls of power. This can be an uncomfortable position for people who might be wary of offending powerful interests and potentially putting themselves at risk for retaliation or punishment. But accepting the current arrangements of society is really no different from questioning them. Recall the words of scholars Justin Lewis and Sut Jhally from their call for a contextual approach to media literacy: "We are advocating a view that recognizes that the world is always made by someone, and a decision to tolerate the status quo is as political as a more overtly radical act."[44] In other words, choosing to ask critical questions is really no different than choosing not to. Questioning and challenging the news and information environment should be accepted as the responsible thing to do for anyone who believes in the principles of democracy.

Questions for Discussion

1. Who and what are the gatekeepers of news and information in the digital age? How has gatekeeping changed since the 20th century? How has it remained the same?
2. What is unique about the news media marketplace as compared to markets for other consumer products like sneakers or toasters?
3. What vestiges of the early 1900s can be found in the structures of news media today? Why does history matter in any attempt to understand today's news environment?
4. What are the pros and cons of a news media system funded primarily by advertising revenue?
5. What are the key differences among global news media systems? Which structures tend to produce the best content for supporting democratic life?

Notes

1. Matthew Ingram, "Here's Why Comcast Decided to Call a Truce with Netflix," *Fortune*, July 5, 2016, http://fortune.com/2016/07/05/comcast-truce-netflix/.
2. Pamela J. Shoemaker and Tim P. Vos, *Gatekeeping Theory* (New York: Routledge, 2009), 1.
3. David Manning White, "The 'Gate Keeper': A Case Study in the Selection of News," *Journalism Bulletin* 27, no. 4 (September 1, 1950): 383–90, https://doi.org/10.1177/107769905002700403.
4. Pamela J. Shoemaker and Stephen D. Reese, *Mediating the Message in the 21st Century: A Media Sociology Perspective*, 3rd edition (New York: Routledge/Taylor & Francis Group, 2014).
5. Keith Payne, Laura Niemi, and John M. Doris, "How to Think about 'Implicit Bias,'" *Scientific American*, March 27, 2018, www.scientificamerican.com/article/how-to-think-about-implicit-bias/.
6. Jaclyn Reiss, "More than 300 Newspapers Join Globe Effort on Freedom of the Press Editorials," *Boston Globe*, August 14, 2018, www.bostonglobe.com/metro/2018/08/14/newspapers-join-globe-effort-freedom-press-editorials/yvvZ0yepu8j1lJ3G3qYbSJ/story.html.
7. James E. Anderson, *Public Policymaking*, 8th edition (Australia: Wadsworth, 2014), 25.
8. Anderson, *Public Policymaking*, 25.
9. Daniel J. Boorstin, *The Image: A Guide to Pseudo-Events in America* (New York: Vintage, 1992), 9.
10. Shoemaker and Reese, *Mediating the Message in the 21st Century*, 124.
11. Daniel C. Hallin, *The Uncensored War: The Media and Vietnam* (Berkeley: University of California Press, 1989), 110.
12. The history of broadcasting covered in this chapter is drawn from several major works on the topic. See Erik Barnouw, *A Tower in Babel: A History of Broadcasting in the United States to 1933, Vol. I* (New York: Oxford University Press, 1966); Susan J. Douglas, *Inventing American Broadcasting, 1899–1922* (Baltimore: Johns Hopkins University Press, 1987); Robert McChesney, *Telecommunications, Mass Media, and Democracy: The Battle for the Control of U.S. Broadcasting, 1928–1935* (New York: Oxford University Press, 1993); Philip T. Rosen, *The Modern Stentors: Radio Broadcasters and the Federal Government, 1920–1934* (Westport, CT: Greenwood Press, 1980). I have also written about the topic myself. See Seth Ashley, "The Closing of the Ether: Communication Policy and the Public Interest in the United States and Great Britain, 1921–1926," *Communication*

Law and Policy 18, no. 1 (January 1, 2013): 1–61, https://doi.org/10.1080/10811680. 2013.746136; Seth Ashley, "A Historical Comparison of the Social Origins of Broadcasting Policy, 1896–1920," *Journal of Radio & Audio Media* 21, no. 1 (January 2, 2014): 134–48, https://doi.org/10.1080/19376529.2014.891210; Seth Ashley, Jessica Roberts, and Adam Maksl, *American Journalism and "Fake News": Examining the Facts* (Santa Barbara, CA: ABC-CLIO, 2018), 47–53.

13. See for example Roland Marchand, *Creating the Corporate Soul: The Rise of Public Relations and Corporate Imagery in American Big Business*, A Director's Circle Book (Berkeley, CA: University of California Press, 1998).

14. Paul Starr, *The Creation of the Media: Political Origins of Modern Communications* (New York: Basic Books, 2004), 363.

15. See Victor W. Pickard, *America's Battle for Media Democracy: The Triumph of Corporate Libertarianism and the Future of Media Reform*, Communication, Society and Politics (New York: Cambridge University Press, 2015).

16. David Foster Wallace, "Host," *The Atlantic*, April 2005, www.theatlantic.com/magazine/archive/2005/04/host/303812/.

17. Pickard, *America's Battle for Media Democracy*.

18. See James L. Baughman, *Same Time, Same Station: Creating American Television, 1948–1961* (Baltimore: Johns Hopkins University Press, 2007).

19. Rodney Benson and Matthew Powers, "Public Media and Political Independence: Lessons for the Future of Journalism from around the World" (Free Press, 2011).

20. George Monbiot, "Neoliberalism—the Ideology at the Root of All Our Problems," *The Guardian*, April 15, 2016, sec. Books, www.theguardian.com/books/2016/apr/15/neoliberalism-ideology-problem-george-monbiot.

21. Reason, "Voices of Reason: Thirty Years of Interviews," *Reason.com*, December 1, 1998, https://reason.com/archives/1998/12/01/voices-of-reason.

22. Ben H. Bagdikian, *The New Media Monopoly* (Boston: Beacon Press, 2004), 3.

23. Dirks, Van Essen, Murray & April, "History of Ownership Consolidation," March 31, 2017, http://dirksvanessen.com/articles/view/223/history-of-ownership-consolidation-/.

24. See Robert W. McChesney, *Digital Disconnect: How Capitalism Is Turning the Internet against Democracy* (New York: The New Press, 2013).

25. Katerina Eva Matsa, "Buying Spree Brings More Local TV Stations to Fewer Big Companies," *Pew Research Center*, May 11, 2017, http://www.pewresearch.org/fact-tank/2017/05/11/buying-spree-brings-more-local-tv-stations-to-fewer-big-companies/.

26. Alex T. Williams, "Newspaper Companies Lag behind Their Broadcast Siblings after Spinoffs," August 9, 2016, www.pewresearch.org/fact-tank/2016/08/09/newspaper-companies-lag-behind-their-broadcast-siblings-after-spinoffs/.

27. See Dallas W. Smythe, "On the Audience Commodity and Its Work," in *Dependency Road: Communications, Capitalism, Consciousness, and Canada* (Norwood, NJ: Praeger, 1981), 22–51; Christian Fuchs, "Dallas Smythe Today: The Audience Commodity, the Digital Labour Debate, Marxist Political Economy and Critical Theory," *TripleC* 10, no. 2 (2012): 692–740.

28. Rob Wile, "The Richest 10% of Americans Now Own 84% of All Stocks," *Money*, December 19, 2017, http://time.com/money/5054009/stock-ownership-10-percent-richest/.

29. See Daniel C. Hallin and Paolo Mancini, *Comparing Media Systems: Three Models of Media and Politics*, Communication, Society, and Politics (Cambridge, UK: Cambridge University Press, 2004); Iyengar, *Media Politics*. I've also written about media system comparisons elsewhere. See Seth Ashley, "Making the Case for War: A Comparative Analysis of CNN and BBC Coverage of Colin Powell's Presentation to the United Nations Security Council," *Media, War & Conflict* 8, no. 1 (April 1, 2015): 120–40, https://doi.org/10.1177/1750635214541031; Seth Ashley, "The Closing of the Ether: Communication Policy and the Public Interest in the United States and Great Britain, 1921–1926," *Communication Law and Policy* 18, no. 1 (January 1, 2013): 1–61, https://

doi.org/10.1080/10811680.2013.746136; Seth Ashley, Jessica Roberts, and Adam Maksl, *American Journalism and "Fake News": Examining the Facts* (Santa Barbara, CA: ABC-CLIO, 2018), 66–72.

30. See Freedom House, "Freedom of the Press 2017," April 18, 2017, https://freedom house.org/report/freedom-press/freedom-press-2017.
31. Freedom House, "Freedom of the Press 2017," April 18, 2017, https://freedomhouse.org/report/freedom-press/freedom-press-2017.
32. Reporters Without Borders, "2017 World Press Freedom Index," *RSF*, 2017, https://rsf.org/en/ranking.
33. Julie Hirschfeld Davis and Matthew Rosenberg, "With False Claims, Trump Attacks Media on Turnout and Intelligence Rift," *The New York Times*, January 21, 2017, sec. Politics, www.nytimes.com/2017/01/21/us/politics/trump-white-house-briefing-inauguration-crowd-size.html.
34. Iyengar, *Media Politics*.
35. "About CPB," September 22, 2014, www.cpb.org/aboutcpb.
36. Benson and Powers, "Public Media and Political Independence: Lessons for the Future of Journalism from around the World."
37. Iyengar, *Media Politics*.
38. See James Curran et al., "Media System, Public Knowledge and Democracy: A Comparative Study," *European Journal of Communication* 24, no. 1 (March 1, 2009): 5–26, https://doi.org/10.1177/0267323108098943; Hallin and Mancini, *Comparing Media Systems*; Iyengar, *Media Politics*.
39. Robert McChesney and John Nichols, *The Death and Life of American Journalism: The Media Revolution That Will Begin the World Again*, 1st Nation Books (Philadelphia, PA: Nation Books, 2010).
40. Benson and Powers, "Public Media and Political Independence: Lessons for the Future of Journalism from around the World," 3.
41. Neil Postman, *Amusing Ourselves to Death: Public Discourse in the Age of Show Business*, Anniversary edition (New York: Penguin Books, 2005).
42. See David Croteau and William Hoynes, *The Business of Media: Corporate Media and the Public Interest*, 2nd edition (Thousand Oaks, CA: Pine Forge Press, 2006). I've also written about this elsewhere in Seth Ashley, Jessica Roberts, and Adam Maksl, *American Journalism and "Fake News": Examining the Facts* (Santa Barbara, CA: ABC-CLIO, 2018), 53–59.
43. See Jürgen Habermas, *The Structural Transformation of the Public Sphere: An Inquiry into a Category of Bourgeois Society*, Studies in Contemporary German Social Thought (Cambridge, MA: MIT Press, 1989).
44. Justin Lewis and Sut Jhally, "The Struggle over Media Literacy," *Journal of Communication* 48, no. 1 (1998): 119.

5

THE POLITICAL ECONOMY OF THE INTERNET

From the moment Mark Zuckerberg called it a "pretty crazy idea" that Facebook could have influenced the outcome of the 2016 U.S. presidential election, critics assailed the Facebook founder and CEO for his naive view of the role of social media in democratic life. While it's impossible to know exactly what effects social media can have on election outcomes, our reliance on social and search platforms for news and information is undeniable, and it's increasingly clear that Facebook and other platforms can have a significant impact on perception, behavior, and judgment. This makes it more important than ever to understand how digital and social media operate, and how the pursuit of private profit in this arena can interfere with the needs of democratic societies.

In theory, the internet has been an enormous boon to civilization. With more access to more information than ever before, humans can learn about anything they want and can create and curate conversations that might have been unavailable before the web. The gatekeepers of traditional news media no longer exert near-universal control over the discourse of society, and traditional news outlets are now often forced to report on and respond to traditionally marginalized voices that can now be heard online. For example, the Black Lives Matter movement in the United States has used social media to offer a stark contrast to coverage of racial conflict on cable television news, and the recent democratic uprisings in the Middle East were undeniably aided by the power of digital technologies.

At the same time, the internet has also made it easier for racist and authoritarian voices to be louder than ever before and to exert their negative influence around the world. White supremacists and religious fundamentalists use the web to spread their messages of hate and to recruit new followers, and authoritarian rulers espouse populist messages that spread lies and fear throughout society. This contrast between pro- and anti-democratic forces illustrates the double-edged sword offered by digital technologies. Often referred to as the *democratization of information*, the loss of traditional gatekeepers theoretically makes it possible for everyone to be heard in the digital age. Democratization is generally thought of as a good thing when applied to society at large—at least as opposed to authoritarianism. But when applied to information, the results are mixed.

The internet celebrant Clay Shirky famously chose *Here Comes Everybody* as the title of his popular 2008 book describing the rise of digital and social media and the accompanying transition from passive consumption to active participation.[1] Shirky showed what digital and social media tools allow groups of individuals to accomplish that couldn't be done by traditional institutions because the costs (both material and immaterial) would be too high. In terms of organizing for everything from mundane tasks to social change, digital tools have a major role to play. But the "everybody" who has come forth in the digital age does not always have good intentions or good motivations or good goals. And despite the revolutionary communication tools at their disposal, the digital masses have not necessarily placed their collective focus on issues that matter most. Thanks to the democratization of information, trying to filter the good from the bad is harder than ever.

Here's the deeper point: the internet doesn't really care what you have to say, only whether you will generate clicks, likes, shares, and thus, profits. In the war between good information and bad, or even between the presence or absence of any information at all, there's often no guiding force that would lead us to relevant, quality information beyond what is profitable for owners and advertisers. As we've explored, this has always been a problem for a commercial media system, but the internet has brought us a market model on steroids. There are two main reasons for this. The online experience has been overtaken by just a few endlessly powerful digital giants, and digital technology makes it easier than ever to generate and promote content that is sure to make a profit. Digital advertisers—primarily Facebook and Google, which make their money by acting as giant advertising firms—do this by learning everything they can about their users—often surreptitiously—and selling those users to others who wish to advertise on their platforms. Under the "old media" of newspapers, radio, and television, at least some degree of human judgment, however flawed, helped to provide accurate information that could be useful to democratic life, and they had limited knowledge about the personal lives of citizens. In the digital era, machines have been enlisted to do most of the sorting for us based on extensive profiles of our lives, and unless we actively engage with those hidden digital forces, our news and information diet will be dominated by content that is first and foremost popular and profitable.

And so the democratizing potential of the internet, once heralded broadly, has turned out to be a mixed bag. While some once-marginalized voices have been able to make themselves heard, the stronger tendency has been to reinforce existing power structures. To be news literate in this environment requires knowledge of those structures and the institutions that keep them in place. Political economy describes the arrangements of power that shape society. Critical news literacy requires an understanding of the political economy of the internet and social media, including the role of mass customization and algorithmic sorting that influence and control news content. The digital landscape must also be considered in the broader context of the tendency toward monopoly capitalism—and the neoliberal policies that make it possible—that has come to dominate much of the global economy. The internet remains only lightly regulated in terms of structure and content, governed by a pseudo-libertarian regulatory philosophy that allows for maximum profits and minimum public service. Finally, the rise of digital and social media and the increase in online participation can be linked to the rise of political polarization and partisanship, which contributes to positive gains for the attention economy even as it fails to serve the public. As conflict and emotion increasingly dominate the participatory news environment, the potential for revenue rises as well.

To understand how we got here, it's useful to consider the origins of the internet, which emerged only with massive public investments due to the needs of military communication and scientific researchers. Following a path similar to other communication technologies such as radio and television, the internet has become an increasingly closed, commercial system dominated by a few powerful giants. Facebook and Google consume most of the digital ad revenue available online. Meanwhile, Amazon, Apple, and Microsoft vie for the distinction of most valuable publicly traded company. As large technology companies come to dominate the information environment, commercialism and profit-making have become even more central to the process by which news is created and distributed.

It's not a pretty picture that emerges when we consider these factors that influence and control the online experience. But that's not where we should stop. Learning about these contexts is the best way to take control of our own information exposure and to harness digital technologies and use them to our advantage. It also helps us learn where we might want to resist or push back against failed algorithms that promote false information or invasions of privacy that abuse personal data for profit. And finally, learning about these contexts can empower us to draw lines and create boundaries for the presence of digital and social media in our lives. More and more, critics promote the idea of deleting our social media accounts and pursuing more meaningful ways to connect with each other. There are ways to engage positively with social media, but we should be able to do it from a position of informed consent.

What Is Political Economy?

Before there was "economics," there was "political economics," which was an outgrowth of moral philosophy dating back to the ancient Greeks that examined the relationships between government and wealth. Only around the 20th century did modern economics emerge as a narrowly focused and coldly mathematical approach to studying the production and distribution of resources and the behavior of consumers in market society. Prior to the invention of modern economics, it was widely recognized that political decision-making could not be separated from economic outcomes, and observers from Adam Smith to John Stuart Mill to Karl Marx based their economic theories—however controversial—on this principle.[2]

When used today, the term *political economy* refers to the relationship between a society's economic and political systems and reflects the idea that competing interests among economic forces must be mitigated by political judgments. It is merely a way of acknowledging that the power dynamics of modern life play a major role in the allocation of resources and the production, distribution, and consumption of goods and services. Political economists recognize that any set of economic arrangements cannot be isolated from the historical developments and social transformations that led up to them. For example, laws and regulations around private property—who can own what—have tremendous effects on the balance of power in society, and so the ways in which property has been privatized and allocated over time cannot be overlooked when examining access to resources. Modern economics is not designed to examine the system as a whole and thus accepts the status quo as the starting point for all analysis. The effect of this is often to ignore questions that are important to democratic life such as the impact of political arrangements on the state of health care or housing markets or public schools. So to take a political economic approach, simply ask: how did we arrive at the current set of political arrangements, and how do they help or hurt economic conditions for the public at large?

As economies and wealth have grown over centuries past, economists have turned away from considerations of the ways in which the exchange of commodities in markets influences and is influenced by larger social forces. In his book *The Political Economy of Communication*, Vincent Mosco describes the many ways in which economics attempts to exist out of context:

> Economics does not take into account many of the significant socio-economic determinants of productivity, including corporate structure and ownership, education and training, and family background. It tends to ignore the relationship of power to wealth and thereby neglects the power of structures to control markets.[3]

As such, today, using standard economic analyses, there is virtually no way to account for a "public good" in the free market, that is, a service that everyone benefits from regardless of who pays for it, like national defense or clean air or water. With no possibility for the consideration of public goods, Mosco suggests there is generally no room for collective decision-making or regulation in the public interest. This is just as true whether the "public good" is clean air and water or the need for quality news and information in the public sphere.

Mosco points out that economics tends to exaggerate the "marketness" of society. Under this view, markets are abstracted from the social, cultural, and political contexts that make them possible. This view neglects considerations of "the vast social system of supports for market activity, such as flexible supply of low-wage labor, unpaid household labor, and a social system of desire that organizes the relationship of want to need in a form amenable to market transactions."[4] The success of a market system is gauged by its efficiency regardless of social consequences such as those related to race, class, gender, power, commodification, consumption, or waste. Thus, political economy strives to situate concerns about these social consequences within the vagaries of markets. Mosco writes: "As political economy has persistently maintained, it is not the pricing system that shapes behavior and gives direction to the economy, but the wider system of values and of power in which the economy is embedded."[5] Thus, rather than being structurally deterministic, research in political economy takes the view that it is possible for the producers of cultural commodities to question and object to mainstream views.

When applied to the news media environment, political economy is a lens through which to view the relationship between news media and power in society. The framework is useful for studying media—especially news and information media—because it encourages a critical approach to examining the interactions of media and power with a focus on the impact of these interactions. That means asking critical questions about who owns news and social media outlets and how they are affected by market structures, government policies, technology, and more. Applying political economy to the study of news and information media also invites us to examine the role of the communication system in supporting or challenging existing political and economic regimes. Examining this complex interplay between content and structure can help us see connections between the quality of our media and the strength of our democracies. As scholar Robert McChesney has noted, "The central question for media political economists is whether, on balance, the media system serves to promote or undermine democratic institutions and practices."[6]

Conducting an analysis of media system structure is not a practice most of us are used to. Until I obtained my first graduate degree in journalism, I certainly did not give much thought to the institutional arrangements of the news media system. Even though I had concerns about the content of the news and media environment, it didn't occur to me to look for deeper underlying explanations for what I saw. My hope is that this chapter (and the book in general) will give you enough of an introduction and invitation to ask these difficult questions that take us beyond a superficial analysis of content and begin to place an emphasis on the contexts in which news and information exist. I do not think a graduate degree in journalism or media studies is necessary to wrap your brain around this stuff. Nor do I think such thinking should be confined to advanced classes on college campuses. Everyone should be empowered to ask critical questions about the political economic arrangements of society, especially those that shape the stories we tell and the ways they are told. This rest of this chapter provides a few ways to get going.

The Origins of the Internet

To begin to apply a political economic approach to studying the internet, we should begin with the beginning. Learning a little history tells us something about the motivations and goals of the people and companies who have developed the web since the infrastructure was created and put in place. To be news literate and understand the contexts in which information is created and shared, it helps to understand the history and origins of the web. Despite some conventional wisdom, the digital revolution didn't begin with Steve Jobs or Bill Gates or Mark Zuckerberg or the guys from Google or anyone else you've heard of. The mythology of the lone innovator working tirelessly in a garage somewhere near San Francisco is wildly overblown. Nerdy guys tinkering with electronics have certainly brought major innovations, but as is typical of the stories we tell about ourselves, we have placed far too much emphasis on the successes of a few individuals without recognizing the significant structures and institutions that made their successes possible.

To put it bluntly, the internet is the result of a massive government project made possible by public investment and long-range research efforts. It's exactly the kind of endeavor that private companies have little interest in. If you need to show quarterly growth and profitability, the last thing you want to do is sink billions into developing some technology that you probably won't even be able to control if it becomes successful at all. So while it's fine to enjoy the latest app and revel in the wealth of digital content online, it's also important to acknowledge how we got here. And know that today's digital giants are reaping massive benefits from decades of investments and expertise that preceded their arrival.

The internet as we know it originated with the Defense Advanced Research Projects Agency, a branch of the U.S. Department of Defense. Variously called DARPA or ARPA for short, the agency was created in 1958 following the launch of the Soviet satellite Sputnik 1 to develop new technologies for use by the U.S. military. DARPA was initially interested in creating a way for sharing access to expensive high-powered computer systems. Meanwhile, researchers at the government-funded RAND Corporation had become interested in developing a communication system that could survive a nuclear attack by the Soviets. The two projects converged on the need to design a system that relied on a distributed, interconnected network rather than a system with a single, centralized hub that could be easily destroyed. This decentralized system, quite different from the IBM mainframes used by corporations at the time, also made it harder to control, a benefit that would help support collaboration and innovation down the line. As James Curran has documented, tax dollars also funded the development of the first digital computers and helped the U.S. computer industry grow. Furthermore, the U.S. space program helped support internet communication by developing the orbiting satellites that would support the growing digital traffic. Curran concludes: "In effect, the American state underwrote a major part of the internet's research and development costs."[7]

What happened next? Major telecommunication companies such as AT&T declined to participate in internet operations in the following decades, and government organizations continued to support research and development, particularly the European Organization for Nuclear Research (CERN) and the National Science Foundation (NSF) in the United States. The NSF established computing centers at research universities in the 1980s with its NSFNET. Eventually, when ARPANET was decommissioned in 1990, the internet had come to represent a robust public sphere that was inclusive, diverse, and noncommercial, and generally was oriented around academic and public service values. In the preceding decades, general etiquette as well as concrete rules forbade commercial activity, as evidenced by a 1982 internet orientation document at MIT: "Sending electronic mail over the ARPANet for commercial profit or political purposes is both antisocial and illegal. By sending such messages, you can offend many people, and it is possible to get MIT in serious trouble with the Government agencies which manage the ARPANet."[8]

By the time the internet was fully commercialized in the mid-1990s, many observers and users saw a golden opportunity. At first, it seemed that the public-spirited "information superhighway" could continue to be a force for enhancing human knowledge and breaking down barriers that existed in the centralized and controlled top-down broadcast technologies of radio and television. But the emerging web soon morphed into a highly commercialized space built around market values for the accumulation of private profit. The entire ethos of the technology shifted as opportunities for profit grew. Even so, government support has continued. For example, an NSF grant supported the work of the founders of Google in creating their PageRank algorithm that made the company enormously profitable. Even Siri is a government-funded creation! That voice on the iPhone originated in the early 2000s as a DARPA project called PAL, or Personalized Assistant that Learns, that could help soldiers in the field. A California company called SRI International received a multimillion-dollar grant from DARPA to create the artificial intelligence program, which later spun off as Siri Incorporated and was sold to Apple for a rumored $200 million.[9] Also, DARPA still exists today and, somewhat ironically, is at the forefront of combating some of the modern abuses of the networking technology it first made possible all those decades ago. The emergence of the "deep fake" video poses an obvious threat to national security and so has drawn the interest of the Department of Defense. The media forensics department of DARPA has a four-year research mandate to develop technologies to detect fake videos and has spent an estimated $68 million on the project so far.[10] Their detection technology will no doubt be a benefit to for-profit services from Facebook to eBay that also have a stake in preserving the veracity of internet content.

Again, what does this have to do with news literacy? None of this history is even terribly surprising; major innovations often start out as public works projects funded by governments and, once developed, are taken over by for-profit entities. First, this is relevant to news literacy as just one example of how historical trends and institutional arrangements have created the media system we have today. Second, this is relevant to news literacy because the internet is the infrastructure that provides access to the wealth of information at our fingertips, and the internet as we know it—a highly commercialized sphere for the accumulation of private profit—did not start out this way. To fully understand the contexts of the digital age, we need to know how we got here and how the original vision for this infrastructure became warped through commercialization. Now try to forget everything you know about the web as it exists and redesign it in a way that would truly enhance human knowledge and improve human existence. Would it look anything like what we have today? Surely some aspects would be worth keeping but there is much we would likely change if we could. The good news is that we still can. Through the spreading of critical awareness combined with citizen participation in the policy-making process, change is possible.

From One Closed System to Another: More Monopoly Capitalism

In the beginning, the idealized internet was heralded for its prospects to improve the conditions of democratic societies and the human experience by opening up new channels of communication and pathways for access. Because of its inherent capacity for openness, its early users and designers had visions of subverting the status quo and challenging the dominant voices and ideologies that ruled society from the top down. But as the digital age has become increasingly commercialized, the power and profits of digital technologies have been unevenly concentrated at the top—just like the old communication systems they were supposed to subvert. Today, the new digital media ecosystem is dominated by a small handful of digital giants that have absorbed the real gains. Understanding some of the nuances of this concentration of power makes us more news literate by challenging much of the conventional wisdom about the free and open internet.

In the modern media environment, most of the gains have gone to the new digital giants. Forecasts for 2019 show that, for the first time, digital ad spending—projected to be $129 billion—will exceed ad spending on traditional media, including television, newspapers, and radio, at only $109 billion.[11] The digital ad industry has exploded in recent years. While traditional news organizations that produce most original reporting have seen continuously declining revenue—like at your local daily newspaper, if you still have one—business is booming at Facebook and Google. These two giants absorb around two-thirds of all digital ad revenue in the United States, and they continue to grow. Total internet advertising revenue grew 22 percent in 2016, up $12.9 billion, but almost all of that growth—99 percent—went to Facebook and Google, according to an industry research report.[12] Of all digital ad revenue, 73 percent goes to the top ten ad-selling companies. That means virtually every penny of new online advertising is going to two companies, and most digital advertising money overall goes to ten companies. If you want to make money online through advertiser-supported content and you are not one of those companies, you are going to struggle.

Most economists would describe this state of affairs as a *monopoly* (or duopoly or oligopoly), which means that the supply of a good or service is controlled by one or two or even a few entities that are so big and dominant that no one else can even attempt to compete. The result is often reduced innovation and progress as well as an increase in prices; there's little reason to innovate if you have no competitors, and there's nothing to stop you from increasing your profits as much as consumers will tolerate. Whether it's one or two or a few companies in control doesn't really matter if the barriers to entry are so high that no one else can come close. And if a competitor does emerge—take Instagram or WhatsApp for example—rather than risk competition, a larger company—Facebook—simply swoops in and buys the company, and now Instagram and WhatsApp are owned by Facebook.

Because a real capitalist economy depends on competition, the existence of monopolies is generally frowned upon, and democratic nations have a long history of making and using laws to prevent them. In the United States, the trust-busting presidents Theodore Roosevelt and William Howard Taft in the early 1900s are famous for enforcing the Sherman Anti-Trust Act of 1890 to break up monopolies in industries such as railroads, oil, and tobacco, where ownership and control had become concentrated in the hands of a few major companies. Industrialization had grown rapidly after the U.S. Civil War in the 1860s, and for the first time in history, market power shifted from small family businesses to major corporations. More recently, in the second half of the 20th century, Xerox, AT&T, and Microsoft all were subjected to legal actions to reduce their domination of their respective industries.

Long-standing critiques of capitalism have focused on the ideas that workers are not compensated for the true value of their productivity (which is absorbed by owners of capital) and that declines in competition would lead to a socialist revolution where workers ultimately became the owners of the fruits of their labor. Karl Marx, for example, is well known for the critical analysis of capitalism he and others established beginning in the 1860s. But in their day, Marx and his contemporaries could not have conceived of the concentration of power represented by today's major corporations thanks to industrialization, technology, financialization, and globalization. As a result, *monopoly capitalism* is a term used to describe a state where a few major corporations become so powerful that competition is impossible, and those companies are so intertwined with government that laws and regulations come to represent corporate interests and preserve monopoly power. The result is not, as Marx predicted, a worker's revolution, but rather a new stage of capitalism where power is even more strongly consolidated and the classes of workers have even less control over the value of their productivity and less freedom in the marketplace.

That's an oversimplified summary of more than a century of economic thought, but it's enough to get us thinking critically about the news and information environment we live in. Generally speaking, as power is concentrated, workers and consumers suffer. Wages stagnate and opportunities dry up. What appears to be a material utopia is really an illusion of choice as a decline in competition leads toward the homogenization of society. That means our news and information environment often comes at a steep cost and offers little of value. Instead, we are overwhelmed with hypercommercialism and cheap entertainment. But it doesn't have to be this way. First of all, by developing our critical awareness, we can resist the low-value instincts this environment encourages. And second, citizens can demand action.

Even today, legislators and regulators are occasionally responsive to citizen demands. That doesn't mean they actually take action, but there is at least a whiff of awareness around the power of the digital giants. For example, in 2018, Facebook founder Mark Zuckerberg was called before the U.S. Congress to explain himself in the wake of the Cambridge Analytica scandal, where millions of Facebook users saw their personal information shared with and used by a political consulting firm to influence the 2016 election. The focus of the inquiry was a concern over privacy, but the issue of monopoly power also came up. Several lines of questioning raised this issue by asking about Facebook's business model. The conservative Republican Senator Lindsay Graham of South Carolina drove the point home when he asked Zuckerberg to name a single competitor to Facebook. Zuckerberg sat dumbfounded and admitted he could not. Graham compared the social media giant to a major car company. "If I buy a Ford, it doesn't work well, I don't like it; I buy a Chevy," Graham said. "If I'm upset with Facebook, what's the equivalent product I can go sign up for?"[13] The fact that there isn't one shows Facebook's anticompetitive dominance of the marketplace.

Under a neoliberal market-oriented approach to governance, legislators are typically reluctant to impose what are considered to be onerous regulations on businesses that should ostensibly be governed by laws of supply and demand, not government intervention in the free market. Furthermore, when regulating media and technology industries, questions of speech and press freedom inevitably arise and make the implementation of regulations even more unlikely. The answer, instead, is self-regulation. It's up to a business such as Facebook to police their own activity and eliminate any abuses of their concentrated power. But even

Senator Graham hinted at the idea that monopoly power removes any impulse to do so. He continued:

> Here's the question that all of us have to answer: What do we tell our constituents, given what happened here, why should we let you self-regulate? What do you tell people in South Carolina that, given all the things we discovered here, it's a good idea for us to rely upon you to regulate your own business practices?

That's a good question.

Of course, the Congressional hearings came and went, and despite the occasionally tough lines of questioning, no new laws or policies have emerged to substantially change the way Facebook operates. At least in the wake of the Cambridge Analytica scandal, the European Union enacted new privacy laws that aimed to increase disclosure and transparency over the collection and use of consumer data. But so far, the consolidated power of digital giants to mostly do as they please remains the effective law of the land. And so just as power was consolidated and controlled in the closed media environments of the pre-digital era, the internet has become similarly closed off to new entrants into the marketplace and new outlets for expression or diversity.

It's easy to imagine that the internet offers a level playing field, but a closer look reveals a highly concentrated business environment. Not only does this reduce consumer choice and encourage abuses of power, this affects the news and information environment because the money going to the digital giants is money that's not going to the individuals and organizations that actually produce news. This creates a serious problem for journalism because companies like Google and Facebook make their money by repackaging and repurposing content that was produced and paid for by other entities. Google and Facebook profit by selling advertising against content that costs them nothing to produce. This is a business model that helps them make lots of money, but it means original news producers are left scrambling to figure out how to remain financially viable in this new media ecosystem.

As a result, news companies are left to practically beg news consumers to pay directly for the services they receive, and in some cases, this has been successful, but mostly with legacy news outlets such as *The New York Times* and the *Washington Post*. Even the supposed digital news innovators such as Buzzfeed (partly owned by Comcast), Vice Media (partly owned by Disney), and HuffPost (owned by Verizon Media) have succumbed to declines in resources and cuts to their reporting staffs. News consumers already pay high prices for access to the web through their internet service providers (another highly concentrated industry dominated by Comcast and Verizon), but none of that money makes its way back to the actual news producers.

And so the political economy of the internet is one of limited competition, high barriers to entry, and homogenized content, which are traits that represent the exact opposite of a dynamic, innovative, and competitive marketplace. The question for citizens is whether we are content with this state of affairs or if we want to demand better.

Here Come the Algorithms

Instead of the idealized level playing field the internet once represented, today's internet is dominated by powerful forces that control what we see by picking and choosing the content available to us. All social and search sites have to have some kind of system for deciding what will show up in news feeds and search results. The answer is an *algorithm*, which is simply a formalized decision-making process. If your car is low on gas, then you go to the gas station. If your algorithm fails, you are stuck on the side of the road. In computers, algorithms are the instructions a computer follows when performing calculations or sorting through data such as web content.

For many web users, the internet's invisible algorithmic decision makers appear to be neutral, benign forces that show us what we want to see. They are dispassionate and agnostic; they just show us what's there. But the reality is that these algorithms are the new gatekeepers, and they often have very different motives from traditional gatekeepers such as newspaper editors who at least exercised some kind of human judgment regarding what is worth sharing and what isn't. To increase your news literacy, you should know a bit about how algorithms work and how they can be manipulated and how they influence your information consumption.

First, algorithms are never neutral. By necessity, the content that shows up in news feeds and search results has to be prioritized in some way. It's possible to simply show every new piece of content in real time, and this was common at one point in time. But most web platforms have moved away from this approach because it's not the best way to keep users' eyeballs on their site. Even Twitter, which comes closest to employing the "real-time" approach, is moving toward ranking and filtering. So the reality is that humans have programmed computers to pick and choose what to share with you. You can see immediately why it matters who is doing the programming and what their motives and priorities might be. You can also see why this leads to inevitable charges of political bias as humans decide what to prioritize in news feeds and search results. Not surprisingly, Facebook and Google are both common targets. While it is always possible for overt political bias to exist, algorithmic bias can be much more subtle.

Through machine learning, otherwise known as artificial intelligence, computers are designed to develop their own systems for deciding what to prioritize. So even though a human might have programmed an algorithm to sort through all the potential content on the web, if the algorithm asks a computer to begin to make its own decisions based on the data it encounters, the machines actually produce their own methods of sorting, which might not have anything to do with what the human programmer initially had in mind. Moreover, this all happens so fast and with such large amounts of data, the programmer might not even know what kind of sorting mechanisms had resulted through the machine-learning process.

As if that weren't enough, here's the real pickle. All of this is hidden from public view. Because the social and search platforms most people use are owned by corporations, their algorithms are proprietary—industry secrets, in other words, hidden inside black boxes. We can make guesses and inferences about how algorithms work based on what shows up on our screens, but we can never know for sure unless companies like Facebook go out of their way to let us know. And you can be sure that they typically don't.

Many people get confused about algorithmic sorting and its apparent neutrality. If a website like Facebook simply chooses to show what is most popular, that can seem like a neutral, market-style solution to giving people what they want. Of course, popularity is not a remotely neutral basis for choosing content—it gives preference to what is popular. Popularity sometimes helps the best content rise to the top, but not always. What is popular can be vile, hateful, misleading, malicious stuff. And what is popular can actually be oppressive and marginalizing to individuals and groups who aren't part of the groups deciding what's popular. For example, in her book *Algorithms of Oppression: How Search Engines Reinforce Racism*, Safiya Noble provides ample evidence of the negative outcomes that result when online searches—far from being neutral—rely on user behavior to predict what people want to search for and what they want to see in the result. For example, Noble observed that a search for "black girls" yielded mostly porn sites and other negative depictions, whereas searches for other racial groups were represented much more positively in search results. Noble concludes that "what we need is a way to reframe, reimagine, relearn, and remember the struggle for racial and social justice and to see how information online in ranking systems can also impact behavior and thinking offline."[14] Since Noble and others have identified these issues, Google and others have begun to take actions to refine their algorithms, but the problems of algorithmic bias—intentional or otherwise—will never go away.

But wait a minute. Is it Google's fault that people can be racist or sexist or hold other antisocial tendencies when conducting their web searches? Does Facebook bear any responsibility for its users who post false or misleading information? Those are fair questions, and maybe your answer is, no, it's up to their users to sort through it all and arrive at a place of truthful information and representational accuracy. But unfortunately, most people give little thought to how information is prioritized online, and even if they have, they might not care one bit. So even if you conclude that private companies bear no responsibility for their users' behavior and its effects on search results and news feeds, at least recognize the inherent structural bias built into a system that bases its decisions on popularity, and that bias gets injected directly into a user's online experience. As tech journalist Laura Hudson has written, "Instead of offering a workaround for human biases, the tools we designed to help us predict the future may be dooming us to repeat the past by replicating and even amplifying societal inequalities that already exist."[15]

We need to dispense with this common notion that because algorithms are simply based on math, there's no way they can be biased or harmful. I've been personally excoriated on Twitter for suggesting otherwise. When pipe bombs were mailed to prominent Democrats and other critics of President Donald Trump in October 2018, I noticed that the first Google autocomplete result was "pipe bombs sent by democrats," which, before a suspect was identified, represented an emerging conspiracy theory that Democrats had sent the pipe bombs to themselves to stir up anti-Trump resentment. I tweeted a screenshot of the result and suggested Google make a correction so as not to spread misinformation, and while I was pleased to see the subsequent interest in my Twittering, the backlash was swift. As one commenter noted, "Dude you dumb as shit. The algorithm is dependent on the most searched term with similar keywords within a span of time, not a bias." Aside from the personal attack, he made my point for me. Of course, bias is exactly what this is, a bias toward the most searched term in a span of time. So let's be clear: popularity is not neutrality.

The problems with algorithms hardly end there. Because savvy website designers can at least begin to guess what kinds of content get prioritized by various algorithms, there are ways to game the system. *Search engine optimization*, or SEO for short, is the practice of influencing where and how a piece of content shows up in search results. Content creators pay large sums of money to digital marketers and developers to help bump their work up to a top position. This works by making the best possible use of stuff that appears on the page like keywords, headlines, and web links, as well as the code you can't see, including tags, metadata, and other behind-the-scenes tricks. Because search algorithms continue to evolve and change, the practice of SEO remains big business. The higher a website appears in organic search results (that is, not paid for), the more legitimacy it appears to have. And almost no one looks beyond the first page of search results, so if your site doesn't appear there, you effectively don't exist. You don't have to know the ins and outs of how SEO actually works, but to be news literate, you do need to be aware that the practice is widespread and has major effects on your exposure to information and other content online. In short, just because something shows up in your search results doesn't mean it has any value at all. And the people who tend to have the most money to spend on SEO are the marketers and advertisers hawking products and services online—not the creators of independent news or journalism that you need to be an informed citizen.

Another issue created by algorithmic sorting is the existence of what's referred to as a *filter bubble*, which is created when your exposure to content online becomes limited by algorithmic sorting that's personalized based on your own online behavior. Algorithms can be programmed to examine a range of factors to determine what content you will see. This can include dozens or even hundreds of factors, including data points such as your geographic location, your browser type, your past search history, and your past clicking behavior. Many of the sites we visit such as Facebook and Google also have extensive profiles on their users that include a surprising range of data including age, race, income, relationship status, political affiliations, and credit card usage.[16] Of course, these profiles are largely hidden from us, and we can never really know what data is being used to shape our online experience. But through these practices of *behavioral targeting* and *data mining*, our digital shadows follow us everywhere we go.

In some ways, the ability to predict what you want to see can be a nice benefit, especially with the surplus of online content. Netflix can steer you toward movies you might like, and Amazon can show you stuff you might want to buy. But there may also be a much more pernicious effect. If your entire online experience is personally tailored by algorithms to their perceptions of you and your interests, you could be massively cut off from much of what is out there and much of what other people are seeing. If so, your worldview is being invisibly shaped by the secret algorithms that rule the web. This process of *mass customization* means manufacturers of technology and creators of digital content can use what they know about you to give you exactly what they perceive to be what you want. Everyone gets their own personalized world of information, entertainment, goods, and services. As the longtime Google CEO Eric Schmidt said as far back as 2010,

> the power of individual targeting—the technology will be so good it will be very hard for people to watch or consume something that has not in some sense been tailored for them. . . . We know roughly who you are, roughly what you care about, roughly who your friends are.[17]

That's some fairly Orwellian talk there—except it's not coming from Big Brother, it comes from one of the world's largest for-profit corporations.

If the web offered any hope for enhancing the prospects of democracy and citizenship by exposing people to diverse information and entertainment, all of this personalization has the potential to effectively remove them. As Eli Pariser concluded in his 2011 book where he coined the term filter bubble, "The era of personalization is here, and it's upending many of our predictions about what the Internet would do."[18] Not only does customization limit our ability to use digital technology to broaden our collective horizons, we need to remember why it's being done in the first place: profit. If we get what we want from a product or service, we are likely to want more of it. For example, Facebook's number one goal is to keep your eyeballs glued to their site. So of course they want to make your experience one that will keep you coming back. It's how they make their money. And there's nothing inherently wrong with that—as long as we remember that the "free" product we get from them is not some benign information service.

It's a vehicle for advertising, and it shapes who we are. We'll learn more about the psychology of all this in the next chapter, but for now, you should know how the political economy of the internet centers on personalization and customization.

Now an important caveat about filter bubbles and the concern about *echo chambers* they can produce, where web users exist in homogenized worlds of their own design and hear mainly their own preexisting views and opinions echoed back at them. Just because our online experience is personalized doesn't mean we are being brainwashed or that we're missing out on alternative points of view. Some research suggests that going online can actually increase the diversity of information someone is exposed to, especially compared to someone who sits down and watches three hours of the same cable news network every night. Talk about an echo chamber! So we should be careful not to overstate the effects of filter bubbles in digital life. We also do a fine job of creating our own filter bubbles—not only online by deciding who to like and follow—but also in real life by deciding who to spend time with and, generally speaking, how to live our lives. But in these contexts, we are able to make these choices at least somewhat freely and independently, and at least occasionally, we are forced to run into people who are different from us. The differences with algorithmic filter bubbles is that the selection process is secret and invisible to us, and its purpose is profit.

Although you can never escape it completely, you can take steps to limit the amount of personalization that happens when you go online. You can make technological adjustments such as using a private or "incognito" browser, deleting your search history, logging out of accounts, deleting or blocking cookies, and using ad blocking software. These changes can affect what you see online and they might also help protect your privacy if that's something you're interested in. But you can fight the forces of personalization by actively resisting them and blowing up the filter bubbles they create. Go out of your way to consult multiple news sources, and become an expert at curating your own online experience to include lots of diverse information. Expose yourself to stuff you're not immediately attracted to and challenge yourself to explore new areas. Finally, get off your devices and talk to real people. Read a physical newspaper or magazine or book and compare it to what you've seen online. Do a digital detox, and try to see the world as it is, not merely as it is presented to you.

Regulation and the Lack Thereof

There were a number of awkward moments during that Congressional hearing where Facebook CEO Mark Zuckerberg testified about a host of issues around privacy and competition in social media. As many observers noted, the Senate's questioners—mostly one old white guy after another—showed their near-complete ignorance of how technology works. As comedian Stephen Colbert put it on Twitter, "Almost feel bad for Zuckerberg. There's no way he left that room full of old people without having to set up their wifi." Not only do most lawmakers have little knowledge of complicated technological operations related to packet switching or IP addressing or end-to-end design or file sharing—who does?—they often have problems contemplating the basic operations of a social media company. Senator Orrin Hatch, an 84-year-old Republican from Utah, noting that Facebook claims its service will always be free, asked, "how do you sustain a business model in which users don't pay for your service?" Zuckerberg appeared to contain his laughter as he paused and replied, "Senator, we run ads."[19] Even the century-old business model of selling eyeballs to advertisers was not evident to Senator Hatch.

While not all of the questioning was this awkward or uninformed, the failure by many lawmakers to understand even the most basic tenets of how a social media company works means any attempt to make rules or laws around their operations are not likely to be very effective. As a former official from the Department of Homeland Security noted after the hearing, "A lot of these members frankly aren't on social media and maybe don't have experience with social media. You need to experience the platform to understand what you're talking about if you do want to challenge the validity of what the company's doing."[20] Without a more thorough understanding of the operations of the companies that control and dominate the internet, lawmakers and regulators can have a hard time making policy that actually works in the best interests of society.

It's worth noting that having difficulty understanding complex phenomena is a common problem in lawmaking. It's not surprising that the average legislator doesn't know enough about every area of legislation to make effective policy. That's just a fact of life in a complex world. But a common result is that the regulations that become law and policy are designed by lobbyists who represent the areas being regulated, as they are the only ones with sufficient technical knowledge to understand the issues at hand (and the ones funding the campaigns of lawmakers). Also, industry specialists are often appointed to serve on the government agencies that make rules and regulations. Not surprisingly, regulations that result—if any—are often highly favorable to the industries being regulated. Called *regulatory capture* by scholars, the process of making law and policy is often controlled by the very entities that need to be reined in to prevent abuses of power. (The FCC, which regulates the media system, represents a classic case of regulatory capture, as its members often come from the telecommunications and media industries the FCC is supposed to regulate.)

Overall, the internet remains only lightly regulated in terms of structure and content, governed primarily by a pseudo-libertarian regulatory philosophy that allows for maximum profits and minimum public service. That means lawmakers have generally opted for what is ostensibly a "hands-off" approach to saying what internet companies and service providers can and can't do. In reality, the laws that get made often protect the power and dominance of companies. For example, Section 230 of the Communication Decency Act (part of the larger Telecommunications Act of 1996) is well known for letting web companies off the hook for the behavior of their users—referred to as "safe harbor" in the law. That is, companies such as Facebook and Google cannot be held responsible for what appears on their sites even if the content violates laws related to libel, copyright, privacy, indecency, or other restrictions on free expression. On the surface, this makes good sense. It helps protect free expression online, and it would be difficult and expensive to police the activity of every user of a website. But nonetheless, this structural feature is exactly what allows these giant companies to exist. The "hands-off" rationale behind this long-standing protection represents a deal commonly offered by lawmakers to industries—we'll protect you from legal action, but we'd like you to regulate yourselves at least a little bit. As Senator Ron Wyden, who co-wrote the law, said in 2018, "the real key to Section 230 was making sure that companies in return for that protection—that they wouldn't be sued indiscriminately—were being responsible in terms of policing their platforms."[21] Of course, without any legal obligation to do so, web companies have not always taken action against socially undesirable content, ranging from simple misinformation to outright falsehoods to violent videos to death threats to terrorist propaganda. So while a rule like this appears to promote a hands-off approach to market activity, it ultimately has the effect of propping up the most powerful entities that dominate the online environment, and it lets them off the hook for spreading misinformation and other types of content that aim to derail the practice of informed self-government.

Free market advocates note that a hands-off approach is still the best way to govern because markets are inherently "self-correcting"; that is, if a company is doing a bad job of meeting consumer needs, it will either change its ways or go away. There are three main problems with this line of thinking. First, consumers have to be aware of the flaws in a product to demand change or alter their consumption. If their television breaks, they can switch brands, but if their water is contaminated with carcinogens that cause cancer after years of drinking that water, it's going to be hard to make a change until it's much too late. With news and information, if you don't know you're being misled or lied to, you might not realize you could do better. Second, just because you're "giving people what they want" doesn't mean much if it's not doing them any good. Lots of people want porn and heroin, but that doesn't mean we want these products sold in an unregulated market. Also, people often don't even know what they want. Think about how much time and money is spent convincing people what they want, such as the millions of dollars spent by marketers to advertise and promote movies, web platforms, and other products, including news media products. Without such promotions, media consumers might have different preferences. Third, change is especially unlikely under the conditions of monopoly capitalism. Internet service providers, for example, are among the most hated companies in the United States, but most households have between zero and two options for true broadband service, leaving little to no room for consumer demand to affect change of any kind.[22] Americans pay among the highest prices for slowest service in the developed world, but what are you going to do about it if you need to use the internet? Similarly, you might have three local television stations that provide daily newscasts, but if they are all basically the same (because they all hire the same industry consultants who give them the same advice), you don't have any other choice if you want to consume local television news.

This is not to say there are no laws governing the internet in the public interest. For example, many governmental bodies have passed laws to outlaw so-called revenge porn, which describes the posting of compromising photos or videos of an individual by a jilted ex-lover. This sort of content restriction is hard to argue with. In the eyes of the law, there is no redeemable social value to be found in this kind of behavior. But there are two important points here. One, it shows that markets don't always self-correct without being forced to. And two, it shows the important role regulations play in protecting consumers from harm. (Think of other types of laws regarding speech and behavior that strive to balance individual freedom with broader societal interests: copyright, defamation, obscenity, property, contracts, and so on.) A supposedly hands-off approach to regulating the internet is bound to cause trouble eventually. The question is: will it be too late to protect consumers from harm if their privacy has already been compromised and their fellow citizens have been fed so much misinformation that their collective decision-making leads to economic and environmental collapse?

In analyzing the evolving media environment of the mid-20th century, media historian Victor Pickard uses the term *corporate libertarianism* to describe the assumption that "the market is the most efficient and therefore the most socially desirable means for allocating important resources."[23] But "maximizing efficiency" is hardly the best way to approach the needs of self-governing citizens. As Pickard points out, this approach puts public goods like the news and information needed in democratic society at a distinct disadvantage, as evidenced by the current crisis in journalism and digital media. In a corporate libertarian context for public goods such as news and information, the result is often market failure—the available supply provided by the market does not meet society's needs. That's where law and policy come in. As Pickard notes, "when market failure is detected, the historical and logical response has been to address it via public policy intervention."[24] The United States and other democratic countries (even more so) have a long history of applying policy solutions—that is, regulations—to strike a balance between unfettered market freedom and the broader needs of society. The question surrounding the internet is whether that balance has been appropriately struck or if more intervention is needed.

Many observers have noted that even though the commercial web grew out of a massive government and academic project, it emerged during an era of increasingly dominant market-oriented regulatory philosophy (that is, neoliberalism), where digital denizens assumed efficiency and innovation would bring massive benefits to society and that this would happen naturally without government intervention. But it's increasingly evident that this approach—despite the benefits it has brought—did not go as planned and that it was a mistake not to treat this major component of daily life like other sectors of industry that are regulated to promote the safety and efficacy of the products and services offered. "The defining fact of digital life is that the web was created in the libertarian frenzy of the 1990s," wrote Franklin Foer in a 2018 article for *The Atlantic* titled "It's Time to Regulate the Internet." "As we privatized the net, releasing it from the hands of the government agencies that cultivated it, we suspended our inherited civic instincts. Instead of treating the web like the financial system or aviation or agriculture, we refrained from creating the robust rules that would ensure safety and enforce our constitutional values."[25] Think of it. The United States once separated commercial and investment banking in order to protect citizens from bankers' gambles. The Food and Drug Administration was created to make sure food and medicine wouldn't be contaminated or deadly. The Environmental Protection Agency was created under President Richard Nixon to help make sure rivers wouldn't catch on fire due to industrial pollution and that the air wouldn't be contaminated with endless toxins. Why not apply a similar regulatory approach to our streams of news and information, the very lifeblood of an informed democratic society?

In the United States, there's an easy answer to this question: the First Amendment. Yes, the First Amendment is foundational to American-style democracy and helps ensure free expression in a wide range of contexts. But it's important to realize that the First Amendment is more than a mere shield against limitations on expression. Scholars like to think in terms of *negative liberty* and *positive liberty*, an idea popularized by political philosopher Isaiah Berlin in the 1950s and 1960s.[26] Negative liberty, broadly, explains that which I am not kept from doing; positive liberty, in general, describes that which I may do in order to fully exercise my "humanness." More specifically, negative liberty keeps the government from interfering with my existence; positive liberty permits the government to create conditions intended to facilitate or enhance freedom or other interests. Writing in the context of World War II, Berlin showed a strong preference for negative liberty. He, like others of the time, feared totalitarianism and communism as massive intrusions into personal freedom by "positive" or active means. These mid-20th-century forms of government employed warped versions of socialist ideals meant to balance negative liberty with other social values such as equality and justice. But through the efforts of totalitarian dictators, personal liberty was ultimately squashed, and individuals ended up with liberty neither negative nor positive. These conditions and Berlin's response illustrate the balance that must be sought between the two concepts of liberty.

Legal scholar Cass Sunstein has written extensively about the clash of positive and negative liberty, especially in the context of media and democracy. In his book *Republic.com 2.0*, he asserts that the fundamental question should not be whether to regulate (indeed, there are always regulations) but rather should ask if a given regulation serves democracy and benefits the social welfare.[27] Historically, courts and policy makers have offered conflicting views of how to properly interpret the

First Amendment, but the absence of an absolutist vision is universal. Fundamentally, Sunstein points out that the media system is built on legal structures that are not unique to media and thus are commonly omitted from discussions of press freedom. Property rights, contracts, tort law, and rights of exclusion are all fundamental legal principles that allow the media system to exist as it does. These are "positive" (meaning active) intrusions of government into public and private life that create capitalist media markets. Copyright law, libel law, and laws designed to protect children are legal intrusions—limits on liberty—that are more specific to media. Even Berlin points to the state's interest in compulsory education and in prohibiting public executions as permissible limits on liberty.[28]

This is not to say that systems of ostensibly free enterprise are not capable of producing public benefits. But the reality is that market economies depend on elaborate and explicit policies that are favorable to business often at the expense of the public. The U.S. system of broadcast licensing, for example, in which broadcasters are granted free use of the supposedly publicly owned airwaves, has been called a $70 billion giveaway.[29] Despite pro-business policies such as this one, market advocates often suggest that the FCC interferes with the workings of the broadcast market by regulating ownership and other structural matters.[30] So when market advocates argue for "deregulation," they are really calling for altering the regulatory scheme from one that places limits on industry to one that supports it. As Sunstein points out, "What 'deregulation' really means is a shift from the status quo to a system of different but emphatically legal regulation, more specifically one of property, tort, and contract rights, in which government does not impose specific public interest obligations but instead sets up initial entitlements and then permits trades among owners and producers. This is a regulatory system just as much as any other."[31] Real regulation is needed to combat market failure and to promote widely shared democratic values that places limits on unbridled profit maximization at the expense of the well-being of society. Sunstein concludes: "The issue is thus not whether to 'deregulate,' but whether one or another regulatory system is better than imaginable alternatives."[32]

Certainly, there is a balance to be struck. Obviously a system of government propaganda would be no more preferable than a purely commercial system. But a public system sufficiently insulated from the whims of politics is in a better position to provide some kind of public benefit. As scholar Owen Fiss notes in *The Irony of Free Speech*,

> We should never forget the potential of the state for oppression, but at the same time, we must contemplate the possibility that the state will use its considerable powers to promote goals that lie at the core of a democratic society—equality and perhaps free speech itself.[33]

These words should be used to guide communication policy today and to create news media structures and institutions that promote democratic values and practices. This approach can be used to break the corporate stranglehold on main-stream news media as well as emerging digital media forms through limits on size, ownership and commercial content.

Once again, objections to interventions in the marketplace for news and infor-mation often rely on the First Amendment's requirement that Congress "make no law" restricting speech or the press. But this argument ignores the fact that many laws have been made and upheld by the courts that embrace this affirma-tive or positive interpretation of the freedoms of speech and the press. And again, it is increasingly clear that journalism—the news and information required by a self-governing society—should be thought of as a public good or "common pool resource," something that everyone benefits from regardless of who pays for it, like clean air or water. Such public goods must be actively protected and promoted by law and policy.

Like other sectors of society, the news media system is constructed through elaborate laws and policies, many of which are not always obvious but are none-theless integral to the structure of the system and the content it produces. And in a democracy, it is not unreasonable to expect those policies to reflect and enhance democratic values. As Sunstein writes: "The question is not whether we will regu-late speech, but how—and in particular how we can do so while promoting the values associated with a system of free expression, emphatically including democratic self-government."[34] To this end, one Supreme Court ruling stands out. In the 1945 case *Associated Press v. U.S.*, the court ruled against the Associated Press due to a set of bylaws that the court deemed in violation of the Sherman Anti-Trust Act because of restrictions placed on access to the news wire service by nonmembers. In the court's opinion, Justice Hugo Black made the case that regulation of media is not a violation of First Amendment protections but rather plays a crucial role in serving a public interest in providing widespread access to reliable news and information:

> It would be strange indeed however if the grave concern for freedom of the press which prompted adoption of the First Amendment should be read as a command that the government was without power to protect that freedom. The First Amendment, far from providing an argument against application of the Sherman Act, here provides powerful reasons to the contrary. That Amendment rests on the assumption that the widest possible dissemination of information from diverse and antagonistic sources is essential to the wel-fare of the public, that a free press is a condition of a free society. Surely a command that the government itself shall not impede the free flow of ideas does not afford non-governmental combinations a refuge if they impose restraints upon that constitutionally guaranteed freedom.[35]

Justice Black's words hint at the predicament we find ourselves in today. The First Amendment clearly is meant to limit the power of government to constrain individual free expression. But that doesn't mean the government can't use its power to help promote free expression especially by the sources of news and information that aim to make useful contributions to society. In fact, individual liberty is at risk when our information environment becomes so concentrated and polluted that we can no longer function usefully as citizens. So the First Amendment is not only about limiting government power to regulate news media but also is about using government power to promote free speech, especially when "nongovernmental combinations," that is, companies like Facebook and Google, have established a monopoly on controlling who gets to speak and who gets to be heard. The *Associated Press* ruling suggests a precedent that would allow the government to break up news and digital media monopolies and to encourage a greater flow of useful information.

Part of news literacy is understanding how Justice Black's words can inform communication policy today in order to create news media structures and institutions that promote democratic values and practices. The positive approach to liberty can be used to break the corporate stranglehold on news and digital media through limits on size, ownership, and commercial content. It can also be used to promote public, nonprofit, nonpartisan, and independent media organizations that can produce positive social benefits by being sufficiently insulated from politics and from markets. If we foster a democratic vision for the First Amendment and for free expression laws around the world, we can see how regulation can play a useful role in helping us survive the messy era of news and information overload. Of course, most people understandably have no interest in the policy-making process. It is arcane and boring. But until we learn the basics about the significance of policy and regulation in shaping the news media system and the content it produces, we will have no hope of understanding why things are the way they are and even less hope of making positive changes. That doesn't mean everyone must learn the ins and outs of every policy question before us—it's enough to know that parts of the system need real change if we want to improve our news and information environment. In our media-saturated age, our ability to facilitate democratic media structures and institutions will play a role in deciding the fate of democracy itself.

The Political Economy of Political Polarization

The rise of digital and social media and the increase in online participation can be linked to the rise of political polarization and partisanship, which contributes to positive gains for digital giants even as it fails to serve the public. As conflict and emotion increasingly dominate the participatory news environment, the potential for revenue rises as well. We still don't know exactly what role news and social media plays in increasing political polarization—more on this in Chapter 6—but we do know that emotions are a great motivator for those who want to make their voices heard online, which means the conflict and animosity the internet can breed often increases user engagement and creates tremendous opportunities for profit-making by the owners of search and social platforms. In short, your deepest passions have been monetized.

We already know that your eyeballs and attention are worth billions of dollars to advertisers and marketers. In the offline world, newspapers and television broadcasters do their best to bring you a product that will attract that attention so it can be converted to revenue. Again, plenty of news organizations are also working hard to fulfill a deeply held public service mission, but without revenue, they can't exist, so with an advertising-based business model, they have to find a way to bring in money somehow. But offline, news producers only know so much about their audience. They collect basic demographic information like age, income, race, and education, but what they know is nothing compared to the amount of data that can be gathered about you online. And the more that's known about you, the easier it becomes to direct you to content that will ignite your passions and keep you engaged.

For some people, a social media company's ability to retain your engagement might actually steer you away from news and information. Maybe Facebook knows you are into Dodgers baseball, Ugg boots, and Beats by Dre headphones, and you actively avoid news and information, especially about politics and policy making. That's a problem in and of itself because these users are being actively discouraged from engaging with civic life and becoming an informed citizen who participates in democratic self-governance. Of course, it's your right to tune out from this stuff, and that's always been true even before the internet, but in this case, the algorithms that are guiding you around the web aren't even giving you a chance to get engaged. And the significant role technology plays in our lives effectively means, for many people, if it's not happening online, it's just not happening.

For now, though, let's assume you are someone who's interested at least to some degree in democratic life, and you like to know what's going in politics, business, and other areas where powerful figures and institutions are influencing the progress of society, and you are at least somewhat intrigued by the competition of interests and the fight over resources that are at the heart of political decision-making. When you go online, search and social algorithms, rather than steering you toward the latest Ugg boots and fashion tips, have an incentive to provide politically oriented content that will ignite your emotions and get you to participate by clicking, liking, sharing, and commenting. These acts of *engagement* are at the core of most online business models. Each bit of engagement not only helps the internet learn more about you, but also creates a revenue opportunity. And if the content you are steered toward is heavily one-sided or full of misinformation or conspiracy theories or worse, you are going deeper and deeper down the rabbit hole of polarization.

Two major caveats here: One, not all internet exposure leads to an increase in polarization, and for some people, it could actually have the opposite effect. But as researchers continue to explore and study these phenomena, we can see at least some emerging evidence that plenty of people are driven further to political extremes based on their online experience. Two, although politics has definitely become more polarized and polarizing over the past few decades, there are plenty of factors that can contribute to these shifts. Some suggest online news and social media play only a small role while others see it as a central driving force in our increasingly combative democracies. Overall, we should be careful not to overstate or overgeneralize about what's happening to our political discourse and what's driving it, but we know enough to be concerned about the role our online experiences play in determining the quality of democratic life.

When you go online, what is exciting and engaging to you might not be the stuff that is more important or most reliable. But because algorithms are the forces deciding what your experience will be, you don't always get the good stuff. This isn't necessarily a malicious act. It's just the natural result of machine learning and computerized decision-making. Of course, the machines have been programmed by humans to find the best ways to get and keep your attention, so if the buck stops somewhere, it's with them. The result of this algorithmic filtering is often to increase your *affective engagement*, or your gut reactions to emotion-laden content. (That's why one of the best pieces of advice for navigating online is to pay attention to your emotional reactions to what you see. If something makes you angry or sad or elated, that's a good time to stop and think before you engage.)

For most internet users, these processes are hidden from view. According to a 2019 survey by the Pew Research Center, most Facebook users (74 percent) do not even know Facebook collects and categorizes data about them, and at least half were uncomfortable with this practice once they learned about it.[36] You can go to the Ad Preferences section on Facebook to catch a glimpse of what Facebook thinks it knows about you. (But also know that they have plenty more data that you are not privy to.) For example, half of Facebook users are given a political affiliation label, and 73 percent of users who have one say it very or somewhat accurately reflects their political views. And that's just the beginning when it comes to the data that's collected and mobilized to get and keep users' attention.

Of course, political polarization is not just a profit-maker for online news and information media. Just look at the enormous profits generated by the cable news channels, especially around the 2016 election, largely thanks to the sensational and polarizing nature of candidate Donald Trump. It's true that Trump did plenty of polarizing on his own, but cable and even broadcast news outlets were well aware that he would bring the eyeballs, and they took full advantage. But the digital environment offers a whole new layer of influence due to the massive amounts of user data that can be collected and exploited, and also due to the pervasive and participatory role of digital and social media in daily life. Online search and social media companies can take a much more targeted approach than traditional media formats, and users can control consumption and distribution of news content in all sorts of new ways that can interfere with democratic imperatives. Ultimately, whether online or offline, polarization can be great for business, but it's terrible for democracy, which will live or die by the ability of citizens to be well informed around a shared set of facts and to be willing to find ways to compromise on workable political solutions.

The profitability of political polarization is especially troubling when it comes to political advertising online. At least on television, everyone watching in a given market has a good chance of being exposed to the same messages, and FCC regulations create a somewhat level playing field for anyone who has the money to buy television airtime for political advertising. But online, particularly on Facebook, people are divided up into targeted audiences—what Facebook calls "Custom Audiences"—in such a way that different groups end up receiving wildly different political messages, and there is little in the way of regulation or transparency around what Facebook charges and what kind of access it provides. And the targeting is effective. A 2018 study concluded that targeted political advertising on social media in 2016 may have increased the number of Donald Trump voters by 10 percent.[37] As Trump digital campaign official Theresa Wong put it, "Without Facebook, we wouldn't have won."[38] Both the Trump and Clinton campaigns spent huge sums on their overall digital strategy—$90 million for the Trump campaign and $100 million for Clinton—but one proved more effective for reasons that remain unclear.[39] It's possible the Trump advertising strategy simply did a better job of creating affective engagement, which helps make sure their ads are seen by more people online. As one digital advertising expert said, "If you have strong opinions on two sides of the same topic, those will typically be more engaging. Even inadvertent controversy can cause a lot of engagement."[40] And of course, Facebook and others can make a fortune from this kind of targeted political advertising.

Another contributor to polarized engagement on Facebook has been foreign entities aiming to either sow disinformation or simply make money from clicks. Much has been made of the Russian Internet Research Agency's role in the 2016 election and the money they spent on Facebook and other digital advertising to reach millions of Americans with divisive messages intended to garner support for the Trump campaign.[41] Also, a number of individuals—even teenagers—in the Balkan region of southeastern Europe, especially in Macedonia, have been identified as purveyors of divisive messages. Initially, it was thought these were just rogue operators out to make a buck off of ill-informed Americans, but now it appears to have been a more coordinated effort with American and Russian agents.[42] In any case, these messages certainly reached far and wide, but it's still not clear how much influence they actually had, particularly compared to the reach of the digital ad strategies of the campaigns themselves and their supporters. Either way, Facebook and others apparently were happy to take money from these people despite the obviously nefarious role they were attempting to play in disrupting American democracy. It's just another reminder that these digital giants are never neutral, benign purveyors of information; they have an agenda, and that agenda is profit.

Over the years, a number of social and tech experts have spoken out about the failure of digital and social media companies to take steps to balance their own revenue and growth imperatives with the needs of their users. As Sandy Parakilas, a former Facebook ad manager told NBC News in 2018, "One of the things that I saw consistently as part of my job was the company just continuously prioritized user growth and making money over protecting users."[43] Another outspoken critic is Tristan Harris, who worked as a design ethicist at Google and has campaigned for a layer of social responsibility at major technology and web companies, particularly in the wake of the misinformation that appeared online around the 2016 election. As Harris has said,

> Facebook is a living, breathing crime scene for what happened in the 2016 election—and only they have full access to what happened. What people don't know about or see about Facebook is that polarization is built in to the business model. Polarization is profitable.[44]

Although we continue to gain a clearer picture of how digital and social media companies operate, critics such as Parakilas and Harris—current and former insiders—are among the few who really know how we got to this point. Increased conversation around these issues have brought light to the problems we face and have encouraged companies to begin to take some corrective actions. While any progress on this is encouraging, many observers remain concerned that such minor corrections are too little, too late, and don't address the fundamental problems that drive the political economy of the internet. For now, the most important thing we all can do is continue to raise awareness around these issues to help news literate citizens learn more about the political economic contexts that influence and even dictate the shape of the digital landscape.

Questions for Discussion

1. What is political economy and how is it different from modern economic analysis?
2. How does the internet encourage democratic participation and reinforce existing power structures at the same time?
3. What hidden forces help make technological advancements possible?
4. In what ways does competition exist in the news and information environment? In what ways is it stifled?
5. What are the pros and cons of mass customization? How can online personalization create problems in a democratic society?

Notes

1. Clay Shirky, *Here Comes Everybody: The Power of Organizing Without Organizations*, Reprint edition (New York: Toronto London: Penguin Books, 2009).
2. See Allan Drazen, *Political Economy in Macroeconomics* (Princeton, NJ: Princeton University Press, 2002).

3. Vincent Mosco, *The Political Economy of Communication: Rethinking and Renewal* (Thousand Oaks, CA: Sage Publications, 1996), 63–64.

4. Mosco, *The Political Economy of Communication*, 64–65.

5. Mosco, *The Political Economy of Communication*, 65.

6. Robert McChesney, *The Political Economy of Media: Enduring Issues, Emerging Dilemmas* (New York: Monthly Review Press, 2008), 12.

7. James Curran, Natalie Fenton, and Des Freedman, *Misunderstanding The Internet* (London and New York: Routledge, 2012), 37.

8. Christopher Stacy, "Getting Started Computing at the AI Lab" (Massachusetts Institute of Technology, September 7, 1982), 9, https://dspace.mit.edu/bitstream/handle/1721.1/41180/AI_WP_235.pdf?sequence=4.

9. Spencer Ackerman, "The IPhone 4S' Talking Assistant Is a Military Veteran," *Wired*, October 5, 2011, www.wired.com/2011/10/siri-darpa-iphone/.

10. Stephanie Kampf and Mark Kelley, "A New 'Arms Race': How the U.S. Military Is Spending Millions to Fight Fake Images," *CBC*, November 18, 2018, www.cbc.ca/news/technology/fighting-fake-images-military-1.4905775.

11. Kurt Wagner, "Digital Advertising in the US Is Finally Bigger than Print and Television," *Recode*, February 20, 2019, www.recode.net/2019/2/20/18232433/digital-advertising-facebook-google-growth-tv-print-emarketer-2019.

12. Tim Baysinger, "Digital Ad Spend Jumps 22 Percent to $72.5 Billion in 2016: Report," *Reuters*, April 26, 2017, www.reuters.com/article/us-digital-advertising/digital-ad-spend-jumps-22-percent-to-72-5-billion-in-2016-report-idUSKBN17S2V3.

13. Gillian Brassil, "Read Sen. Graham's Blistering Line of Questioning for Mark Zuckerberg," April 10, 2018, www.cnbc.com/2018/04/10/read-sen-grahams-blistering-line-of-questioning-for-mark-zuckerberg.html.

14. Safiya Umoja Noble, *Algorithms of Oppression: How Search Engines Reinforce Racism* (New York: New York University Press, 2018), 117–18.

15. Laura Hudson, "Technology Is Biased Too. How Do We Fix It?," *FiveThirtyEight* (blog), July 20, 2017, https://fivethirtyeight.com/features/technology-is-biased-too-how-do-we-fix-it/.

16. Caitlin Dewey, "98 Personal Data Points That Facebook Uses to Target Ads to You," *Washington Post*, August 19, 2016, www.washingtonpost.com/news/the-intersect/wp/2016/08/19/98-personal-data-points-that-facebook-uses-to-target-ads-to-you/.

17. Jason Deans, "Google Chief Warns on Social Networking Dangers," *The Guardian*, August 18, 2010, sec. Media, www.theguardian.com/media/2010/aug/18/google-facebook.

18. Eli Pariser, *The Filter Bubble: How the New Personalized Web Is Changing What We Read and How We Think*, Reprint edition (Penguin Books, 2012), 15.

19. Chris Cillizza, "How the Senate's Tech Illiteracy Saved Mark Zuckerberg," *CNN*, April 11, 2018, www.cnn.com/2018/04/10/politics/mark-zuckerberg-senate-hearing-tech-illiteracy-analysis/index.html.

20. Shara Tibken, "Questions to Mark Zuckerberg Show Many Senators Don't Get Facebook," *CNET*, April 11, 2018, www.cnet.com/news/some-senators-in-congress-capitol-hill-just-dont-get-facebook-and-mark-zuckerberg/.

21. Alina Selyukh, "Section 230: A Key Legal Shield for Facebook, Google Is About to Change," *NPR.org*, March 21, 2018, www.npr.org/sections/alltechconsidered/2018/03/21/591622450/section-230-a-key-legal-shield-for-facebook-google-is-about-to-change.

22. Jon Brodkin, "50 Million US Homes Have Only One 25Mbps Internet Provider or None at All," *Ars Technica*, June 30, 2017, https://arstechnica.com/information-technology/2017/06/50-million-us-homes-have-only-one-25mbps-internet-provider-or-none-at-all/.

23. Victor Pickard, "Social Democracy or Corporate Libertarianism? Conflicting Media Policy Narratives in the Wake of Market Failure," *Communication Theory* 23, no. 4 (2013): 337, https://doi.org/10.1111/comt.12021.

24. Pickard, "Social Democracy or Corporate Libertarianism?," 339.

25. Franklin Foer, "It's Time to Regulate the Internet," *The Atlantic*, March 21, 2018, www.theatlantic.com/technology/archive/2018/03/its-time-to-regulate-the-internet/556097/.

26. Isaiah Berlin, "Two Concepts of Liberty," in Isaiah Berlin, Henry Hardy and Ian Harris, eds., *Liberty: Incorporating Four Essays on Liberty* (Oxford: Oxford University Press, 2002).

27. See Cass R. Sunstein, *Republic.com 2.0* (Princeton: Princeton University Press, 2007).

28. Berlin, "Two Concepts," Conclusion.

29. Sunstein, *Republic.com 2.0*, 154.

30. Mark S. Fowler, "A Marketplace Approach to Broadcast Regulation," *Texas Law Review* 60, no. 2 (1982): 207.

31. Cass R. Sunstein, "Television and the Public Interest," *California Law Review* 88, no. 2 (2000): 512–13.

32. Sunstein, "Television and the Public Interest," 512–13.

33. Owen Fiss, *The Irony of Free Speech*, Reprint edition (Harvard University Press, 1998), 26.

34. Sunstein, *Republic.com 2.0*, 219.

35. *Associated Press v. U. S.*, 326 U.S. 1 (1945).

36. Paul Hitlin and Lee Rainie, "Facebook Algorithms and Personal Data," *Pew Research Center*, January 16, 2019, www.pewinternet.org/2019/01/16/facebook-algorithms-and-personal-data/.

37. Universidad Carlos III de Madrid, "A Study Analyzes the Impact of Targeted Facebook Advertising on the Election," *ScienceDaily*, accessed February 15, 2019, www.sciencedaily.com/releases/2018/11/181119155940.htm.

38. Casey Newton, "How Facebook Rewards Polarizing Political Ads," The Verge, October 11, 2017, www.theverge.com/2017/10/11/16449976/facebook-political-ads-trump-russia-election-news-feed.

39. Deepa Seetharaman, "Made You Click: How Facebook Fed You Political Ads for Less Than a Penny," *Wall Street Journal*, September 15, 2017, sec. Tech, www.wsj.com/articles/made-you-click-how-facebook-fed-you-political-ads-for-less-than-a-penny-1505476808.

40. Seetharaman, "Made You Click."

41. Craig Timberg and Tony Romm, "New Report on Russian Disinformation, Prepared for the Senate, Shows the Operation's Scale and Sweep," *Washington Post*, December 17, 2018, www.washingtonpost.com/technology/2018/12/16/new-report-russian-disinformation-prepared-senate-shows-operations-scale-sweep/.

42. Craig Silverman, "Macedonia's Pro-Trump Fake News Industry Had American Links, And Is Under Investigation for Possible Russia Ties," *BuzzFeed News*, July 18, 2018, www.buzzfeednews.com/article/craigsilverman/american-conservatives-fake-news-macedonia-paris-wade-libert.

43. Jo Ling Kent et al., "Zuckerberg's Former Mentor Says Facebook Puts Profits and Growth First," *NBC News*, January 16, 2018, www.nbcnews.com/tech/tech-news/facebook-living-breathing-crime-scene-says-one-former-manager-n837991.

44. Kent, "Zuckerberg's Former Mentor Says Facebook Puts Profits and Growth First."

6

HUMAN PSYCHOLOGY AND THE AUDIENCE PROBLEM

Think for a minute about how far humans have come since our prehistoric ancestors spent much of their time figuring out where their next meal would come from and thinking up ways to outwit the next saber-toothed tiger to come wandering by. It was probably a pretty harrowing existence most of the time. Today, we live relatively comfortable lives compared to those of our primitive ancestors. But here's the trouble. While our societies have progressed at light speed over the past century, the brains we use to navigate the world around us still have a lot in common with those of our prehistoric ancestors and haven't changed that much over the 10,000 or so years of evolution since our particular species—*Homo sapiens*—became the only brand of human around. While our brains do continue to evolve, possibly even at a speed that's increasing, we are still built for a life of hunting and gathering and fending off saber-toothed tigers, which requires vastly different skills compared to how most of us spend our days in the 21st century.[1]

Even 10,000 years is a mere blip on an evolutionary timescale, so this isn't surprising. Also, recent science has shown that brains are remarkably pliable with an ability to adapt to the demands of their environment. But still, it's important to remember that we continue to rely on some of the basic structures of our primitive monkey brains—especially the fear and reward centers—to figure out how to navigate Facebook or work an iPhone or make peace among nations or try to agree on a way to address climate change. On one hand, we should cut ourselves a break and marvel at what we have been able to do with the big ball of mush between our ears, considering how it was crafted by evolution primarily to make quick fight-or-flight decisions based on gut reactions. On the other hand, this is exactly why we have such a hard time navigating the modern news and information landscape. If sorting through all the content out there depends on slow, deliberate evaluation of complex and interconnected facts and data, we are built to do the exact opposite.

So far in this book, we've taken a sociological look at the contexts that create and influence the news and information environment—that is, we've explored the role organizations, institutions, and social structures play. At this point, we'll turn inward to explore what happens at an individual level that shapes our thinking and behavior as we encounter all sorts of content across the news media landscape. Most proponents of news literacy these days have at least something to say about the importance of understanding the role our brains play in navigating the news landscape, but most content-oriented approaches to news literacy don't go far enough to help us understand how human psychology contributes to our problems or what we can do to make improvements. This chapter will reach far and wide to gather wisdom and insights from a range of fields and experts who are only beginning to understand our complicated relationships with how we consume and process news and information. Social, political, moral, and evolutionary psychology can help us understand our desire to reduce the unpleasant sensations that accompany challenging information, and learning about various kinds of cognitive bias can help explain our reactions to overwhelming choice. Thus, while all this psychology might seem tangential to news literacy, it is central. Understanding our own motivations and desires is part of the critical, contextual approach to news literacy.

Recent research in political and moral psychology can also help us understand how we perceive and respond to social reality. This includes theories of confirmation bias, motivated reasoning, selective exposure, and the backfire effect. The rise of digital and social media and the increase in online participation can be linked to the rise of political polarization and partisanship, which contributes to positive gains for the attention economy even as it fails to serve the public. As conflict and emotion increasingly dominate the participatory news environment, the potential for revenue rises as well.

Not only does the wiring of our brains have major implications for democracy and informed self-government, it also can have a big impact on how we live our daily lives. Particularly, as we live our lives online, citizens must understand the basic psychological tendencies that the internet and digital technologies exploit. Digital technologies such as smart phones have created new generations of information addicts, constantly seeking the next fix regardless of how useless or even toxic it may be. Blurring lines between producer and consumer also make it important to consider how the limitations of human cognition affect our agency in managing our news consumption. And knowing how other people respond emotionally to information can help us as we shape our own communication, whether we're having a family conversation at dinner, working for a major news outlet, or creating messaging strategies for a political campaign.

And finally, we must recognize the way our brains respond to the overwhelming amount of choice we have in today's news and information environment.

When broadcast television consisted of only three channels and little opportunity for viewer feedback, news audiences had little choice regarding their exposure to information. You might not agree with what you saw, but as long as you were watching, at least you saw it. Today's high-choice digital environment changes everything, making it easier than ever to tune out entirely from news media or to recede into a comfortable bubble of like-minded thinking. Ultimately, our news literacy is not complete until we understand the psychological contexts that humans operate in when attempting to navigate the news and information environment.

One caveat: Much of the science around human psychology is still emerging, particularly as scientists develop new ways to read and interpret how the brain works and how neural networks affect cognition, attitudes, and behaviors. We've learned a great deal in recent years, and we are likely to see new developments in years to come. But for now, I've tried to focus on providing the broad strokes of well supported ideas while letting you know where uncertainty lies.

Our Quest to Eliminate Unpleasant Sensations

It's no coincidence that the emotional center of our brain is housed in our amygdala at the core of our brain stem. It's one of the "older" parts of our brains on an evolutionary time frame along with the rest of the limbic system, which helps manage emotion, motivation, attention, memory, and automatic functions like sleeping and breathing. Similarly, the cerebellum, a part of the hindbrain, has also been around since our early days and is responsible for motor control as well as some fear and pleasure responses. Contrast this with the evolutionarily "newer" parts of the brain in the large cerebrum, especially the frontal lobe, where more complex thinking and reasoning take place. It's not a dichotomy—for example, the frontal cortex also helped to expand our emotional capacity—but there's still a significant difference between old and new.[2]

Understanding a little brain anatomy and the evolutionary process that got us to where we are—and I do mean "a little" because I'm being quite general here—helps us think about how we respond to the cues we encounter in the news and information environment. Why do we have the reactions we have? Why do some things make us have such strong emotional reactions? Why do we feel joy or fear or pleasure or anxiety? Why do we feel negative emotions and sensations at all? Why can't we just be happy all the time? In short, because the brain is designed to leave us unsatisfied and wanting more. These brains of ours evolved through the process of *natural selection*, where traits that contribute to survival are passed along to the next generation. The main thing natural selection hopes to accomplish is getting your genes passed along. So our brains and our bodies have evolved to reward us for doing things that will accomplish this, such as eating, reproducing, trying not to get killed. But while we are wired to seek the pleasures and thrills that come with these things, our brains also don't want us to get complacent, so at some point, the pleasure fades.

Natural selection ultimately doesn't care if you're happy or satisfied or pleasured. It just cares that you pass those genes along. So as we try to figure out what to do with these brains of ours, it's worth remembering the goals of our brains and bodies are not necessarily the goals we have for ourselves. Humans are wired to resist unpleasant sensations and to seek pleasant ones, and because pleasure is fleeting, the pursuit never ends. Psychologists have described the theory of *hedonic adaptation* that brings us back to a base level of contentment after experiencing highs or lows. If hedonism is the pursuit of pleasure, the adaptation that accompanies the pursuit is what balances us out. That's why buying a new gadget or item of clothing can bring an immediate thrill, but that high typically fades over time and we are left wanting more. This is even true for big things like winning the lottery, getting a job promotion, or buying a brand-new car. Psychologists even use the term "hedonic treadmill" to describe the phenomenon because of the endless chase that's involved. Fortunately, the phenomenon is thought to work in both directions; even when we are devastated by terrible experiences, we are capable of adapting and returning to a happiness set point.[3]

From an evolutionary perspective, this makes sense. For our genes to be passed along, we need to feel a desire to be proactive about making that happen. If we were blissed out all the time, we would be less effective at this, and our genes would not get passed on. So natural selection has gotten us to this point by weeding out those who are unable to successfully produce another successful generation. Sorry if that sounds cold; evolution is brutal. But in modern life, we don't have to work as hard as our ancestors did to pass our genes along, and some of us don't even want to. In general, we live relatively comfortable, easy lives, and that leaves us with a lot more time on our hands to seek feelings of pleasure. Furthermore, our thinking and behavior can also be influenced by the simple process of learning—what psychologist B.F. Skinner called *operant conditioning*, where rewards or punishments can produce more or less of a behavior. If smoking cigarettes, for example, can help a teenager get in with the "cool" crowd, she might want to do more of it even if it's bad for her health.

Now add technology and other trappings of modern life. These days, we have become so used to being entertained and stimulated almost constantly that we often find it torturous if we are not consistently inundated with something that will dull the pain of simply existing. Consider a remarkable 2014 study that found not only did participants dislike sitting alone in a room with only their thoughts, but many preferred to administer electric shocks to themselves instead of being left alone with their thoughts. This was particularly true for men, who are typically more sensation-seeking. The researchers concluded: "Most people seem to prefer to be doing something rather than nothing, even if that something is negative."[4] In our plugged-in cultures, we often use media and technology to escape the unpleasantness of doing nothing even when this produces negative consequences. Researchers attribute this to a "scanner hypothesis," where we are meant to constantly watch out for danger and opportunity rather than sitting around navel-gazing all day. As one researcher told *The Atlantic*, "It would be a little odd to see a chimpanzee posed like Rodin's thinker for extended periods of time."[5]

Another aspect of our quest to avoid unpleasant feelings includes our tendency to resist emotions that make us second-guess ourselves or otherwise eat away at our self-concept. Once again, we can blame natural selection. Our memories and emotions are often inaccurate or misguided because a little self-deception is sometimes necessary to stay focused on the task at hand—passing on those genes. Sticking with our tribe on an issue—no matter what the facts are—is a major evolutionary advantage; we need that tribe to help take care of us so we can pass on our genes. Because thinking hard and sorting through complicated data is mentally and emotionally unpleasant and possibly even counterproductive if you need to act quickly, natural selection has wired us to generate false perceptions to make life a little easier. But that means we don't always perceive reality accurately. Our memories are notoriously uneven when it comes to remembering the past accurately, and memory often overexaggerates or misdirects us toward what will make us happy, toward what will bring us pleasure. So avoiding unpleasant feelings not only keeps us chasing highs, but also encourages us to avoid the lows we experience when we think too much. Our addiction to stimulation especially by media and technology and our resistance to information we don't like both have major implications for how we navigate the news and information environment. Ultimately, we have to remember that even though brains are malleable and adaptable, we are wired for addiction, and we have to consider how the arrival of technology fuses with our naturally designed inclinations to react in ways that make us feel good—even if they are ultimately bad for us.

The impulse to chase highs and avoid lows has meant serious problems for heavy users of media and technology. It's well documented that internet and social media use have contributed to a wide range of mental health problems, including anxiety, depression, addiction, loneliness, isolation, low self-esteem, self-harm, and even suicide.[6] Psychologist Sherry Turkle has been at the forefront of identifying the "illusion of companionship" that technology can provide, which ultimately makes people more disconnected and dissatisfied. Turkle uses the phrase "alone together" to describe the way people become more isolated through the use of technology. She writes, "We think constant connection will make us feel less lonely. The opposite is true. If we are unable to be alone, we are far more likely to be lonely."[7] While these are problems for our relationships with media and technology broadly, the implications are important for our news literacy as well. We can easily see how important it is to be deliberate about our media use and to make sure we are using it to meet clearly defined goals. And we can see the significance of unplugging and making sure we are interacting with real humans in the real world in order to become better informed about the actual lived experience of our fellow humans.

Another consequence of technology's takeover is the one described by Nicholas Carr in his book *The Shallows: What the Internet Is Doing to Our Brains*. In his view, the web and digital technology have significantly reduced our ability to think deeply. As our brains gradually adapt to our new environment where we are inundated with constant stimuli, we lose our ability to pay attention for the long periods of time that are necessary for us to engage in slow, creative thinking. Carr draws on the work of media theorist Marshall McLuhan, who famously declared in a 1964 book that "the medium is the message."[8] The gist of his point was that the method used to deliver a message matters more than the content itself. Think of it: A bumper sticker on your car can only convey so much information. Similarly, television has a bias toward compelling visual imagery, which in part, dictates what content it will offer.

By itself, this argument smacks of *technological determinism*, which means media messages are predetermined by the format in which they are delivered. Of course, we know there is more to the process of shaping content, but it's also undeniably true that the choice of medium does influence a message. When applied to the internet, we can see how McLuhan's idea helps us understand why our online experience often feels superficial and inconsequential. As Carr concludes,

> Our focus on a medium's content can blind us to these deep effects. We're too busy being dazzled or disturbed by the programming to notice what's going on inside our heads. In the end, we come to pretend that the technology itself doesn't matter.[9]

As technology helps us chase the highs and avoid the lows of being human, it's important for us to pay attention to the contexts where information is created and presented and to consider how our brains react. With so much information at our disposal, it's easy to understand why we might be getting worse at sorting through it all or resisting its potentially harmful allure.

In our quest to avoid unpleasant sensations, in some cases, we deal with the hard work of decision-making by deciding not to decide and tuning out entirely. In some ways, this makes sense. Being constantly inundated with negative news is almost certainly bad for you. It can make the world seem a lot worse than it really is, it can make you worry more about personal issues, and it can even exacerbate physical ailments.[10] Knowing that humans have a built-in *negativity bias* shows how easy it is for us to be taken in by bad news; we are prone to be influenced by and to rely on negative information and emotions than those that are neutral or positive.[11] This wasn't such a big deal when news was only available once or twice a day in a physical newspaper or an evening newscast. But with 24-hour access, it's easy to get sucked in and spiral downward. To avoid this, some people just ignore news altogether, or worse, they find one or two preferred sources that speak to their preexisting view of the world and block out other important information. So again, we should all strive to be deliberate about what we consume, making sure our consumption is time-limited and is directed at sources that will actually help us achieve the goals we have for ourselves, especially those related to the important role we all play in democratic society.

Since we can't control most of what happens around us, learning to control where we choose to direct our attention and how to react to what we experience is crucial to our ability to navigate modern life, and that includes the news and information environment. Recently, there has been tremendous interest in learning to tame our relentless "monkey minds." The practices of meditation and mindfulness go back centuries, but now it has become mainstream to seek out ways to gain better control over our thoughts and to learn to resist the urges that we are wired for. Practicing these techniques can even lead to structural changes in the brain over time and can change the ways we process and react to our emotions. That doesn't mean you have to become a monk or sit cross-legged on top of a mountain. But it does stress the importance of being aware of how our minds and emotions work and making sure that we are controlling them, not the other way around.

How We Perceive Social Reality

While there is much about the world that we can know for certain through the examination of evidence and the application of reason, the way we see the world depends heavily on our own mental filters—the preconceived notions we have that we bring to each difficult question and decision we face.[12] As Shakespeare famously wrote in the tragedy of *Hamlet*, "There is nothing either good or bad; but thinking makes it so." That is, we decide how we will see the world when we apply our own personal lenses, which each have been colored by a lifetime of socialization. In other words, the world often looks like we want it to look; bias is in the eye of the beholder.

Our perceptions of reality are filtered through a tremendous number of *cognitive biases*, which is the umbrella category for all kinds of errors in thinking that occur when people are processing and interpreting information in the world around them. When it comes to the news and information we need to be capable of democratic self-government, we can do a better job of seeking out and making use of good information if we have an understanding of how our cognitive biases influence our perceptions of reality. The mediated world, especially in an online environment, takes advantage of the basic human tendencies that stem from our cognitive biases that lead us to stick with our group, reinforce our prior beliefs, ignore or reject conflicting information, and to be influenced by emotion over reason or logic.

The bias that's probably most well known and most closely associated with news consumption is *confirmation bias*, which refers to our penchant to see and remember things in ways that confirm our preestablished beliefs and to ignore or reject alternative ideas or information. If I've spent years convincing myself that my dog is a perfect angel in every way, I'm going to be less likely to believe someone who tells me my dog was the instigator in a scuffle with a neighbor dog. Similarly, if I'm convinced that childhood vaccinations will make my child autistic, information I encounter that suggests otherwise can be met with my resistance. Confirmation bias is the logical outgrowth of the well-known phenomenon of *cognitive dissonance*, which is the discomfort we experience when we are forced to hold two or more competing ideas in our head at the same time, first documented by the social psychologist Leon Festinger in 1957.[13] As we've learned, our brains are wired to get us out of such unpleasant situations as much as possible, so it makes sense that we are eager to perform the necessary mental gymnastics to reject one set of information—even if it's the ugly truth—in order to return to a mental set point we can handle.

The mental gymnastics we're capable of performing are impressive. For decades, psychologists have studied the phenomenon of *motivated reasoning*, which describes the mechanisms we use to escape the uncomfortable condition of cognitive dissonance. When our personal goals lead us in a particular direction, we undergo a thinking process that will get us there. Just as you might find a way to rationalize an expensive purchase when you are short on money, it can be easy to convince our brains to reach a conclusion that fits with our preexisting beliefs, like the idea that climate change is a hoax even in the face of mountains of evidence to the contrary. A central figure in understanding this process is the social psychologist Ziva Kunda, who proposed that "when one wants to draw a particular conclusion, one feels obligated to construct a justification for that conclusion that would be plausible to a dispassionate observer. In doing so, one accesses only a biased subset of the relevant beliefs and rules."[14]

Contorting our minds into believing false information can help explain how misinformation runs rampant even in the information age. Even after five centuries of discovering and celebrating the benefits of using science and reason to establish knowledge, we are still chasing our tails on so many topics. Of course, it's always good to be skeptical and to challenge our observations, but at some point, we have to stop ignoring what science and reason tell us is true. For example, it's estimated that 6 percent of Americans still believe astronauts never landed on the moon and that Neil Armstrong's famous appearance there was an elaborate hoax.[15] That's the kind of denialism you can shake your head and chuckle at, but sometimes the consequences of the rejection of evidence extend beyond mere personal ignorance. For example, many new parents began opting out of childhood vaccines after being wrongly convinced that they are linked to the onset of autism. As a result, measles—a potentially serious and highly contagious disease that was declared eliminated from the United States in 2000 thanks to a rigorous 20-year vaccination program—has returned in early 2019 with 159 confirmed cases across 10 states, creating a real public health problem.[16] Not only does the return of this easily preventable disease put others at risk, it wastes public resources and attention that could be better used on other pressing matters. I don't think it's dramatic to say that our failure to embrace an evidence-based consensus on a range of issues threatens our ability to survive and thrive as a species.

We might be inclined to dismiss those who don't see things accurately as fringe idiots, but this is a bad idea for two reasons. First, their vote counts just as much as anyone else's, so what they think matters to the rest of us. Second, we can all become fringe idiots. Believe it or not, you don't have to be a science-denying nut-job to be taken in by false information that doesn't fit with your preferred version of reality. As the political communication scholar R. Kelly Garrett has written, anyone can be "prone to embrace claims for which there is little evidence, and to defend those claims in the face of contradictory evidence. This is particularly likely when stakes are high, when outcomes are hard to explain or accept, or when a claim is consistent with one's political values."[17] We are also particularly likely to embrace false information through repeated exposure, as any marketing expert knows. Even hearing a false claim once can give it the ring of truth and plant it as a seed in our minds, but hearing it over and over is what really makes it sink in. You can imagine what a particular disaster this is on social media, where it's easier than ever to make false claims appear over and over simply by liking, sharing, retweeting, and so on. And the repeated misinformation becomes even more convincing when it's repeated by trusted sources. That could include friends, family, news outlets, celebrities, political leaders, and others.

Once we've embraced a false claim, it can be even harder to get rid of it. The *backfire effect* is the idea that attempting to correct misinformation can lead to even stronger endorsement. In other words, trying to set the record straight can lead someone to dig in their heels even more. Consider this often-cited 1994 study about the innocuous question of the origin of a warehouse fire: Participants in the study maintained their certainty that old paint in a storage room was the cause of the warehouse fire even when they were later told that the storage room had been empty.[18] In this study, researchers attributed the acceptance of misinformation to the *continued influence effect*, where a compelling narrative, once cemented in the mind, is difficult to shake. The continued influence of misinformation rears its head again and again in democratic discourse. In a 2015 poll, 42 percent of Americans still believed that weapons of mass destruction were found in Iraq after the 2003 U.S. invasion, a false claim used extensively to make the case for the war.[19] Similarly, as of September 2016, only 62 percent of Americans correctly said President Barack Obama was born in the United States despite widespread evidence of his 1961 birth in Hawaii.[20] Some Americans still subscribe to the conspiracy theory that the September 11, 2001, attacks were orchestrated by the U.S. government, and a small but newly vocal minority have come to accept that the earth is actually flat.

Misinformation and continued influence have been studied widely as researchers attempt to understand how false beliefs persist even in the face of conflicting evidence, but there is still much to learn. In some cases, experimenters were unable to produce a backfire effect and have rejected the idea that individuals are overwhelmingly resistant to factual information. In one study, researchers tested 52 polarizing issues across 10,000 subjects and found no evidence of a backfire effect in the face of corrections. In their explanation, they suggest that most people are uninterested in engaging in the kind of cognitive effort that's required to develop the counterarguments that would be necessary to resist competing claims, so they are likely to simply accept the correction and move away from the original false claim. The researchers also note that a good deal of the research in this area relies on college students as subjects, and they are known to be more inclined toward cognitive effort than most people. As the study concludes, "Research that claims to show widespread democratic incompetence may mistake the snapshot that any one study represents for the sum total of citizens' abilities."[21] On the other hand, this study did not test for lasting effects of corrected information, and even though it relied on a broad set of participants, this study, like most experiments, was removed from real-world settings where results could differ. And finally, these findings fly in the face of decades of research on confirmation bias and cognitive dissonance that lead us to opposite conclusions.

While the specific mechanisms of the acceptance of misinformation remain contested, we certainly have enough evidence to know that it's hard to get people to change their minds. But as numerous scholars and practitioners have shown, a number of potentially successful strategies for correcting misinformation do exist. The Australian psychologist Stephan Lewandowsky and colleagues have documented a number of these.[22] First, it helps to head off misinformation before it starts. Letting people know that a false claim is swirling can avoid backfire. Second, repeating a correction can strengthen it, just as a false claim gathers steam through repetition. Third, it's important to create an alternative narrative that's plausible to a believer of misinformation. Rather than simply stating the correction, it can help to provide context that shows why the false claim might have originated. For example, explaining that an Iraqi site thought to house weapons of mass destruction was indeed a chemical plant even though no weapons were present. It can also help to explain the rationale behind the misinformation, such as the important role suspected Iraqi weapons played in the case for the 2003 war, especially for some leaders who had a well-known and long-standing interest in an invasion. Finally, it's best to keep it simple. Too many counterarguments or over-explanation can increase the potential for backfire. People who believe false information can actually be quite knowledgeable about the topic in general, so getting too deep into the weeds over specifics can lead to increased resistance.

When it comes to our individual news consumption, the mental processes that distort our thinking play out in interesting ways that help us limit our exposure to challenging information and convince ourselves that everyone else is wrong and we are right. First, there's the well-documented *hostile media effect*, where people with strong political views tend to think media content is always biased against their own positions. That is, news media is always "hostile" to their point of view. The really fascinating thing about this is that two people with opposed political views can watch the exact same news report and both conclude that the report was biased against their position. Another relevant phenomenon is the *third-person effect*, where we overestimate how much other people are subject to an outside influence and we underestimate how much something affects ourselves. For example, people are likely to believe that while others are easily duped by tricky marketing messages, they themselves can see right through the same attempt to influence their behavior. Applied to social media, people often think they can spot and reject "fake news" more easily than others who encounter it.

Finally, there's the problem of *selective exposure*, where individuals limit their consumption of news and information to the kind of stuff they already know they are likely to agree with. This is why Fox News and MSNBC have been wildly successful business ventures; they take advantage of the fact that citizens are interested in seeing a picture of the world that fits with their preexisting notions. And of course, digital and social media can take this a step further, since these platforms make it easier than ever to filter out anything you don't want to see. That's how we get filter bubbles and echo chambers, where we tend to hear the same messages over and over without being challenged with other points of view or being exposed to new ideas. Like the backfire effect, there is some dispute over whether online echo chambers are really as bad as some critics think they are.[23] Some scholars have noted that most people actually consume a fairly diverse media diet, and only the most extreme partisans are trapped in their bubbles. Also, while most people follow news to some extent, it's often only at critical moments or superficial levels. Finally, people are not particularly trusting of social and online news media, which could help reduce any echo chamber effects. Ultimately, it may be the offline world where people are less likely to experience competing points of view—which brings us back to Fox and MSNBC and, crucially, our own friends, family, and neighbors. It's clear that the phenomenon of selective exposure is complicated, but for most people, our exposure to news and information is likely shaped at least to some extent by our preexisting preferences and our desire to avoid challenging information.

All of this fancy psychological jargon aside, the overall point and the overwhelming conclusion here is that understanding our brains and the ways we consider and process information is central to our news and information consumption. If we want to bring an impartial perspective to the news we consume, there are many forces working against us, which means we have a lot of work to do. As the social psychologist Jonathan Haidt has said, "Reasoning, when we do it, is mostly to find justification for what we already believe."[24] To sum things up, Haidt has provided a nice, simple metaphor in his work where he differentiates between our rational selves and our emotional selves. Haidt imagines himself as a rider on an elephant, where his rational mind is represented by the rider and his emotions are represented by the elephant. As Haidt explains, "I'm holding the reins in my hands, and by pulling one way or the other I can tell the elephant to turn, to stop, or to go. I can direct things, but only when the elephant doesn't have desires of his own. When the elephant really wants to do something, I'm no match for him."[25] Finally, to put in another way, Haidt's metaphor maps nicely onto the work of behavioral economist Daniel Kahneman, who in his 2011 book, *Thinking, Fast and Slow*, describes human thinking in terms of two main systems: System 1, like the elephant, is fast, unconscious, intuitive, and emotional. System 2, like the rider, is slow, controlled, logical, and rational.[26] Decades of research in judgment, decision making, and even human happiness confirms this basic dichotomy. It doesn't mean we are destined to be the helpless victims of the unwieldy elephant, but it does mean we need to know what's going on in our heads when we attempt to make sense of the world around us.

Technologies of Addiction and the Attention Economy

Considering what we know about the downsides of technology and the mental processes that it can easily exploit, it's not surprising that many critics have rung alarm bells about its potentially harmful effects. First of all, the technologies are undoubtedly pervasive. In 2018, an average American adult spends 11 hours a day interacting with media in some form, especially video and smartphone apps.[27] One survey found that 85 percent of Americans have smartphones and check them an average of 52 times a day, more than ever before.[28] A Gallup poll in 2015 found that 81 percent of users say they keep their phones near them at all times, and most people also say they check their phones less than other people (remember the third-person effect?).[29]

Second, the problems of tech addiction—depression, anxiety, loneliness, and so on—are real.[30] In recent studies, researchers have found that keeping your smartphone out of your bedroom even for just a week can lead to increased happiness and improved sleep, relationships, focus, and well-being.[31] Another found that ignoring someone in a face-to-face encounter to look at your phone—called "phubbing," or snubbing with your phone—leads to decreased relationship satisfaction and increases feelings of depression and alienation.[32] Even the mere presence of a phone can have a negative effect on social interaction,[33] and the ding of a phone notification can cause "significantly disrupted performance on an attention-demanding task."[34] Research has found that having pervasive technology in our lives has led us to have shorter attention spans, worse memories, and lower levels of productivity.

Smartphones and other digital technologies certainly can have enormous benefits. They can help us stay connected and informed, and they can offer new ways to participate in democratic and civic life. But the dark side of tech is not only that it can be addictive and harmful, but also that it serves as a massive distraction machine, and one that is operated for profit. That's why it's a supreme irony that many of the creators and purveyors of digital technology and social media are among those who are most opposed to its presence, especially in the lives of their own children. According to numerous reports, a consensus is emerging around Silicon Valley—home to Google, Facebook, and a range of other tech companies—that the tools they've created have serious dark sides for developing brains. As one former Facebook employee told *The New York Times*, "I am convinced the devil lives in our phones and is wreaking havoc on our children."[35] Some Silicon Valley families have nannies who are hired largely to keep kids away from screens and must even sign contracts to that effect.[36]

As Adam Alter documents in his 2018 book, *Irresistible: The Rise of Addictive Technology and the Business of Keeping Us Hooked*, a number of tech pioneers are quite cautious about the use of technology in their own homes. As Alter put it, "It seemed as if the people producing tech products were following the cardinal rule of drug dealing: never get high on your own supply."[37] Alter found that video game designers avoid the very games they create, that Twitter founder Evan Williams filled his home with books for his kids but no iPad, and that even Steve Jobs said his kids had never used an iPad. Alter quotes design ethicist Tristan Harris, who suggests willpower is no match for addictive technologies: "There are a thousand people on the other side of the screen whose job it is to break down the self-regulation you have."[38]

In a *New York Times* article titled "A Dark Consensus About Screens and Kids Begins to Emerge in Silicon Valley," tech pioneer and former editor of *Wired* magazine Chris Anderson expressed similar concerns about the screens in our lives: "On the scale between candy and crack cocaine, it's closer to crack cocaine." As Anderson went on to say, "We thought we could control it. And this is beyond our power to control. This is going straight to the pleasure centers of the developing brain. This is beyond our capacity as regular parents to understand.[39] And ex-Google strategist James Williams has called the global search advertising business the "largest, most standardized and most centralized form of attentional control in human history." Williams concludes that not only are digital technology and search and social media companies changing how we think and act, but also that they are leading to the destabilization of democracy. "The dynamics of the attention economy are structurally set up to undermine the human will," he said in the *Guardian*. "If politics is an expression of our human will, on individual and collective levels, then the attention economy is directly undermining the assumptions that democracy rests on."[40] And some concerned observers suggest that if something is to be done to correct this course, now is the time to do it, because pretty soon, no one alive will remember what life was like before technology came to dominate our lives.

Is all this alarmism warranted? Time will tell. We should try to be nuanced not absolutist in our approach to the effects of technology. But we do know enough to be concerned about what's happening around us. In the *attention economy*, our ability to focus on any one thing is viewed as a scarce resource that must somehow be captured. As we learned earlier, this is not a new idea. Trading our attention for something we want is the original business model for broadcasting, stretching back at least a century. But the difference today is that there are so many new ways to capture and monetize our attention, and that has negative effects on our daily experience. Nicholas Carr saw this way back in 2008 when he wrote his famous *Atlantic* article titled "Is Google Making Us Stupid?" Carr wrote:

> When the Net absorbs a medium, that medium is re-created in the Net's image. It injects the medium's content with hyperlinks, blinking ads, and other digital gewgaws, and it surrounds the content with the content of all the other media it has absorbed. A new e-mail message, for instance, may announce its arrival as we're glancing over the latest headlines at a newspaper's site. The result is to scatter our attention and diffuse our concentration.[41]

More than a decade later, this description of competing stimuli sounds quaint compared to life today. And we adapt by learning to "multitask," which isn't actually a real thing in the way most people think. Instead, we engage in *task switching*, where our attention jumps rapidly from one task to another, decreasing our focus on each individual activity, making us less productive and more error-prone.[42]

As we live our lives through modern media, every second we are glued to a screen of some kind is an opportunity for someone to make a buck. So while our attention is scarce, it is also lucrative, which creates a motivation to do whatever it takes to get it. As Tim Wu writes in his 2017 book, *The Attention Merchants: The Epic Scramble to Get Inside Our Heads*, the basic mode of operation is to "draw attention with apparently free stuff and then resell it."[43] The goal of an attention merchant is to gather a crowd to the point where the attention of the crowd becomes profitable. Wu calls this the process of "harvesting" our attention, intentionally choosing a crop metaphor to help paint a picture of attention as a commodity like wheat or corn. But this process has consequences for the nature of the "stuff" used to get our attention. Wu continues,

> But a consequence of that model is a total dependence on gaining and holding attention. This means that under competition, the race will naturally run to the bottom; attention will almost invariably gravitate to the more garish, lurid, outrageous alternative.[44]

To be sure, the appeal commonly made by the attention merchant is to our emotional brains, not our rational ones.

The race for our attention means at least three things. One, the content used as "bait" is far less likely to be the kind of news and information, delivered calmly and rationally, that we need to function in democratic societies. Instead, we get flash over substance, entertainment over information, and if we do get news, it's more likely to be the kind that gets us riled up rather than dispassionately engaging our critical faculties. Again, this is not new. An old cliché about broadcast news is "if it bleeds, it leads," suggesting that news producers emphasize gory scenes of death and destruction at the top of the newscast to grab viewers' attention. What's new in the digital age is that this mentality is not confined to the six o'clock news; it defines every second of our lives.

Second, looking beyond the actual content that the attention economy tends to prefer, we can see a host of mechanisms, some subtle, some overt, used to capture our attention. The content that attracts us is one thing, but in today's attention economy, coders, designers, and analysts are always looking for new tricks to reel us in. That doesn't mean these are evil people who have set out to manipulate the masses; rather, they are diligent workers who are simply doing their jobs. Like so many of us, their jobs just happen to have some potentially serious side effects. As technologist Tobias Rose-Stockwell has written about the design of addictive technologies, "These decisions are not made with malice. They are made behind analytics dashboards, split-testing panels, and walls of code that have turned you into a predictable asset—a user that can be mined for attention."[45]

So what mechanisms are we actually talking about here? Everyone knows the allure of a smartphone's ding or vibration. Russian psychologist Ivan Pavlov is famous for teaching dogs to salivate at the sound of a metronome simply by associating the sound with food, a process called *classical conditioning*. Like Pavlov's dogs, we have become classically conditioned to salivate—or at least perk up—when triggered by the phone because each ding feels like a little reward. Just knowing that this stimulus could come at any moment leaves us in a state of *continuous partial attention*, where we pay unconscious attention to the devices around us. Already our resources are being drained at least a little bit just by having the technology around. Now think about those ubiquitous little red notification dots and squares that are carefully designed to get your attention based on your learned associations.

The dings and dots that notify us are especially engaging because they offer small, frequent rewards rather than a bigger, delayed payoff. A bigger reward might bring more pleasure, but the consistency of a small reward is a more effective attention-getter. A host of other mechanisms grab our attention in countless subtle ways. For example, the infinite scroll of most webpages and smartphone apps is far more effective at keeping us hooked because there is no end point or exit point. Sites that are broken up into distinct pages makes it easier to disengage. Similarly, the auto-play feature that now appears on most platforms is a relatively recent invention. It's easier to stay engrossed in YouTube or Netflix if you don't have to do anything to keep the entertainment coming, making it that much easier to binge on your favorite shows and clips.

Social media takes advantage of other components of human psychology such as *social reciprocity*, or the idea that if I scratch your back, you should scratch mine. Because humans are inherently social creatures capable of communication and cooperation, we evolved to depend on each other for our survival. Social media and digital communication in general exploit this by making it easy to reciprocate: we "follow" and "friend" each other, we "like" each other's photos, we reply to each other's emails. And notifications make it easy to see whether the other person has reciprocated appropriately or not.

The science on media and technology addiction is still emerging, but the neurotransmitter dopamine is often implicated in these contexts because of its reputation for producing pleasure and causing addition. Dopamine plays many roles in the brain, but it doesn't appear to actually cause the pleasure or "rush" we feel from the ding of a phone or a shot of heroin. Instead, it does let us know when we can anticipate a reward, and that's what makes us feel good.[46] In other words, it tells us what to pay attention to. And remember, as humans, we are not mainly chasing pleasure but rather we are avoiding displeasure. So we do not get addicted to technology mainly because of the pleasure it brings, but rather because of the unpleasant sensations it soothes. Distress, anxiety, boredom, and other unpleasant conditions lead us to the technologies of addiction.[47]

A third problem in the attention economy is the sheer volume of bids for our attention it produces. Advertisers and marketers sometimes talk about "cutting through the clutter"; that is, they need to find a way to make their message rise above all the other messages out there. The problem is that this produces even more clutter. Clutter begets clutter. And digital technology makes it easier than ever to produce clutter. So our mediated worlds are flooded with an exponentially increasing amount of stuff desperately seeking our attention. This makes it harder than ever to sort through everything out there, separating the useful stuff from the misinformation, lies, and propaganda. It also means we are overwhelmed with commercialism. Nothing is truly "free" online, so we are often trading our attention for advertising messages telling us what to buy, what to do, where to go, what to look like, how to dress, and who to be. An already hypercommercial society combined with digital technology and the ongoing war for our attention is a clear detriment to our democratic life.

All of this is to say nothing of the privacy issues raised by digital technology and social media, but that is beyond the scope of this book. Let us just say we should all be concerned about the amount of information that's being collected and traded about us and the implications for our independence and agency as humans, not to mention the basic "right to be left alone" that is central to our flourishing as individuals. One way to reduce the flood of commercial messaging and the invasions of our privacy both online and offline is to pay directly for the content we consume and avoid trading our identities for the stuff we want. Another approach is to provide robust public funding for quality news and information so citizens have access to reliable sources without shelling out a fortune. All of this is easier said than done, but it will take these kinds of public and private investment to improve the news and information environment.

For now, let's consider a few simple ways we can break free from the exploitation of the attention economy and from the cycles of addiction it can produce.

First of all, always think of the words of technology historian Melvin Kranzberg: "Technology is neither good nor bad; nor is it neutral."[48] We can decide how to use the tools before us, but it's important to also remember that they have been designed in certain ways that produce certain outcomes, whether intentional or not. Knowing how the technology exploits your vulnerabilities and weaknesses is the first step in resisting their allure. Second, make the tools of technology work for you rather than the other way around. Remove the temptation and put your phone away when you don't really need it. Turn off all notifications or at least most of them. Use internet and app blockers when you need to focus and remain productive. When you are tempted to check your phone or engage in an endless scroll on your computer, ask yourself what else you could be doing with that time. If you decide to go ahead, you can also decide in advance how much time you will devote and stick to a reasonable limit. Slow your consumption and don't be afraid of missing out on something; everything will still be there when you return, and you won't be any less complete from not being the first to know.[49]

Many good books and articles exist to help you find a healthy balance, and I've provided only a few basic tips here to get you started. But I hope what you've learned here gets you thinking about the bigger picture around our devices and platforms: why they exist, how they hook us, and whether we are really using them to our advantage and to the benefit of society at large. Author Catherine Price, writing in *The New York Times*, advises us to "get existential about it":

> If all else fails, consider your own mortality. How many people on their deathbeds do you think are going to say, "I wish I'd spent more time on Facebook"? Keep asking yourself the same question, again and again and again: This is your life. How much of it do you want to spend on your phone?[50]

To sum up, Price, who runs an online service called "Screen/Life Balance"—her slogan is "scroll less, live more"—also advises asking three simple questions when you are tempted to reach for your devices: "What for? Why now? What else?" When technology beckons, pause for a minute, consider these questions, take a few deep breaths, look around you, and make a deliberate choice.

News Literacy and Political Polarization

Considering all the complexities of the inner workings of our brains, the messiness of our news and information environment, and the difficult political questions of our times, it's no surprise that social and digital media get implicated in causing the recent rise in political polarization. We already learned in Chapter 5 that polarization can be profitable. Getting people fired up about social and political issues increases their engagement, which means more clicks, more likes, and more profit. But how do our brains actually respond to polarizing triggers, and how does this contribute to problems in our news and information environment that limit our capacity as participants in democratic life?

First of all, we know political polarization has been on the rise in the United States since the 1990s as political partisans—those who say they are aligned with one political party—have become more ideologically separated as they sort themselves into increasingly distinct camps.[51] More people express consistently conservative or liberal opinions, especially people who are most active and engaged in political life. These are the people who are most likely to vote, write letters to officials, and give money to political candidates and groups, which gives them an outsized influence over political life and also makes their voices stronger and louder. They surround themselves with like-minded individuals. We also know they live in different media worlds with little overlap in the sources they consume. Liberals tend to consume a variety of mainstream sources such as CNN, NPR, and *The New York Times*. Conservatives are tightly clustered around Fox News, with some additional consumption of far-right outlets including *The Blaze*, *Breitbart*, and Rush Limbaugh.[52]

The conventional wisdom says that partisan media outlets and social media are to blame for the rise in polarization, but this is probably only part of the explanation. Consuming partisan media such as Fox and MSNBC certainly can increase partisanship in certain individuals.[53] But research also suggests those who consume partisan news media are already polarized, and their news sources don't seem to have much of an effect on their views.[54] In many ways, this is a chicken-egg question. For example, are people more likely to watch Fox because they are conservative, or does watching Fox make them more conservative? Scholar Marcus Prior points out that certain people have always been highly polarized, so now that we live in an age of increased media choice, it makes sense that those polarized individuals would gravitate toward partisan news options.[55] There also appears to be an age gap. Polarization is increasing fastest among older Americans who don't use social media but mainly get news from cable news and talk radio. Social media users, who tend to be younger, are more likely to see a varied mix of political and nonpolitical news and information.[56]

Prior and others also note that a potentially bigger problem in a high-choice media environment is that it's easier than ever to tune out of news altogether. That means more people are disengaged from the political process, and those who remain—the most intense and vocal partisans—are the ones who get the most attention. As Prior has written, "The main danger of this more partisan media environment is not the polarization of ordinary Americans but a growing disconnect between increasingly partisan activists and largely centrist and modestly involved masses."[57] Think about the fact that the largest voting bloc in the United States consists of nonvoters. When politically moderate individuals do tune into news, they consume sources that are varied and relatively centrist. It's also possible that news media in general might have little to do with increasing polarization. Other cultural and demographic changes taking place in the United States and elsewhere could be bigger contributors. In the United States, this includes shifting views about race, religion, and social issues such as gay marriage, and widening gaps in education and wealth, as well as structural issues across the political system such as the gerrymandering of congressional districts, the increasing significance of the primary process, and changes to election laws. And in the United States, we have a fairly unique winner-take-all, two-party system, which means there is little incentive for compromise.[58]

This isn't to say the internet and digital and social media have not played a significant role in the coarsening of political discourse and the difficulties of reaching political consensus. As a *Wired* magazine article titled "Your Filter Bubble Is Destroying Democracy" declared after the 2016 election, "The global village that was once the internet has been replaced by digital islands of isolation that are drifting further apart each day."[59] Similarly, even filter bubble skeptics have noted that the news and information environment can still have a significant influence on the citizens who happen to be most politically active. As Princeton University professor of politics and public affairs Andrew Guess has written,

> Even if echo chambers are not widespread, partisan media can still disseminate misinformation and increase animosity toward the other party among a highly visible and influential subset of the population. In this sense, the danger is not that all of us are living in echo chambers but that a subset of the most politically engaged and vocal among us are.[60]

If that's the case, it's likely that there is at least some amount of trickle down to the rest of us even if news and social media are not the primary messenger.

The science on the mechanisms of political polarization remains unsettled, but we have learned a fair amount about why we respond the ways we do to messages that are more likely to separate us than bring us together. We already know we are all prone to avoiding the unpleasant feeling of cognitive dissonance, to hold a confirmation bias, and to engage in selective exposure. But where do we come up with the positions we hold and why are we so darn devoted to them? It all goes back to natural selection and those pesky unpleasant sensations. Our political positions are informed by our moral judgments, and when it comes to staking out a moral position, we're not as interested in what's right or wrong as we are in exercising our emotional brains and sticking with our tribe. Why? Because it feels good, or more likely, because it relieves the unpleasant sensations of feeling bad—loneliness, isolation, fear, and so on. Our moral decision-making is motivated by a host of overlapping and sometimes even conflicting goals, but that's because we are always seeking to balance competing interests.

Social psychologist Jonathan Haidt makes a convincing case about the messiness of our moral decision-making in his book *The Righteous Mind: Why Good People Are Divided by Politics and Religion.* Building on the work of other psychologists and anthropologists, Haidt finds a mix of genetics, upbringing, socialization, and instinct that inform our moral reasoning, which is really a retroactive process of justifying our emotional reactions. In this sense, returning to Haidt's metaphor of the elephant and the rider, it is the job of the rider to serve the elephant. Because the elephant—the emotional brain—is pretty much going to do what it wants, the rider—the thinking, reasoning brain—has to come up with justifications for what the elephant has already done. That's why Haidt concludes, "If you want to change people's minds, you've got to talk to their elephants."[61]

How do we do that? In his work, Haidt identifies a handful of foundations for our moral reasoning and shows that significant differences exist for liberals and conservatives. The main foundations we rely on are care (protecting the vulnerable and preventing harm), liberty (resisting dominance or bullying), fairness (preventing cheating and not being exploited), loyalty (maintaining coalitions and punishing betrayal), authority (respecting social rank or status), and sanctity (preserving cleanliness and purity). Think for a moment about which of these traits resonate most strongly with you. What Haidt and others have found is that conservatives are more likely to exercise all six moral foundations to some extent, but liberals are more heavily focused on three main traits—care, liberty, and fairness. When you start to map these moral foundations onto policy preferences, it starts to make sense. Liberal policy preferences are often more devoted to promoting equality, opportunity, and care for all (such as universal health care or social safety nets), and conservative policy preferences can be geared toward preserving social hierarchies and traditional approaches to human relationships. Of course, there is plenty of overlap along a spectrum here, but it's at least a starting point for thinking beyond narrow ideologies and partisan talking points.

It's not going to be easy. Haidt and others have identified differences in genetics and brain structures that reflect real differences in how we see the world.[62] But there is certainly some value to be found in this diversity. Haidt ultimately defines morality in terms of complex systems that include a mix of mechanisms and motivations: "Moral systems are interlocking sets of values, virtues, norms, practices, identities, institutions, technologies, and evolved psychological mechanisms that work together to suppress or regulate self-interest and make cooperative societies possible."[63] The "evolved" part is key—we got to this point because natural selection brought us here, so it is part of our shared humanity going forward.

Now let's get back to news literacy. While this might have seemed like a departure, knowing how we process information and how it influences our behavior is actually central to our engagement with the news and information environment and our participation in democratic life. If we are truly interested in self-government, our tribalism is a major obstacle. We have to find those common areas where we can move forward and achieve shared goals based on shared facts. We have to learn to communicate in ways that can help us orient ourselves toward those shared goals, and we have to learn how our brains—and those of our fellow humans—work for and against us. Whatever the processes are that guide our thinking, it's important to make sure we don't let the news messages we consume exploit or distort our reasoning. So I hope it's clear how our shared psychology is a key context for news literacy and our hope for preserving and promoting a shared democratic society.

Questions for Discussion

1. What role does human psychology play in how we consume news and information? How do our brains sometimes work against us?
2. How does the constant connection offered by modern communication serve to support human relationships? How does it undermine them?
3. Review your own news and information consumption habits. Can you identify a pattern of selective exposure? What does your filter bubble look like?
4. What role does the attention economy play in democratic life? How does it support or detract from democratic participation?
5. How do you know whether you are a well-rounded citizen or a narrow-minded partisan? Is it possible to hold strong convictions without closing yourself off to other points of view?

Notes

1. See Yuval Noah Harari, *Sapiens: A Brief History of Humankind*, Reprint edition (New York: Harper, 2015).
2. Jonathan Haidt, *The Happiness Hypothesis: Finding Modern Truth in Ancient Wisdom* (New York: Basic Books, 2006), 10.
3. P. Brickman, D. Coates, and R. Janoff-Bulman, "Lottery Winners and Accident Victims: Is Happiness Relative?," *Journal of Personality and Social Psychology* 36, no. 8 (August 1978): 917–27.
4. Timothy D. Wilson et al., "Just Think: The Challenges of the Disengaged Mind," *Science* 345, no. 6192 (July 4, 2014): 75–77, https://doi.org/10.1126/science.1250830.
5. Matthew Hutson, "People Prefer Electric Shocks to Being Alone with Their Thoughts," *The Atlantic*, July 3, 2014, www.theatlantic.com/health/archive/2014/07/people-prefer-electric-shocks-to-being-alone-with-their-thoughts/373936/.
6. Alice G. Walton, "New Studies Show Just How Bad Social Media Is for Mental Health," *Forbes*, November 16, 2018, www.forbes.com/sites/alicegwalton/2018/11/16/new-research-shows-just-how-bad-social-media-can-be-for-mental-health/.
7. Sherry Turkle, "The Flight From Conversation," *The New York Times*, April 21, 2012, sec. Opinion, www.nytimes.com/2012/04/22/opinion/sunday/the-flight-from-con versation.html.
8. Marshall McLuhan and Lewis H. Lapham, *Understanding Media: The Extensions of Man* (Cambridge, MA: The MIT Press, 1994).
9. Nicholas Carr, *The Shallows: What the Internet Is Doing to Our Brains* (New York: W. W. Norton & Company, 2011), 3.
10. Markham Heid, "You Asked: Is It Bad for You to Read the News Constantly?," *Time*, January 31, 2018, http://time.com/5125894/is-reading-news-bad-for-you/.
11. Amrisha Vaish, Tobias Grossmann, and Amanda Woodward, "Not All Emotions Are Created Equal: The Negativity Bias in Social-Emotional Development," *Psychological Bulletin* 134, no. 3 (2008): 383–403, https://doi.org/10.1037/0033-2909.134.3.383.
12. See for example Haidt, *The Happiness Hypothesis*.

13. Leon Festinger, *A Theory of Cognitive Dissonance*, A Theory of Cognitive Dissonance (Stanford: Stanford University Press, 1957).
14. Ziva Kunda, "The Case for Motivated Reasoning," *Psychological Bulletin* 108, no. 3 (1990): 480–98, https://doi.org/10.1037/0033-2909.108.3.480.
15. John Schwartz, "The Vocal Minority: Moon Landing Was a Hoax," *The New York Times*, July 13, 2009, sec. Space & Cosmos, www.nytimes.com/2009/07/14/science/space/14hoax.html.
16. CDC, "Measles Cases and Outbreaks," February 25, 2019, www.cdc.gov/measles/cases-outbreaks.html.
17. R. Kelly Garrett, "Making Sense of the Scalia Conspiracy Theory," *The Conversation*, February 22, 2016, http://theconversation.com/making-sense-of-the-scalia-conspiracy-theory-55083.
18. Hollyn M. Johnson and Colleen M. Seifert, "Sources of the Continued Influence Effect: When Misinformation in Memory Affects Later Inferences," *Journal of Experimental Psychology: Learning, Memory, and Cognition* 20, no. 6 (1994): 1420–36, https://doi.org/10.1037/0278-7393.20.6.1420.
19. Kendall Breitman, "Poll: Half of Republicans Still Believe WMDs Found in Iraq," *Politico Magazine*, January 7, 2015, www.politico.com/story/2015/01/poll-republicans-wmds-iraq-114016.html.
20. Kyle Dropp and Brendan Nyhan, "It Lives. Birtherism Is Diminished but Far from Dead," *The New York Times*, January 20, 2018, sec. The Upshot, www.nytimes.com/2016/09/24/upshot/it-lives-birtherism-is-diminished-but-far-from-dead.html.
21. Thomas Wood and Ethan Porter, "The Elusive Backfire Effect: Mass Attitudes' Steadfast Factual Adherence," *Political Behavior* 41, no. 1 (March 1, 2019): 161, https://doi.org/10.1007/s11109-018-9443-y.
22. Stephan Lewandowsky et al., "Misinformation and Its Correction: Continued Influence and Successful Debiasing," *Psychological Science in the Public Interest* 13, no. 3 (December 1, 2012): 106–31, https://doi.org/10.1177/1529100612451018.
23. Andrew Guess, "Avoiding the Echo Chamber about Echo Chambers," *Trust, Media and Democracy* (blog), February 13, 2018, https://medium.com/trust-media-and-democracy/avoiding-the-echo-chamber-about-echo-chambers-6e1f1a1a0f39.
24. Patricia Cohen, "Counseling Democrats to Go for the Gut," *The New York Times*, July 10, 2007, sec. Arts, www.nytimes.com/2007/07/10/arts/10west.html.
25. Haidt, *The Happiness Hypothesis*, 4.
26. Daniel Kahneman, *Thinking, Fast and Slow* (New York: Farrar, Straus and Giroux, 2011).
27. Nielsen, "Time Flies: U.S. Adults Now Spend Nearly Half a Day Interacting with Media," *Nielsen*, July 31, 2018, www.nielsen.com/us/en/insights/news/2018/time-flies-us-adults-now-spend-nearly-half-a-day-interacting-with-media.html.
28. Andy Meek, "Survey: Americans Now Check Their Smartphones a Whopping 52 Times a Day," *BGR* (blog), November 13, 2018, https://bgr.com/2018/11/13/smartphone-addiction-survey-data/.
29. Frank Newport, "Most U.S. Smartphone Owners Check Phone at Least Hourly," Gallup.com, July 9, 2016, https://news.gallup.com/poll/184046/smartphone-owners-check-phone-least-hourly.aspx.
30. Alice G. Walton, "New Studies Show Just How Bad Social Media Is for Mental Health," *Forbes*, November 16, 2018, www.forbes.com/sites/alicegwalton/2018/11/16/new-research-shows-just-how-bad-social-media-can-be-for-mental-health/.
31. Nicola Hughes and Jolanta Burke, "Sleeping with the Frenemy: How Restricting 'Bedroom Use' of Smartphones Impacts Happiness and Wellbeing," *Computers in Human Behavior* 85 (August 1, 2018): 236–44, https://doi.org/10.1016/j.chb.2018.03.047.
32. Varoth Chotpitayasunondh and Karen M. Douglas, "The Effects of 'Phubbing' on Social Interaction," *Journal of Applied Social Psychology* 48, no. 6 (2018): 304–16, https://doi.org/10.1111/jasp.12506.

33. Andrew K. Przybylski and Netta Weinstein, "Can You Connect with Me Now? How the Presence of Mobile Communication Technology Influences Face-to-Face Conversation Quality," *Journal of Social and Personal Relationships* 30, no. 3 (May 1, 2013): 237–46, https://doi.org/10.1177/0265407512453827.

34. Cary Stothart, Ainsley Mitchum, and Courtney Yehnert, "The Attentional Cost of Receiving a Cell Phone Notification," *Journal of Experimental Psychology. Human Perception and Performance* 41, no. 4 (August 2015): 893–97, https://doi.org/10.1037/xhp0000100.

35. Nellie Bowles, "A Dark Consensus About Screens and Kids Begins to Emerge in Silicon Valley," *The New York Times*, October 26, 2018, sec. Style, www.nytimes.com/2018/10/26/style/phones-children-silicon-valley.html.

36. Nellie Bowles, "Silicon Valley Nannies Are Phone Police for Kids," *The New York Times*, October 26, 2018, sec. Style, www.nytimes.com/2018/10/26/style/silicon-valley-nannies.html.

37. Adam Alter, *Irresistible: The Rise of Addictive Technology and the Business of Keeping Us Hooked*, Reprint edition (Penguin Books, 2018), 2.

38. Alter, *Irresistible*, 3.

39. Bowles, "A Dark Consensus About Screens and Kids Begins to Emerge in Silicon Valley."

40. Paul Lewis, "'Our Minds Can Be Hijacked': The Tech Insiders Who Fear a Smartphone Dystopia," *The Guardian*, October 6, 2017, sec. Technology, www.theguardian.com/technology/2017/oct/05/smartphone-addiction-silicon-valley-dystopia.

41. Nicholas Carr, "Is Google Making Us Stupid?," *The Atlantic*, July 1, 2008, www.theatlantic.com/magazine/archive/2008/07/is-google-making-us-stupid/306868/.

42. American Psychological Association, "Multitasking: Switching Costs," www.apa.org, accessed February 28, 2019, www.apa.org/research/action/multitask.

43. Tim Wu, *The Attention Merchants: The Epic Scramble to Get Inside Our Heads*, Reprint edition (New York: Vintage, 2017), 16.

44. Wu, *The Attention Merchants*, 16.

45. Tobias Rose-Stockwell, "This Is How Your Fear and Outrage Are Being Sold for Profit," *Medium* (blog), July 14, 2017, https://medium.com/@tobiasrose/the-enemy-in-our-feeds-e86511488de.

46. Alex Korb, "Expectations, Dopamine and Louis CK," *Psychology Today*, March 3, 2016, www.psychologytoday.com/blog/prefrontal-nudity/201603/expectations-dopamine-and-louis-ck.

47. See Alter, *Irresistible*, 61–89.

48. Melvin Kranzberg, "Technology and History: 'Kranzberg's Laws,'" *Technology and Culture* 27, no. 3 (1986): 545, https://doi.org/10.2307/3105385.

49. See Tristan Harris, "How Technology Hijacks People's Minds—from a Magician and Google's Design Ethicist," May 19, 2016, www.tristanharris.com/2016/05/how-technology-hijacks-peoples-minds%e2%80%8a-%e2%80%8afrom-a-magician-and-googles-design-ethicist/; Catherine Price, "How to Break Up With Your Phone," *The New York Times*, February 24, 2018, sec. Well, www.nytimes.com/2018/02/13/well/phone-cellphone-addiction-time.html.

50. Price, "How to Break Up With Your Phone."

51. Pew Research Center, "Political Polarization in the American Public," *Pew Research Center*, June 12, 2014, www.people-press.org/2014/06/12/political-polarization-in-the-american-public/.

52. Amy Mitchell et al., "Political Polarization & Media Habits," *Pew Research Center*, October 21, 2014, www.journalism.org/2014/10/21/political-polarization-media-habits/#.

53. Matt Levendusky, "Are Fox and MSNBC Polarizing America?—The Washington Post," February 3, 2014, www.washingtonpost.com/news/monkey-cage/wp/2014/02/03/are-fox-and-msnbc-polarizing-america/?utm_term=.a1dd09956ec4.

54. See Kevin Arceneaux and Martin Johnson, *Changing Minds or Changing Channels? Partisan News in an Age of Choice* (Chicago and London: The University of Chicago Press, 2013).
55. Markus Prior, "Media and Political Polarization," *Annual Review of Political Science* 16, no. 1 (2013): 101–27, https://doi.org/10.1146/annurev-polisci-100711-135242.
56. Levi Boxell, Matthew Gentzkow, and Jesse M. Shapiro, "Is the Internet Causing Political Polarization? Evidence from Demographics," Working Paper (National Bureau of Economic Research, March 2017), https://doi.org/10.3386/w23258.
57. Prior, "Media and Political Polarization," 123.
58. See Jacob S. Hacker and Paul Pierson, *Winner-Take-All Politics: How Washington Made the Rich Richer--and Turned Its Back on the Middle Class* (New York: Simon & Schuster, 2011).
59. Mostafa M. El-Bermawy, "Your Filter Bubble Is Destroying Democracy," *Wired*, November 18, 2016, www.wired.com/2016/11/filter-bubble-destroying-democracy/.
60. Guess, "Avoiding the Echo Chamber about Echo Chambers."
61. Jonathan Haidt, *The Righteous Mind: Why Good People Are Divided by Politics and Religion* (Vintage, 2013), 57.
62. Haidt, *The Righteous Mind*, 365.
63. Haidt, *The Righteous Mind*, 314.

PART III

The Future of News Literacy

7

MAKING NEWS LITERACY WORK FOR DEMOCRACY

If democratic societies are to thrive or at least survive, it will depend on the quality of news and information citizens consume. The commonly noted paradox of the information age is that we have more of it than ever but we have an unprecedented struggle to find our way to accurate, reliable information. To navigate this environment, we need news literate citizens who can not only analyze content for accuracy and relevance but also examine and interpret the broader social, historical, political, and economic contexts that influence the news and information that surrounds us. The point of this book is to make the case for the inclusion of these critical contexts in news literacy education and to provide a basic introduction to some of the major forces that influence our consumption and participation in the news media environment. First, I hope readers will come away with an understanding of the importance and significance of the broader forces that influence news content. Second, I hope readers now have a grasp of what some of those forces are and are prepared to dig deeper.

In this book, I've suggested we look beyond the problem of "fake news" and focus more deeply on its underlying causes including the barriers posed to traditional journalism due to economic and technological changes over the past three or four decades as well as the institutional and structural forces that have shaped the modern news environment running back at least a century or more. I've also covered the contemporary digital news landscape with a focus on the political economy of the internet and the way we interact with it. This includes the operations of the companies that dominate the web as well as some of the basic psychology that gives the digital world its enormous power. Certainly, there is more to learn, and this book has provided only a general overview of some of the important issues and contexts. But my hope is that there is enough here to get readers thinking more critically about how news is produced and consumed and, most importantly, asking questions of their own and becoming motivated to seek out their own answers. In Table 7.1, I've summarized what I hope are the main takeaways we can all work to incorporate in our daily lives right away.

That leads us to one final piece to this puzzle that needs some attention, and that's the call to action that news literacy requires. Just as I don't think it's enough to passively analyze news content, I also don't think it's enough to develop a thorough understanding of the contexts of news production and consumption and then just sit back and watch the world go by. There's a final step and that's the process of getting engaged with the news environment, the political landscape,

TABLE 7.1 A news literacy agenda: getting engaged with news and democracy.

A News Literacy Agenda: Getting Engaged With News and Democracy

Curate Your News Diet
- Get in the habit of consuming news every day
- Identify the gatekeeping forces that influence what you read, see, and hear
- Choose news sources carefully and make sure they are meeting your needs
- Limit your exposure to news and information so you are not overwhelmed

Cultivate Your Critical Mind
- Increase the amount of thinking you do overall
- Seek knowledge and understanding, not confirmation of preexisting views
- Rely on evidence-based knowledge and allow for uncertainty

Build Your Knowledge
- Learn about news media systems, structures, institutions, and routines
- Examine historical and cultural influences that shape news media systems
- Understand the limits of human cognition and its role in news consumption
- Explore the tensions between democracy and capitalism

Exercise Your Sociological Imagination
- Ask why things are the way they are
- Look beyond individual experience to see how social structures shape daily life
- Examine socially constructed representations of reality for accuracy and truth

Spread Critical Awareness
- Let others know what you're learning and why it matters
- Help others who want to know more
- Explore questions that lack simple, easy answers
- Create and share information responsibly

Participate in Civic Life
- Get informed and vote in every election
- Learn about your local communities and find ways to get involved with others
- Reject cynicism and apathy
- Embrace empathy and engagement
- Create and support social structures that enhance democratic life for all

and civic life in general. *Civic life* means the affairs of our communities, which can range from local to global, and our role as citizens in the social spheres that make up our civilization. Our role in this environment can range from the simple activity of voting and the practice of becoming a well-informed citizen to more involved forms of participation such as educational outreach, political activity, or community organizing—both online and offline. In short, we all need to help spread the word about critical news literacy and the important role informed citizens play in democratic life.

This final chapter reviews some of the ways we can do this and some of the obstacles we need to overcome. The good news about the increasing messiness of the news environment is that it has brought an increase in awareness of the challenges we face in democratic life. This is a great time to harness the growing attention to news and media literacy and spread critical awareness in order to help promote pro-social outcomes such as commitments to evidence-based knowledge, rational thought, and a tolerant, inclusive society. Critical news literacy is a prerequisite for developing a more democratic news media system, that is, one that provides a sufficient quantity and quality of public service journalism and works to represent all citizens. Viewed in the context of public health, bad information can work like a virus, spreading and infecting unsuspecting consumers who go on to express poorly informed policy choices that can end up harming society at large as well as their own personal interests. News literacy is not a simple antidote to all that ails us, but it can help provide a sort of "herd immunity" to those who would otherwise become victims of toxic information. Awareness of issues surrounding the production, distribution, consumption, and sharing of news and information media can equip citizens with the knowledge they need to successfully navigate the digital media landscape and participate in civic life. In this sense, the future of news literacy is inextricably linked to the future of democratic life.

Civic Engagement and Social Capital

Social capital is the value created by networks between humans who interact in meaningful ways and produce outcomes that are broadly beneficial to society. To be sure, the use of the word *capital* here can be a crude metaphor that potentially belittles the worth of a human by comparing human connection to mere economic output. The idea can also be criticized for placing too much focus on the behavior of individuals and not enough on the influence of social structures and the inequalities they produce. However, if we dig a bit deeper and take a nuanced view of the concept, I think it can be a useful way to think about the idea that news literacy is something we do together. A holistic news literacy that includes an understanding of critical contexts can help us all broaden our horizons and make us more accepting and tolerant and empathetic, all of which will be necessary for what is inevitably a global, pluralistic future.

Social capital and the civic life it enables are fuzzy concepts, but they can have real meanings with real applications. Social capital is the engine behind the collective efforts of members of a society, and democratic life and stable societies are only possible with broad trust and reciprocity among citizens. The idea of social capital has been around since at least French democratic theorist Alexis de Tocqueville's discussions of civic life and collective effort in his 1835 book, *Democracy in America*.[1] Noting the positive effects of civic participation, Tocqueville famously wrote, "Sentiments and ideas renew themselves, the heart is enlarged, and the human mind is developed only by the reciprocal action of men upon one another."[2]

The idea of social capital became prominent in the 1990s as many theorists and observers helped popularize the idea. Harvard political scientist Robert Putnam is perhaps best known for drawing attention to social capital, particularly in his 2000 book, *Bowling Alone: The Collapse and Revival of American Community*, where he argued that the decline of participation in civic life was to blame for a decline in democratic engagement.[3] Putnam cited declining political activism as well as more subtle forms of civic engagement, such as participation in parent-teacher associations, membership in civic groups like the League of Women Voters, Elks, and Shriners, and as his title indicates, instead of joining organized bowling leagues, bowling alone. To explain his observations, Putnam somewhat arbitrarily blamed generational change and watching too much television. His book faced criticism for focusing on out-of-date organizations while neglecting to consider new and emerging forms of civic participation and demographic changes and that he was overly nostalgic about the 1950s. Scholars also noted that "Putnam implicitly suggests that being powerless is a result of not having enough capital rather than a structural problem of society."[4] Putnam later reversed his views himself, citing a strengthened civic conscience in young people after the September 11, 2001, terrorist attacks (although the strengthening was concentrated around upper-middle-class youth, while poor and working-class youth were increasingly left out).[5] But in any case, his approach to the concept of social capital remains useful, especially in the context of critical news literacy.

Social capital and civic life are generated through interactions between citizens that occur outside of the market and the state. Sort of like Habermas's public sphere, that means they don't center on commercial exchange—that is, no one is seeking personal gain or profit, nor do they occur because government creates them. The hue of individual empowerment for a greater good behind social capital has appeal for people across the political spectrum. Conservatives might like the emphasis on individual behavior and the exclusion of government intervention, while liberals and progressives might see appeal in the collectivist impulse behind social organizing. At the same time, it's not all about individuals. What we do together is only possible under certain social conditions.

Society requires strong political, social, and economic institutions to support the development of social capital. If an oppressive neoliberal ideology creates conditions where workers struggle to get by—living paycheck to paycheck on minimum wage, lacking access to quality health care, barely being able to put food on the table—then it's no surprise that individuals don't have loads of free time or energy to participate in civic life in meaningful ways. Thus, the idea of social capital is rightly criticized if it fails to account for the structural problems of society that inhibit the accumulation and exercise of social capital. Note also that social capital is distinct from human capital, which is an even cruder measure of the ability of an individual to create economic value—that is, a purely private resource that contributes only to private gain. There's also negative social capital, where people get together to do terrible things, like gang violence or racist hate-mongering, which we should always be on guard against. A weak political state in 1930s Germany encouraged the formation of strong civic connections that supported Hitler's rise to power. So negative social capital can be a path to tyranny and oppression. I hope it's clear that's not what I'm talking about here.

Critical news literacy has the potential to create social capital and improve civic connections, especially when it occurs beyond the confines of the market or the state. Although news literacy is taught in government-supported classrooms, it's not a government institution like elections or courts, and outside of the requirements of educational policy, it is often up to individual schools and teachers to decide whether to teach news literacy and how to do it. Beyond the classroom, news literacy is something we can share with each other in our interpersonal lives and daily discourse (online and offline) as well as through political activism and advocacy work. We can help each other become inspired to learn about news literacy and to link it to various forms of civic engagement. The social capital we build can even be good for our health; developing positive social connections has been linked to a variety of positive health outcomes and providing reductions in stress, loneliness, depression, illness, and even early death.[6] Maybe developing social capital and participating in civic life can literally save your life!

Perhaps this all sounds too touchy-feely, partly because there's no good way to measure it or account for it. But I think social capital creates substantive benefits for both individuals and society at large, and I think you know it when you see it. News literacy can help generate a range of forms of social capital and civic engagement, ranging from simple online participation such as forming groups on Facebook and following hashtags on Twitter, or it could be linked to volunteering in your community, working with nongovernmental organizations, participating in get-out-the-vote efforts, attending political events, and even talking with your family about political and social issues at holiday dinners. Building these connections—especially when based on a holistic explanation of the critical contexts of news literacy and their importance to democratic life—can ultimately help break down barriers between citizens and help everyone appreciate more complicated forms of identity, multiculturalism, and pluralism.

The connections forged through the development of social capital can be broken down into what sociologists have called *strong ties* and *weak ties*, part of social network theory. Strong ties are the powerful interpersonal relationships that influence us most; these are the people you call when you need help. Weak ties are the kind you have across social media; you might have 1,000 "friends" on Facebook, but they can't all be friends in the true sense. (It's been suggested that humans can only maintain up to 150 meaningful relationships.[7]) Weak ties have been praised for their ability to create new connections and provide access to information, but they've also been derided for their superficiality and inability to produce meaningful action. As Malcolm Gladwell wrote in *The New Yorker*,

> Our acquaintances—not our friends—are our greatest source of new ideas and information. The Internet lets us exploit the power of these kinds of distant connections with marvelous efficiency. It's terrific at the diffusion of innovation, interdisciplinary collaboration, seamlessly matching up buyers and sellers, and the logistical functions of the dating world. But weak ties seldom lead to high-risk activism.[8]

Gladwell points to the protests that led to the civil rights movement, which relied on strong ties between participants to create social change. But if weak ties help us encounter new ideas and point us toward new opportunities that might lead to the development of strong ties, then they have obvious value. Developing our news literacy and its role in democratic life can help us develop both.

News itself is a public good that helps us develop social capital and civic engagement, and thus news literacy is key to our ability to engage with news in productive ways that will help create larger social benefits. Unfortunately but unsurprisingly, as American journalism declines, especially at the local level, it becomes harder to generate those benefits as communities become more disconnected and more polarized. In one recent study, increased concentration of television news station ownership was associated with more national news coverage and less attention to local news as well as an ideological shift toward more right-leaning partisan content. Viewership also declined, which is not surprising if viewers are not getting the local content that they come to local news to find.[9] In another study, a decline in the availability of local news was linked to more polarized voting behavior, identified by a decrease in split-ticket voting across party lines. As Americans become more reliant on national news outlets, especially overtly partisan ones on cable television, they tend to see local politics through a similar lens, which contributes to an increase in polarization.[10] These findings are significant because researchers at the University of North Carolina have found that roughly 20 percent of all local newspapers have gone out of business since 2004, a loss of about 1,800 news outlets. The decline has left 1,300 American communities with no news coverage at all, creating vast "news deserts." Virtually all remaining newspapers have scaled back their operations, many to the point that their product is almost nonexistent; researchers labeled these outlets "ghost newspapers." As their report concludes,

> The stakes are high, not just for the communities that have lost newspapers—or are living with the threat of losing a local newspaper—but also for the entire country. Our sense of community and our trust in democracy at all levels suffer when journalism is lost or diminished. In an age of fake news and divisive politics, the fate of communities across the country—and of grassroots democracy itself—is linked to the vitality of local journalism.[11]

At the same time, it's worth noting that, despite all the talk about widespread polarization and antipathy, most Americans are actually quite united on a range of important issues, and all the talk about strident divisions can be quite discouraging for those who might otherwise make investments in their communities and increase their civic engagement. For example, as Columbia University law professor Tim Wu pointed out in *The New York Times*, most Americans favor higher taxes for the superrich, support paid maternity leave, want stronger privacy laws, and back strong net neutrality regulations. Wu writes:

> The defining political fact of our time is not polarization. It's the inability of even large bipartisan majorities to get what they want on issues like these. Call it the oppression of the supermajority. Ignoring what most of the country wants—as much as demagogy and political divisiveness—is what is making the public so angry.[12]

Why can't Americans get what they want? Two political scientists, Martin Gilens and Benjamin Page, have documented a massive gap between citizen policy preferences and actual policy making. Their studies have found that policy makers are mostly receptive to elite special interest groups while virtually ignoring citizens and citizen-based groups.[13] This can be attributed at least in large part to the iron grip of money in politics and a flawed campaign finance system. It can also be attributed to the fact that elite interests have come to dominate the policy-making process so much that citizens have little influence. These larger structural issues might be beyond the scope of news literacy, or they might not. Either way, understanding problems with our political system can be linked to our ability to understand and engage with information about it. Ultimately, social capital and civic engagement can only be generated with a well-educated, well-informed citizenry.

Critical Awareness and Critical Apathy

Learning about some of the ugly realities of our news and information environment—and the political and democratic life it is meant to support—can be a real downer. That's why we have to find joy in generating and spreading critical awareness, and we must veer far away from the dreadful condition of critical apathy, where we get stuck in a rut that leaves us feeling powerless and hopeless. Critical news literacy cannot be gained without a willingness to embrace a broad critical perspective toward life in general. In this sense, "critical" means the ability to question and examine the underlying forces that we often take for granted and assume to be natural and inevitable. Critical questioning can pose challenges for modern discourse, especially in classrooms, but a decision not to examine broader contexts is just as value-laden as a decision to include them. To return to the words of Justin Lewis and Sut Jhally regarding media literacy, "We are advocating a view that recognizes that the world is always made by someone, and a decision to tolerate the status quo is as political as a more overtly radical act."[14] In other words, choosing to not ask critical questions is really no different from asking them; both approaches involve taking a position. It is a fundamental problem with our depoliticized cultures if we pretend to discuss and understand news media messages without discussing the contexts and structures that produce them. Indeed, tolerating the status quo—or worse, altogether ignoring that there is a status quo—is a failure to recognize a fundamental truth about reality and a missed opportunity to engage students in the world they seek to know.

Let's start with the value of critical, analytical thinking in general. Recent research has shown that good analytical thinking is associated with having a higher degree of skepticism about a range of topics and to be less likely to have delusional beliefs or to endorse conspiracy theories and other forms of misinformation.[15] This also holds true for fake news. Two studies involving more than 900 participants found that delusion-prone individuals who were more likely to believe fake headlines also demonstrated thinking that is less "actively open-minded" (i.e., searching for alterative explanations and establishing evidence-based beliefs) and less analytical, that is, relying on deliberate thought processes rather than intuition alone.[16] Another study found that individuals with weak analytical skills were more likely to find randomly generated sentences to be profound and meaningful (e.g., "We are in the midst of a high-frequency blossoming of interconnectedness that will give us access to the quantum soup itself.").[17] Studies like this are often based on narrow psychological measures. For example, one measure of analytical thinking is the well-established Cognitive Reflection Test, which includes questions like this: "A bat and ball cost $1.10 in total. The bat costs $1.00 more than the ball. How much does the ball cost?" The common gut-level response is that the ball costs 10 cents, but a little analysis shows how that would make the bat $1.10 and the total would have to be $1.20. (The correct answer is 5 cents.) You might deride this as a trick question, but a large body of research based on measures like this paints a compelling picture of the significance of different analytical styles in our ability to use reason and evidence to reach accurate conclusions.

Findings like this add complexity to some of what we learned in Chapter 6 about our ability to rationalize our way to information that sits well with our preconceived notions—the process of motivated reasoning. Instead, these studies show that we are just as likely to fall prey to false information because we're simply lazy thinkers who tend to avoid cognitive effort. Basically, thinking is hard, and if we can avoid it, we tend to do so. Another study found that, regardless of their political beliefs, participants with poor analytical thinking skills were less likely to spot fake news, while better analytical thinking was tied to an increased ability to spot fake news.[18] This makes sense in light of other findings that show everyone is just as likely to fall for misinformation regardless of political ideology. In other words, the best explanation for reaching inaccurate conclusions is mostly due to a failure to think rather than prior political beliefs. At the same time, other research has found a "political asymmetry" where certain categories of voters were more likely to be taken in by false information than others. This is a thorny topic that needs more investigation, but the findings so far should be taken seriously.

Another interesting connection is the idea that people who "overclaim"—they pretend to know more than they do about a topic—are also more likely to believe fake news.[19] This relates to other findings that people who hold strong beliefs on a topic—called "belief superiority"—are likely to think they know more about it when actually they know less than people whose beliefs are less strong.[20] And this is consistent with the well-established *Dunning–Kruger effect*, a type of cognitive bias where people think they are smarter than they actually are.[21] That is, ignorant people are often unaware of their own ignorance. These overconfident individuals don't engage in a lot of self-reflection or deep thinking, they're bad at spotting their own mistakes, and they're bad at recognizing the actual skills and knowledge of other people. As psychologist David Dunning wrote in an article called "We Are All Confident Idiots,"

> An ignorant mind is precisely not a spotless, empty vessel, but one that's filled with the clutter of irrelevant or misleading life experiences, theories, facts, intuitions, strategies, algorithms, heuristics, metaphors, and hunches that regrettably have the look and feel of useful and accurate knowledge.[22]

Dunning points out that we can all fall victim to this effect because it's easier to spot someone else's ignorance than to recognize our own. The best way to challenge it is to be your own devil's advocate. Don't be too proud to interrogate your own beliefs and ask why you believe what you believe—and whether it's based on good evidence or just good feelings.

Overconfidence is also a problem for news and media literacy. Emerging research suggests that people who have greater confidence in their own levels of news literacy are the same people who actually know less about news media. All of this points to obvious issues for our consumption of news and our role in democratic society. As if the messy media landscape weren't enough to make it harder than ever to be an informed citizen, we also have a lot of work to do to battle our own human tendencies. But there is a silver lining in this otherwise dark cloud. The picture painted here suggests that what people need to become better citizens is more knowledge and better analytical skills. That's no easy task, but it is easier than changing people's political beliefs or getting them to adjust their entire worldview. Maybe they will end up adjusting their beliefs based on increased literacy, but the thing that must come first is the knowledge and the thinking. If we want to improve the news and information environment and work to combat the problem of misinformation, that's something society can actually set out to accomplish—by improving the conditions and quality of education for everyone, and ensure that critical news literacy is a universal component. Gordon Pennycook and David Rand, two of the leading psychologists who study the connections between analytical thinking and belief in fake news, have concluded that their work

> suggests that the solution to politically charged misinformation should involve devoting resources to the spread of accurate information and to training or encouraging people to think more critically. You aren't doomed to be unreasonable, even in highly politicized times. Just remember that this is also true of people you disagree with.[23]

When it comes to critical thinking, what we need is more *critical loyalty*, or the idea that a person can hold strong beliefs but maintain a critical orientation to evidence and argument whether the conclusion fits with their preexisting views or not.[24] This is similar to the idea of "intellectual humility," or simply "the recognition that the things you believe in might in fact be wrong," according to psychologist Mark Leary.[25] It's easier said than done, but examining our own potential cognitive blind spots is a good start. I'd also like to draw attention to the work of education psychologist William G. Perry, whose theory of intellectual and ethical development might be helpful here.[26] Perry studied the intellectual journey of students to find three distinct phases most pass through, which are simplified here. The first is a position of "dualism," where the world appears to be black and white and absolute, the answers are out there, and you just have to learn them from an authoritative source. The second phase is "relativism," where we learn that knowledge is relative and contextual, and we start to see the complexity of knowledge and how it is created. How can we really know anything if there are so many different perspectives or ways of answering questions? This is an important step to move beyond mere black-and-white absolutism, but the risk at this point is that we can feel unstable, alienated, or overwhelmed by the difficulty of knowing what is true and real and from seeing the challenge of arriving at useful understanding. We may want to escape from the unpleasantness of relativism by retreating back toward dualism or by giving up on knowledge altogether. But if we stick with it, we progress to the third phase of "evolving commitments," where we appreciate that knowledge generation is difficult and contextual and socially constructed, but we realize we can commit to certain ways of knowing the world, and we can find ways to establish a worldview based on a tolerance for uncertainty and ambiguity and an ability to absorb new information and adapt accordingly.

News literacy requires a similar journey. At first, "news" is just something out there to be consumed and then internalized or rejected. But if we can escape this limited perspective, we can see how different kinds of news and information can be valid in different ways and for different reasons, and we can see how news is constructed and influenced by outside forces. The world becomes messy at this point and we may want to give up—Everyone is lying! How can I believe anyone?—or we may retreat to a dogmatic position of blind acceptance of the authorities we recognize and reject other information. But if we push on, we can arrive at a third phase where we start to embrace the messiness and appreciate different ways of knowing while remaining committed to our own experiences and understandings. We can understand and even seek out information that challenges our perceptions, and we can keep an open mind and a critical orientation toward everything we see and hear. Completing this journey is crucial to realizing our full potential in democratic life as well as our full potential as humans. Consider the words of sociologist Stuart Ewen, who has written about the role of media literacy in democratization and social progress:

> Media literacy cannot simply be seen as a vaccination against PR or other familiar strains of institutionalized guile. It must be understood as an education in techniques that can democratize the realm of public expression and will magnify the possibility of meaningful public interactions.[27]

Without this journey, we risk falling prey to a condition of *critical apathy*, where, even when we are armed with critical news consumption habits, we are still fundamentally consumers, powerless to affect change. This is why focusing narrowly on news content is not sufficient for developing news literacy. It is one thing to take apart the news and information we see and hear to test for accuracy, relevance, and reliability—we may even get really good at this. But when we bring this savviness to news content alone, we risk engaging only on a superficial level where we fail to see or address the larger political or social contexts that prefer some types of content over others and that play a central role in the construction of the social world. This steers us away not only from deeper thinking but also from the political and social engagement that could otherwise follow. We are positioned as consumers, not citizens. The idea of critical apathy comes from media studies scholar Jan Teurlings, who built on the work of Mark Andrejevic's investigations of reality television (e.g., "Survivor," "Big Brother," and "The Bachelor"), where savvy viewers could see through the constructed nature of the mediated experience and were able to critique the whole contrived and often absurd premises. But they still tuned in.[28] As Teurlings puts it, under conditions of critical apathy, the "savvy viewer is not duped but instead analyses and understands—often endlessly so—but sees no way in which things could be different."[29]

Many programs in news literacy and media education in general focus so heavily on the analysis of content that it becomes easy to internalize the forms and formats of media to such an extent that alternatives are cut off or seem like a waste of time—like a kind of hegemony of the imagination, where things as they are come to be seen as the natural and inevitable way for them to be. Teurlings says this viewing position

> engages our critical faculties, yet does so by directing us away from political action instead of towards it. It is, so to speak, the televisual equivalent of conspiracy theories: nothing is what it seems, everything is being manipulated, thus let us abolish politics.[30]

This also plays out in the consumption of news, as frequent exposure to conflict, poverty, and other bad news can leave people feeling both powerless and miserable. *Learned helplessness* is the psychological term for this and can lead to depression and low performance. As Shawn Achor and Michelle Gielan wrote in *Harvard Business Review*,

> We believe that negative news influences how we approach our work and the challenges we encounter at the office because it shows us a picture of life in which our behavior does not matter. The majority of news stories showcase problems in our world that we can do little or nothing about. We see the market dropping 500 points or ISIS poised to attack, and we feel powerless to change those outcomes.[31]

You can see how this overlaps with Perry's second phase of intellectual development—relativism—where we might be inclined to give up when we see how messy things can be. That's why we need to go further to be an engaged and empowered participant in democratic life.

In some ways, this is what *postmodernism* has done to us. The postmodern movement is known for its critique of objective reality and the supposed progress of society and often highlights the socially constructed nature of knowledge and institutions. This approach emerged after the rise of totalitarianism and the two world wars of the first half of the 20th century—which created the perception that human progress and its attendant values had largely failed. This reaction is understandable, considering the horrors people had lived through during that period. Since then, postmodern ways of thinking about human progress have been hugely instrumental in challenging and replacing outdated structures of power. But the double-edged sword of postmodernism is that it risks creating a false equivalence across all ways of knowing and learning, and it might suggest to some that antisocial tendencies have as much value as their pro-social counterparts. We have done this to ourselves by embracing the validity of multiple perspectives, which is part of the postmodern condition, often viewed as a positive result of the rejection of the narratives and ideologies of industrialization that characterized the modern era. So there is a balance to be struck here: Maintaining critical awareness without getting bogged down by feelings of helplessness and avoiding the pit of relativism and apathy. Finding this balance is something we all must do to support our meaningful engagement with democratic life.

Improving the News Media Environment

So let's get cracking. There are many things we can do right now to improve the news media environment—some easy and some hard—from both the supply side and the demand side. The supply side includes the people and organizations behind the news production and distribution process, and it also includes the economic, political, and legal contexts that influence the process. The demand side includes those of us who consume news of all kinds and share it with others using digital media. The line between demand and supply is not totally black and white, of course, because digital tools empower all of us to create and share our own news. This is an important point, but for purposes of this discussion, we'll approach things from these two general perspectives. News literacy is something that happens on the demand side, where we learn to become more critical and empowered as informed, self-governing citizens.

Starting with the demand side, we need to increase our critical awareness and knowledge—basically all the stuff I've covered in this book—and we need to encourage others to do the same. We need to get really good at the critical analysis of content that we reviewed in Chapter 1, but we really need to dig deeper and understand the contexts that create and shape the news media environment. As individuals, we need to learn which news sources are most insulated from commercial and political pressures and seek them out and support them financially as best we can. We need to recognize the fundamental role of politics and policy making in daily life, and we need to embrace and discuss the difficult issues that democratic societies must grapple with as they are represented to us through mediated formats. To help make all of this happen, we need to spread the word about news and media literacy and make sure it's being offered to students everywhere so they are prepared to navigate today's news media landscape.

While news literacy is still an emerging domain, media literacy has caught on around the world and is a well-established educational practice in many developed and even developing nations. Some governments require formalized media education in primary and secondary schools, but others—notably the United States—have yet to do so, so only some students have access to the smattering of inconsistent approaches that exist. A handful of states have introduced or passed laws requiring media education in schools, but these remain the exception. One problem is that while media literacy plays a central role in improving the conditions of the news and information environment, educational initiatives are often offered as solutions but are not supported in meaningful ways. As scholar Sonia Livingstone has written,

> Call it what you will—media literacy, digital literacy, critical literacy, news literacy—educational alternatives to the regulation of the digital environment are suggested on all sides. Yet oddly, this rarely results in concrete policies or resources to increase the media literacy of the public. It seems the mere suggestion is enough to deflect attention from the politically undesirable or practically-challenging. Media literacy, conveniently, is someone else's responsibility.[32]

As a result, media literacy education is just as likely to reach the public informally through librarians, community organizations, public scholarship, and sometimes, the news itself. Even where media literacy does reach students and the public, it often covers a broad swath of material and tends to focus on media content at large. These are important components of media education, but students and citizens need more. We all need a concentrated introduction to the important role of news—not just media generally—in democratic life, and we need to understand that news is not just something to be passively consumed and analyzed, but also is a system of education in itself that needs to be broken apart and understood at institutional and structural levels, including the influences of market forces, technology, algorithms, communication routines, and consumption habits.

Beyond passing legislation to improve access to media education, news and media literacy advocates have authored a range of reports and policy papers to lay out plans for making media education broadly available and accessible. These reports cover different domains of media education and literacy, but they call for common efforts to put resources to work. For example, media literacy scholar Renee Hobbs laid out a number of these in her 2010 report for the Knight Foundation called "Digital and Media Literacy: A Plan of Action." Hobbs notes that we need to support the demand side of news literacy education by funding a range of initiatives and partnerships, including those that support local and community journalism and outreach; education and professional development for teachers, journalists, and civic leaders; and public service announcements and educator conferences.[33] Some of these recommendations have been realized, but more work remains.

In addition to supporting and improving news literacy and media education—the demand side of news—much work remains on the supply side. For starters, there's a great deal that can be done by individual news producers and the outlets they work for. Reporters, editors, and producers should do more to take an evidence-based approach to representing the world, and they should reject the false equivalence that gives equal attention to uninformed or misinformed opinions and ideologies. For example, it was significant in December of 2018 when NBC's "Meet the Press"—the longest running show in television history—devoted an entire episode to climate change and noted there would be no time for those who reject the basic science of climate change. As moderator Chuck Todd said at the outset,

> We're not going to debate climate change, the existence of it. The Earth is getting hotter. And human activity is a major cause, period. We're not going to give time to climate deniers. The science is settled, even if political opinion is not.[34]

Similarly, those who create the news should focus their attention on the important policy issues that affect citizens—all citizens, not just the affluent—and avoid the allure of scandal, intrigue, and horse race politics. The primary goal of news should be to educate citizens, not just convey the empty "both sides" rhetoric of politics.

The supply side also needs major structural change. We need a rebirth of local journalism, which has been devastated by economic and technological changes. This means subsidies and tax breaks for independent, noncommercial, nonpartisan news producers. We need meaningful investments in politically independent public media to provide real alternatives to commercial programming. We need to use anti-trust laws to break up too-powerful media and technology giants, and we need to force the social media and digital technology companies to contribute to the information needs of society rather than profiting off the labor of others and facilitating the spread of misinformation. We need to reform election campaign coverage and give free airtime to qualified candidates. We need to consider ways to incentivize or require commitments to public service by powerful media owners. And in the United States, we need to realize the hard truth that, despite the power of the First Amendment, some kinds of speech truly are more valuable than others, and we need to use the force of law to limit the spread of misinformation and hate speech, as some other developed nations have already done. (Note that in the United States "hate speech" still has no legal meaning and receives the same First Amendment protection as other forms of speech.)

These are just a few of things regulators and policy makers could do to improve the conditions of the news landscape, but they will only do so if consumers and citizens demand it. One caveat here: it's been suggested that media literacy should not be conflated with media reform efforts because media education is already fraught with political challenges, and advocating for change pushes the limits of what educators should be trying to do. Perhaps the same is true for news literacy. But there's only so much we can do as individuals if we want to have power over the news and information environment, and I do think it's incumbent upon us to learn about and advocate for structural reforms to the system that would help improve the quality, reliability, and usefulness of the news available to us. And there's no reason it needs to be the political hot potato some see it as. All kinds of people of all political stripes agree that the news and information environment is seriously flawed and in need of real reform. We won't necessarily agree on every solution, but I'm confident that it's possible to find consensus on this issue if we try.

Revolutions in communication like ours don't come along very often, and the decisions we make during windows like this one will have long-lasting effects. (Just think about the basic regulatory structure for broadcasting that was created in the 1930s that we are still living with today.) We face a *critical juncture* where we have the option to shape communication policy and the news media environment for decades to come. Media scholar Robert McChesney says a critical juncture in media and communication requires at least two of three main criteria: existing communication technology is undermined by a revolutionary new system, news content is discredited or viewed as illegitimate, and a major political crisis leads to a breakdown of the social system and to social reform movements.[35] The first two criteria are easily met at the present moment, and we've at least seen signs of the third if not outright confirmation. Even without a political crisis, it's clear that the upheaval caused by the digital revolution and the decline of journalism puts us at an important moment in time. If this is indeed a critical juncture, we need to do everything we can to make sure we come out on the other side with a more democratic news media system that serves the needs of all citizens.

While we wait on the major structural changes we need, we can see positive signs in other areas of the supply side. Even though the news industry has seen substantial decline in the 21st century, plenty of exciting experiments to help it rebound are already in the works. For example, a range of new nonprofit news outlets have emerged, such as ProPublica and the Center for Public Integrity, which have a national focus, as well as outlets with a local or regional focus, such as *The Texas Tribune* and Voice of San Diego. Nonprofit investigative outlets such as the Center for Investigative Reporting and *Mother Jones* have been doing similar work for decades, but this work and this business model have taken on new importance as commercial journalism has declined. Other newly developed nonprofit outlets have directed their attention to specific issues, such as criminal justice for The Marshall Project, state policy for Stateline, and environmental issues for InsideClimate News. Similar to public media, nonprofits rely on a mix of individual contributions, private donors, foundations, and grants. Alternative funding sources like these can help support valuable public service journalism.

At the same time, some have raised concerns that such funding sources can be unreliable, and can produce outlets with a narrow focus and limited reach.[36] The same can be true for outlets that are supported by a single wealthy individual, such as Amazon owner Jeff Bezos who owns *The Washington Post* or casino magnate Sheldon Adelson who owns *The Las Vegas Review-Journal*. In some cases, benevolent billionaires can provide much-needed support, but in other cases, an "oligarchy media model" runs the risk of putting too much power in the hands of an unaccountable few.[37] This also goes for the venture capitalists of Silicon Valley who have offered cash infusions to support digital media start-ups, such as Vox Media and Buzzfeed. While some of these new arrivals have shown promise, it's also possible that funding sources can influence news content in negative ways, such as reproducing the same market pressures that have harmed other outlets. Ultimately, when it comes to the supply side, we should remember that reliable, independent news is an unqualified public good in democratic life, and like police departments, national parks, and clean air and water, we should find ways to support news accordingly.

#DeleteFacebook?

Then there's the question of what to do about social media. Social media platforms and networks such as Facebook, Twitter, Snapchat, Instagram, and YouTube have provided enormous benefits to many individuals who are now empowered in ways they could not have been before the digital age. But these platforms have created real costs for society. As media scholar Siva Vaidhyanathan notes in his extensive study of Facebook called *Antisocial Media: How Facebook Disconnects Us and Undermines Democracy*, "Facebook likely has been—on balance—good for individuals. But Facebook has been—on balance—bad for all of us collectively."[38] The digital tools at our disposal are helpful for staying connected, sharing our experience, and hearing from others, especially those we might not otherwise get a chance to interact with. But then there are the downsides, and it's possible that the costs to society outweigh the benefits to individuals. As Vaidhyanathan concludes,

> If you wanted to build a machine that would distribute propaganda to millions of people, distract them from important issues, energize hatred and bigotry, erode social trust, undermine journalism, foster doubts about science, and engage in massive surveillance all at once, you would make something a lot like Facebook.[39]

The hashtag "#DeleteFacebook" took off on Twitter in 2018 as more and more people began to learn about the company's deceptive practices, especially in the wake of the Cambridge Analytica scandal. There's an obvious irony of using social media to advocate for ditching social media—and even bragging about it on social media—but this is just one example of people turning on social media or at least having real conversations about whether their life is better with or without it. I'm not here to tell you to delete your social media accounts. Like the misguided "kill your television" bumper stickers that were popular in the 1990s, technology— from television to social media—can be used deliberately with the goal of improving the conditions of democracy. Television offers lots of great learning opportunities, and as long as we limit our exposure and avoid hypercommercial garbage, anyone can benefit. At the same time, social media can offer benefits if we use it well. Unfortunately, this is not how most of us use and understand Facebook and other platforms. That's why news literacy needs to help us understand how and why digital media companies operate as they do, and we need to learn to treat them like the for-profit corporations they are rather than the benign public utilities we sometimes mistake them for. We certainly need to continue to call for more democratic, user-centered control of social and search platforms as well as tighter regulations over data collection, privacy, and marketing practices.

Plenty of other people actually do want you to quit social media, or at least take a good long break. That includes tech insiders and pioneers, such as computer scientist Jaron Lanier, a leader in the creation of virtual reality technology. In his book *Ten Arguments for Deleting Your Social Media Accounts Right Now*, Lanier makes his case that social media is making us lose our free will, undermining truth, destroying our capacity for empathy, making us less happy, taking away our economic dignity, and making politics impossible.[40] Lanier, like others who have seen the tech industry from the inside, point to the commodification of our attention and our behavior as the central problem created by social media. As Lanier has written,

> The issue isn't only that internet users are crammed into environments that can bring out the worst in us, or that so much power has concentrated into a tiny number of hands that control giant cloud computers. A bigger problem is that we are all carrying around devices that are suitable for mass behaviour modification. . . . In short, your behaviour has been turned into a product—and corporate and political clients are lining up to modify it.[41]

Basically, it's the business model that turned social media into the menace it has become.

The potential for mass manipulation is real and well documented. For example, one of Facebook's own studies with researchers from Cornell and the University of California manipulated people's newsfeeds to explore "emotional contagion effects," or the influence of other people's emotions and behavior on our own. In this case, the study showed some users more positive posts, which led the user to produce more positive posts and fewer negative posts; other users saw more negative posts, which had the opposite effect.[42] The researchers wanted to know if a person's behavior could be altered simply by observing another person's experience as opposed to having the actual face-to-face verbal and nonverbal cues that were assumed to be necessary for emotional contagion. Was this a simple social science experiment or mass manipulation of an unsuspecting population? The backlash was swift. Critics cited a violation of basic research ethics by failing to get the informed consent of participants. The Facebook researcher who led the study later apologized, saying, "In hindsight, the research benefits of the paper may not have justified all of this anxiety."[43]

Furthermore, Facebook researchers have found that they can actually influence voting behavior. In a widely cited 2012 study published in the scientific journal *Nature*, Facebook manipulated the news feeds of 61 million users of the site and found a simple message showing which of a user's "friends" had indicated they had voted made the user more likely to vote. Researchers used publicly available voting records to see if the manipulation worked, and it did. An estimated 340,000 additional people voted in the 2010 midterm election as a result.[44] Maybe this kind of get-out-the-vote peer pressure is not so bad, but if this kind of manipulation works, so can all sorts of other efforts that might not be so positive. Facebook and other social and search companies are constantly running subtle manipulations to improve the user experience and, of course, keep people on the site, but because it all happens behind closed doors inside of a private company, we'll never know what they're doing to us unless they go out of their way to tell us. Facebook won't share its data with independent researchers, so what we know about Facebook comes from Facebook. It's a little disconcerting to imagine what kinds of manipulations and experiments they are running behind those closed doors that we'll never know about.

At the same time, social and digital media companies occasionally do take steps to improve the content on their sites and platforms. For starters, it's worth noting that Facebook alone has a reported 15,000 content moderators around the world. They often work for third-party vendors, such as Cognizant, which Facebook contracts with to police the site for the really bad stuff—pornography, hate speech, violent attacks, even murder.[45] (The job of moderator has gotten more attention lately mainly because of the devastating impact it can have on workers, causing anxiety and PTSD.) When it comes to the trickier content area of misinformation, Facebook has toyed with efforts to let users mark certain posts as "disputed," having third-party fact-checkers offer "related articles" to challenge or debunk possible misinformation, and simply demoting potentially false or harmful content so it's less likely to appear in news feeds.[46] In late 2018, Twitter removed 50 fake accounts attributed to Republican state lawmakers, and Facebook said it would remove 559 pages and 251 accounts it had identified that amplified misinformation.[47] (In both cases, the accounts and pages were run by Americans, demonstrating that domestic disinformation campaigns are at least as great a threat as foreign ones.) Facebook also has made use of third-party fact-checkers to limit the spread of false news across Africa and has sponsored public service announcements to help teach people to spot misinformation.[48]

Finally, digital giants Facebook, Pinterest, and YouTube are reportedly taking some responsibility and working to crack down on the spread of misinformation that has been pervasive on their platforms and presumably has helped to discourage some parents from vaccinating their children, creating a dangerous situation for public health. It's great news anytime these powerful platforms that have helped create problems like this are finally trying to do something about it, but at the same time, it's sort of hard to take these moves seriously considering what a drop in the bucket they are compared to all the damage that's been wrought by social media. And finally, all of this belies a central point about social and search companies: whether they like it or not, moves like this amount to an admission of guilt, demonstrating their recognition that they are not merely benign technological utilities but rather are publishers of information. They might not create the information themselves, but their decisions over what to pass along makes them culpable for the results. Facebook and others have long insisted that they are mere technology companies, not media or publishing companies. This helps them avoid a host of thorny legal complications, but it also ignores the reality of their impact. Of course they are publishers, picking and choosing what kinds of news and information dominate public dialogue and discourse.

The digital media landscape is full of moving targets. It's hard to keep up with all the new developments, changes, fallout, and consequences. It's possible that protective measures will help reduce the spread of misinformation, but it's also possible that it's too little too late. Just remember that while Facebook and other platforms might seem great for you as an individual, they run the risk of infecting society with misinformation and distraction, and they do it to protect their profits. We should continue to call for more democratic control and regulatory measures and do our best to use digital platforms for good, but there is a lot to be concerned about, and until there is a sweeping change to the basic business model of digital advertising, we should be cautious.

News Literacy As Public Health Problem

As I write this, the myth that childhood vaccines cause autism has been debunked by yet another study, this time a massive ten-year investigation of more than half a million people.[49] Will studies like this one ever be enough to reverse the anti-vaccination trend that has taken hold in some parts of the world over the past decade, or will some individuals continue to embrace the conspiracy theory and put others at risk? Public health depends on the broad understanding and agreement that what we do as individuals affects not only ourselves but other people as well. News literacy is no different. It is something we do together because a successful democratic society relies on a well-informed and well-educated citizenry at large. What good does it do if some of us are informed and engaged but many of us are not? All it takes is a small resistance to put the whole population at risk. In this sense, news literacy—and its counterpart, news illiteracy—can be viewed as a public health problem.

The rise of anti-vaxxers presents its own public health problem and offers a useful analogy here. The myth of a vaccine-autism link originated from a single scientific study published in 1998 in a British medical journal called the *Lancet*, where a British gastroenterologist named Andrew Wakefield and his coauthors suggested there could be a link between the vaccine for the measles, mumps, and rubella diseases—the MMR vaccine—and the disruption of intestinal tissue, which could lead to bowel disease and neuropsychiatric disease, namely autism. In the ensuing years, not only could other researchers not replicate this tentative finding but also investigations revealed his use of fraudulent data to make the case as well as an undisclosed financial conflict of interest on Wakefield's part—he wanted to help peddle an alternative vaccine.[50] The *Lancet* finally retracted the original article in 2010, writing in an editorial that the study was "utterly false" and that the journal had been "deceived." Wakefield was banned from practicing medicine in the UK due to his "serious professional misconduct."[51] What a jerk, right? But I doubt even Wakefield could have imagined the sensation his malfeasance would cause. Today, measles is on the rise due to declining vaccination rates—due partly to access and cost issues for certain people who lack quality health care—but also because of the anti-vaccine hysteria Wakefield triggered.

Vaccinations work only when large majorities of populations receive them, a phenomenon called *herd immunity*. This is relevant for two reasons: one, the anti-vaccination crisis could not have occurred without the help of both traditional and digital forms of media, and two, it provides a helpful analogy for understanding how news literacy works much like the vaccines that prevent contagious diseases—as long as we reach an appropriate level of herd immunity. The good news about the Wakefield debacle is that the scientific process worked. Science is built on observation, experimentation, and replication, and without consistent patterns of evidence, scientific findings must be revised or rejected. And like good journalism, science requires transparency and accountability that helps the public identify conflicts of interest and errors. This is true whether the issue is vaccines, climate change, tobacco smoking, pharmaceuticals, hydrofracking, and so on. It's hard enough to do good science in the first place, so it really doesn't help when propaganda and misinformation are spread by those who aim to sow confusion and advance their own interests. Science historians Naomi Oreskes and Erik M. Conway showed in their book *Merchants of Doubt* how special interests such as the tobacco industry have worked for decades to suggest that there is a lack of settled science on a range of issues when scientific consensus is well established.[52]

So not only does public health desperately need quality news content that can use an evidence-based approach to parse and explain important issues, we desperately need a citizenry that can understand the contexts in which news is produced and consumed in order to do their part with the process of sorting good information from bad. Another comparison can be made to the American obesity epidemic and the attendant rise of metabolic disease due to terrible diets and sedentary lifestyles. Like news literacy, the problem of obesity should be dealt with on two fronts: what we can do as individuals on the demand side—avoiding processed foods, eating fruits and vegetables—and what society needs to provide on the supply side—stronger oversight and regulation of the food industry, better and more affordable access to healthy food. If we think about the news and information environment in a similar way, we need to educate and empower individuals on the demand side, and we need to improve the supply side through structural and regulatory changes.

When news literacy is viewed as a public health problem, we can see how important it will be to make sure citizens are knowledgeable about the news and information environment, especially as civilization is forced to grapple with a host of difficult issues going forward. Scientists and other advocates of evidence-based reasoning sometimes point out that the scientific method, which relies on experiment and observation, and gave us electricity, computers, cars, and medicine, is no different from the scientific method that helps us understand climate change. It's also how we know that cigarettes and sugar are harmful to our health and that genetically modified food and vaccinations are safe. It's how we know our microwave will reliably heat a frozen burrito and that our car is not likely to explode on our way to work. It's how we know the earth is round and gravity makes things fall. On these and many other issues, we can either trust the science or not, but we can't pick and choose which science to believe. Of course, like any human endeavor, science is imperfect, and we should certainly be skeptical of any findings until they are thoroughly vetted and have gained broad support from knowledgeable experts. But once issues are generally settled by well-trained experts, if we believe in some science, we should believe in all science—whether we like the conclusion or not. Understanding these principles is central to navigating the news and information landscape so we do not succumb to misinformation, conspiracy theories, fake news, and other information that interferes with our ability to make good decisions for ourselves and for society.

News Literacy and Democratic Life

If we understand news literacy is a public health issue, we can see it's not just about our own individual experience in the world as people often assume. Savvy students often profess to know all that they need to know to navigate the news environment and be well informed. Even if that's true, they must recognize that news literacy is not just about them; it's about the democratic life we all share and our ability to navigate its difficult waters together. Consider the timely and analogous issue of climate change, which can be mitigated in part with individual-level solutions: change our light bulbs, ride a bike, maybe even install solar panels on the roof. But that's not going to be anywhere near enough. We need widespread social, political, and economic change to make a real difference in how much average global temperatures will rise in the coming decades. As one writer in *The Guardian* has pointed out, suggesting that we deal with climate change strictly on an individual level is a disastrous idea, spawned by a neoliberal orientation to policy making that prevents us from employing the collective action efforts and public works projects that are necessary to address large-scale social problems.[53] It's certainly great if we all could ride our bikes to work and ditch our cars, but moves like this are a drop in the bucket compared to the real causes of climate change and the real solutions that are needed to combat it. We know that fossil fuels and agricultural practices are among the leading causes, yet we continue to subsidize dirty energy and factory farming while ignoring opportunities to transform energy production to renewables.[54] We know we are facing a major social transformation if climate change does its worst. If we're facing transformation anyway, why not seize the opportunity to do things that will actually address the problem?

Climate change, public health, wealth inequality, automation of the workforce, terrorism, human rights abuses, artificial intelligence, rising authoritarianism—the list of topics that threaten social stability and progress is endless. But it will only be harder to deal with these without a broad news literacy that educates and empowers people by dealing with both the content and contexts of the news environment. As I've suggested earlier, there can actually be joy and meaning to be found in the work we do together to make ourselves and our societies more news literate and more prepared for the future. That might be little comfort when there's so much doom and gloom to consider, but if we get serious about what needs to happen to educate and empower a global citizenry, we can all celebrate our shared humanity and enjoy the fruits of our collective efforts. And it's especially important to look back and see all the accomplishments of humanity, such as reducing global poverty, hunger, and child labor, and increasing leisure time, life expectancy, public safety, and education.[55] That's not to say these problems are totally solved, but looking at what we've done can help remind us what we can do. Critical news literacy can help us see the dark spots but can also help light the way forward.

Democratic life also needs to be broadly inclusive in order to support our increasingly diverse and pluralistic societies. News literacy efforts can support this by helping citizens see the contexts that influence news and sometimes lead to incomplete or inaccurate mediated representations of reality. Understanding these connections can help burst our bubbles—our mediated bubbles and our real-life bubbles—with the hope that we can better understand each other and solve problems based on our shared goals and values.

The future of democracy remains uncertain. Some believe we need to prepare for a future with less participation, not more. In this view, we need to accept the reality that most people aren't really interested in public affairs, and when they are, they make gut decisions based on their feelings about life in general, especially the economy at the time, and on ideological orientations they gained as far back as childhood.[56] All of this may be true but that doesn't make news any less important to our lives. It still shapes our reality, tells us how to view ourselves and others, and influences our behavior in both our public and our private lives. And just because we have created depoliticized societies where citizens are broadly uninvolved in public life doesn't mean we should be satisfied with that. I think we can do better. To live meaningful lives of fulfillment, humans need to feel that their voice matters, that they have some agency in determining how society operates, that they possess political self-efficacy and have the opportunity to exercise it. And for those who do participate in public life, it's important to note that helping people become better informed can be best accomplished by teaching them about the structures of the news media environment, which is likely to be more doable and more effective than asking people to reorient their entire ideological outlook. Because it does not undermine or challenge our basic view of the world, changing knowledge appears to be easier than changing beliefs.

So where does that leave us? What can we reasonably expect for news literacy and democratic life going forward? I don't think anyone expects to generate a world of *omnicompetent citizens* (to borrow a term from Walter Lippmann in *Public Opinion*), where everyone is fully informed on every subject and prepared to make rational decisions based on a full accounting of the best available evidence. But reaching toward a democratic ideal is possible, where citizens work together to make good decisions based on accurate portrayals of reality. Finally, the means for reaching this end are as important as the end itself. In that sense, news literacy is a process, not a product. It's something we do together to create more meaningful lives and a better society. But the process must be oriented around a holistic approach to understanding and interacting with the news media environment, which requires broad foundational knowledge like the kind I've described in this book, along with a critical orientation toward not just what we see on the surface of our mediated reality but toward what lies beneath. As we face the uncertain future, let's make the most of the opportunity of the present to broaden our horizons, increase our knowledge, and improve the conditions of democratic life for all.

Questions for Discussion

1. Where can social capital be found today? How can news literacy enhance social capital and civic life?
2. How has the decline of journalism contributed to an erosion of social capital and civic engagement?
3. Is challenging the status quo any different from accepting it? What are the best ways to pursue social change?
4. How can you harness the power of digital and social media without succumbing to its negative effects?
5. What structural changes are necessary to improve the conditions of news, education, and democracy for all?

Notes

1. See Paul Lichterman, "Social Capital or Group Style? Rescuing Tocqueville's Insights on Civic Engagement," *Theory and Society* 35, no. 5/6 (2006): 529–63.
2. Alexis de Tocqueville, *Democracy in America* (Chicago: University of Chicago Press, 2000), 491.

3. Robert D. Putnam, *Bowling Alone: The Collapse and Revival of American Community*, 1st edition (New York: Touchstone Books by Simon & Schuster, 2001).

4. Emanuele Ferragina and Alessandro Arrigoni, "The Rise and Fall of Social Capital: Requiem for a Theory?," *Political Studies Review* 15, no. 3 (August 1, 2017): 363, https://doi.org/10.1177/1478929915623968.

5. See Thomas H. Sander and Robert D. Putnam, "Democracy's Past and Future: Still Bowling Alone?—The Post-9/11 Split," *Journal of Democracy* 21, no. 1 (January 21, 2010): 9–16, https://doi.org/10.1353/jod.0.0153.

6. Kristian Bolin et al., "Investments in Social Capital—Implications of Social Interactions for the Production of Health," *Social Science & Medicine* 56, no. 12 (June 1, 2003): 2379–90, https://doi.org/10.1016/S0277-9536(02)00242-3.

7. NPR Staff, "Don't Believe Facebook; You Only Have 150 Friends," June 5, 2011, www.npr.org/2011/06/04/136723316/dont-believe-facebook-you-only-have-150-friends.

8. Malcolm Gladwell, "Small Change," *The New Yorker*, September 27, 2010, www.newyorker.com/magazine/2010/10/04/small-change-malcolm-gladwell.

9. Gregory J. Martin and Joshua McCrain, "Local News and National Politics," *American Political Science Review*, February 19, 2019, 1–13, https://doi.org/10.1017/S0003055418000965.

10. Joshua P. Darr, Matthew P. Hitt, and Johanna L. Dunaway, "Newspaper Closures Polarize Voting Behavior," *Journal of Communication* 68, no. 6 (December 1, 2018): 1007–28, https://doi.org/10.1093/joc/jqy051.

11. "The Expanding News Desert" (University of North Carolina Center for Innovation and Sustainability in Local Media, 2018), www.usnewsdeserts.com/reports/expanding-news-desert/.

12. Tim Wu, "Opinion | The Oppression of the Supermajority," *The New York Times*, March 5, 2019, sec. Opinion, www.nytimes.com/2019/03/05/opinion/oppression-majority.html.

13. Martin Gilens and Benjamin I. Page, "Testing Theories of American Politics: Elites, Interest Groups, and Average Citizens," *Perspectives on Politics* 12, no. 3 (September 2014): 564–81, https://doi.org/10.1017/S1537592714001595.

14. Justin Lewis and Sut Jhally, "The Struggle over Media Literacy," *Journal of Communication* 48, no. 1 (1998): 119.

15. Gordon Pennycook, Jonathan A. Fugelsang, and Derek J. Koehler, "Everyday Consequences of Analytic Thinking," *Current Directions in Psychological Science* 24, no. 6 (December 1, 2015): 425–32, https://doi.org/10.1177/0963721415604610.

16. Michael Bronstein et al., "Belief in Fake News Is Associated with Delusionality, Dogmatism, Religious Fundamentalism, and Reduced Analytic Thinking," *SSRN Scholarly Paper* (Rochester, NY: Social Science Research Network, September 14, 2018), https://papers.ssrn.com/abstract=3172140.

17. Gordon Pennycook and David G. Rand, "Who Falls for Fake News? The Roles of Bullshit Receptivity, Overclaiming, Familiarity, and Analytic Thinking," *SSRN Scholarly Paper* (Rochester, NY: Social Science Research Network, May 23, 2018), https://papers.ssrn.com/abstract=3023545.

18. Gordon Pennycook and David G. Rand, "Lazy, Not Biased: Susceptibility to Partisan Fake News Is Better Explained by Lack of Reasoning Than by Motivated Reasoning," *SSRN Scholarly Paper* (Rochester, NY: Social Science Research Network, 2018), https://papers.ssrn.com/abstract=3165567.

19. Pennycook and Rand, "Who Falls for Fake News?"

20. Michael P. Hall and Kaitlin T. Raimi, "Is Belief Superiority Justified by Superior Knowledge?," *Journal of Experimental Social Psychology* 76 (May 1, 2018): 290–306, https://doi.org/10.1016/j.jesp.2018.03.001.

21. Justin Kruger and David Dunning, "Unskilled and Unaware of It: How Difficulties in Recognizing One's Own Incompetence Lead to Inflated Self-Assessments,"

Journal of Personality and Social Psychology 77, no. 6 (1999): 1121–34, https://doi.org/10.1037/0022-3514.77.6.1121.

22. David Dunning, "We Are All Confident Idiots," *Pacific Standard*, October 27, 2014, https://psmag.com/social-justice/confident-idiots-92793.

23. Gordon Pennycook and David Rand, "Why Do People Fall for Fake News?," *The New York Times*, January 25, 2019, sec. Opinion, www.nytimes.com/2019/01/19/opinion/sunday/fake-news.html.

24. Howard G. Lavine, Christopher D. Johnston, and Marco R. Steenbergen, *The Ambivalent Partisan: How Critical Loyalty Promotes Democracy* (New York: Oxford University Press, 2012), 11.

25. Brian Resnick, "Intellectual Humility: The Importance of Knowing You Might Be Wrong," *Vox*, January 4, 2019, www.vox.com/science-and-health/2019/1/4/17989224/intellectual-humility-explained-psychology-replication.

26. William G. Perry, *Forms of Ethical and Intellectual Development in the College Years: A Scheme*, 1st edition (San Francisco, CA: Jossey-Bass, 1998).

27. Stuart Ewen, *PR!: A Social History of Spin*, 1st edition (New York: Basic Books, 1996), 414.

28. Mark Andrejevic, *Reality TV: The Work of Being Watched* (Lanham, MD: Rowman & Littlefield Publishers, 2004), 135.

29. Jan Teurlings, "Media Literacy and the Challenges of Contemporary Media Culture: On Savvy Viewers and Critical Apathy," *European Journal of Cultural Studies* 13, no. 3 (August 1, 2010): 368, https://doi.org/10.1177/1367549410363202.

30. Teurlings, "Media Literacy and the Challenges of Contemporary Media Culture," 368.

31. Shawn Achor and Michelle Gielan, "Consuming Negative News Can Make You Less Effective at Work," *Harvard Business Review*, September 14, 2015, https://hbr.org/2015/09/consuming-negative-news-can-make-you-less-effective-at-work.

32. Sonia Livingstone, "Media Literacy—Everyone's Favourite Solution to the Problems of Regulation," *London School of Economics Media Policy Project* (blog), May 8, 2018, https://blogs.lse.ac.uk/mediapolicyproject/2018/05/08/media-literacy-everyones-favourite-solution-to-the-problems-of-regulation/.

33. Renee Hobbs, "Digital and Media Literacy: A Plan of Action" (Knight Foundation, 2010), https://knightfoundation.org/reports/digital-and-media-literacy-plan-action.

34. Ian Schwartz, "Chuck Todd: 'We're Not Going to Give Time to Climate Deniers,'" January 2, 2019, *Real Clear Politics*, accessed March 13, 2019, www.realclearpolitics.com/video/2019/01/02/chuck_todd_im_not_going_to_give_time_to_climate_deniers.html.

35. Robert McChesney, *Communication Revolution: Critical Junctures and the Future of Media* (New York: New Press, 2007), 10.

36. Victor Pickard, "Can Charity Save Journalism from Market Failure?," *The Conversation*, 2017, http://theconversation.com/can-charity-save-journalism-from-market-failure-75833.

37. Rodney Benson and Victor Pickard, "The Slippery Slope of the Oligarchy Media Model," *The Conversation*, 2017, http://theconversation.com/the-slippery-slope-of-the-oligarchy-media-model-81931.

38. Siva Vaidhyanathan, *Antisocial Media: How Facebook Disconnects Us and Undermines Democracy* (New York: Oxford University Press, 2018), 18–19.

39. Vaidhyanathan, *Antisocial Media*, 18–19.

40. Jaron Lanier, *Ten Arguments for Deleting Your Social Media Accounts Right Now* (London: Henry Holt and Co., 2018).

41. Jaron Lanier, "Six Reasons Why Social Media Is a Bummer," *The Observer*, May 27, 2018, sec. Technology, www.theguardian.com/technology/2018/may/27/jaron-lanier-six-reasons-why-social-media-is-a-bummer.

42. Booth, Robert. "Facebook Reveals News Feed Experiment to Control Emotions." *The Guardian*, June 29, 2014, sec. Technology. www.theguardian.com/technology/2014/jun/29/facebook-users-emotions-news-feeds.

43. Vindu Goel, "Facebook Tinkers With Users' Emotions in News Feed Experiment, Stirring Outcry," *The New York Times*, December 20, 2017, sec. Technology, www.nytimes.com/2014/06/30/technology/facebook-tinkers-with-users-emotions-in-news-feed-experiment-stirring-outcry.html.
44. Corbyn, Zoe. "Facebook Experiment Boosts US Voter Turnout." *Nature News*, September 12, 2012. https://doi.org/10.1038/nature.2012.11401.
45. Casey Newton, "The Secret Lives of Facebook Moderators in America," *The Verge*, February 25, 2019, www.theverge.com/2019/2/25/18229714/cognizant-facebook-content-moderator-interviews-trauma-working-conditions-arizona.
46. Daniel Engber, "Facebook's Revamp Is Also an Effort to Fight Fake News. Will It Work?," *Slate Magazine*, January 12, 2018, https://slate.com/health-and-science/2018/01/facebooks-revamp-includes-an-effort-to-fight-fake-news.html.
47. Sheera Frenkel, "Facebook Tackles Rising Threat: Americans Aping Russian Schemes to Deceive," *The New York Times*, October 12, 2018, sec. Technology, www.nytimes.com/2018/10/11/technology/fake-news-online-disinformation.html.
48. Nwafor Polycarp, "How Facebook Is Mitigating Fake News in Africa," *Vanguard News Nigeria* (blog), February 27, 2019, www.vanguardngr.com/2019/02/how-facebook-is-mitigating-fake-news-in-africa/.
49. Jan Hoffman, "One More Time, With Big Data: Measles Vaccine Doesn't Cause Autism," *The New York Times*, March 7, 2019, sec. Health, www.nytimes.com/2019/03/05/health/measles-vaccine-autism.html.
50. Sarah Boseley, "Andrew Wakefield Case Highlights the Importance of Ethics in Science," *The Guardian*, May 24, 2010, sec. Society, www.theguardian.com/society/2010/may/24/andrew-wakefield-analysis-ethics-science.
51. Sarah Boseley, "Lancet Retracts 'utterly False' MMR Paper," *The Guardian*, February 2, 2010, sec. Society, www.theguardian.com/society/2010/feb/02/lancet-retracts-mmr-paper; Fiona Godlee, Jane Smith, and Harvey Marcovitch, "Wakefield's Article Linking MMR Vaccine and Autism Was Fraudulent," *BMJ* 342 (January 6, 2011): c7452, https://doi.org/10.1136/bmj.c7452; James Meikle and Sarah Boseley, "MMR Row Doctor Andrew Wakefield Struck off Register," *The Guardian*, May 24, 2010, sec. Society, www.theguardian.com/society/2010/may/24/mmr-doctor-andrew-wakefield-struck-off.
52. Naomi Oreskes and Erik M. Conway, *Merchants of Doubt: How a Handful of Scientists Obscured the Truth on Issues from Tobacco Smoke to Global Warming* (New York: Bloomsbury Press, 2011).
53. Martin Lukacs, "Neoliberalism Has Conned Us into Fighting Climate Change as Individuals | Martin Lukacs," *The Guardian*, July 17, 2017, sec. Environment, www.theguardian.com/environment/true-north/2017/jul/17/neoliberalism-has-conned-us-into-fighting-climate-change-as-individuals.
54. Dana Nuccitelli, "America Spends over $20bn per Year on Fossil Fuel Subsidies. Abolish Them | Dana Nuccitelli," *The Guardian*, July 30, 2018, sec. Environment, www.theguardian.com/environment/climate-consensus-97-per-cent/2018/jul/30/america-spends-over-20bn-per-year-on-fossil-fuel-subsidies-abolish-them; Georgina Gustin, "Industrial Agriculture, an Extraction Industry Like Fossil Fuels, a Growing Driver of Climate Change," *InsideClimate News*, January 25, 2019, https://insideclimatenews.org/news/25012019/climate-change-agriculture-farming-consolidation-corn-soybeans-meat-crop-subsidies.
55. Dylan Matthews, "23 Charts and Maps That Show the World Is Getting Much, Much Better," *Vox*, November 24, 2014, www.vox.com/2014/11/24/7272929/global-poverty-health-crime-literacy-good-news.
56. See Christopher H. Achen and Larry M. Bartels, *Democracy for Realists: Why Elections Do Not Produce Responsive Government* (Princeton: Princeton University Press, 2017).

INDEX

Note: Page numbers in *italics* indicate figures and those in **bold** indicate tables.